Frommer's®

IRREVERENT guide to Paris

Frommer's®

IRREVERENT guide to Paris

6th Edition

By

Darwin Porter & Danforth Prince

Wiley Publishing, Inc.

other titles in the

IRREVERENT GUIDE

series

Irreverent Amsterdam

Irreverent Boston

Irreverent Chicago

Irreverent Las Vegas

Irreverent London

Irreverent Los Angeles

Irreverent New Orleans

Irreverent Paris

Irreverent Rome

Irreverent San Francisco

Irreverent Seattle & Portland

Irreverent Vancouver

Irreverent Walt Disney World®

Irreverent Washington, D.C.

About the Authors

Darwin Porter, a native of North Carolina, and **Danforth Prince** lived in France for many years. Darwin worked in television advertising and as a bureau chief for the Miami Herald. Danforth, who began his association with Darwin in 1982, worked for the Paris bureau of the *New York Times.* They are also the authors of *France For Dummies, Frommer's Paris 2006,* and *Frommer's France.*

Published by:
Wiley Publishing, Inc.

111 River St.
Hoboken, NJ 07030-5774

ISBN-13: 978-0-471-77336-8
ISBN-10: 0-471-77336-0

Interior design contributed to by Marie Kristine Parial-Leonardo

Editor: Matthew Brown
Production Editors: Bethany J. André & Katie Robinson
Cartographer: Anton Crane
Photo Editor: Richard Fox
Production by Wiley Indianapolis Composition Services

For information on our other products and services or to obtain technical support, please contact our Customer Care Department within the U.S. at 800/762-2974, outside the U.S. at 317/572-3993 or fax 317/572-4002.

Wiley also publishes its books in a variety of electronic formats. Some content that appears in print may not be available in electronic formats.

Manufactured in the United States of America

5 4 3 2 1

A Disclaimer

Prices fluctuate in the course of time, and travel information changes under the impact of the varied and volatile factors that influence the travel industry. We therefore suggest that you write or call ahead for confirmation when making your travel plans. Every effort has been made to ensure the accuracy of information throughout this book and the contents of this publication are believed correct at the time of printing. Nevertheless, the publishers cannot accept responsibility for errors or omissions or for changes in details given in this guide or for the consequences of any reliance on the information provided by the same. Assessments of attractions and so forth are based upon the author's own experience and therefore, descriptions given in this guide necessarily contain an element of opinion, which may not reflect the publisher's opinion or dictate a reader's own experience on another occasion. Readers are invited to write to the publisher with ideas, comments, and suggestions for future editions.

Your safety is important to us, however, so we encourage you to stay alert and be aware of your surroundings. Keep a close eye on cameras, purses, and wallets, all favorite targets of thieves and pickpockets.

CONTENTS

INTRODUCTION

Paris: Few words evoke more emotion and promise than this one. Paris, the capital of France, the northern border of the Latin spirit. Paris, where the clichés are so potent that they ultimately become the real thing. Paris—briefly challenged in the early 1990s by Prague as the world's finest hangout for English-speakers looking for high-quality lifestyles—has never lost, and will never lose, its place in the world as the Capital of Sophistication and the Hormonal City-State of Desire. It is here that you can best contemplate what it is you want from life.

People come to Paris for all kinds of reasons. They come to hold hostage the banality of their daily lives back home. They come to compare and complain. They come to repair love that is ailing or to find love that is missing. They come to treat themselves to the guilt of calories that they usually deny themselves. They come to re-ingest the buzz of recognizing the details they discovered, the tastes they recall, and the waiter who charmed them when they visited 8 years ago as a student, or last summer with their children. The intensity of Parisian feelings multiplies on the return. There is the visit, and there is the return, the tiny thrill of reconnecting with the person you were in Paris. The person in you that you like best and can't always be.

Paris is a tumultuous contradiction of pleasures and annoyances, and it almost seems as though one feels the power of the other. Traffic, pollution, quick tempers, bitchiness, high-mindedness taken for arrogance, a natural unwillingness to comply, and lofty prices all lock horns day and night with the unfaltering beauty of the Seine, the attractiveness of Parisian women and men, the attention the city's residents devote to their flowers, their hair, their window displays, their shoes (but not always their sidewalks).... If you pay attention to language and dig into the collective history of words, spoken French itself becomes your mistress or lover, and the inelegant attempts of Parisians to take on the Americanness of global contemporary life absolutely lose importance. Forget the last 20 years of the 20th century when you're in France. Just let it go. Often in denial, the real place lives elsewhere in time.

And that's the irreverent message: Even in the throes of everything you think you know and believe, in Paris the ultimate mystery of existence and lower levels of surprise are always present. Being here is as much about you as it is about the city. Paris is not surreal or weird or hedonistic. It is not Amsterdam or Shanghai, nor Rio de Janeiro or Kiev. It simply is inexhaustible in its ability to charm, to seduce, to please, and to invite you to search deeper and with more intensity into everything. The *café noisette* or the flute of kir that you nurse on any great boulevard terrace is really defined by the time you take to do nothing, by the plans you make for the afternoon or for the next 30 years, and by the little nods you exchange with strangers too Parisian to say hello outright. For the true visitor in you, Paris is about love, about memory, about the broader history of which you and the city are both part, and, of course, the flush of delight that lives in realizing this. The rest is, well, irrelevant.

Map 1: Central Paris Neighborh

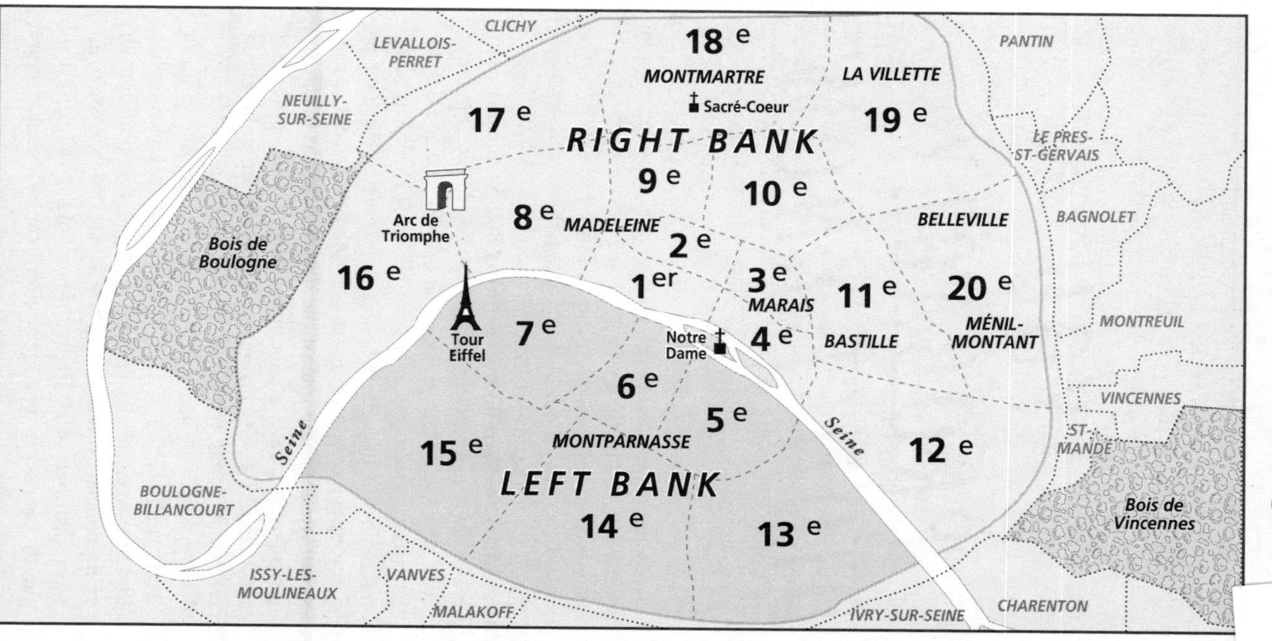

YOU PROBABLY DIDN'T KNOW

Where do you think you're going?... No major city in the world is as misperceived as Paris. People get all moony-eyed about the place just looking at their airplane tickets, fantasizing about romantic sidewalk cafés (with accordion music in the background, of course), incredible food at fancy restaurants, and perhaps a stolen kiss from a new *amour* while leaning against the side of an idyllic bridge on the Seine. Ah, Paris. Pure romance, right? Well, maybe and maybe not. The city inarguably offers a beautiful backdrop for handholding and secret trysts, and being a foreigner here makes it all that much more romantic. But the cold truth is that Paris is a staid, grandmotherly city with a highly conventional bourgeois sense of decorum and an aging population that mostly lives alone. (Singles make up more than half of all Parisian households.) Take a seat in the Parc Monceau on a sunny afternoon and you'll be more likely to observe a strict code of conduct than rampant displays of public affection. If Gene Kelly were to dance down the street at night the way he did in the movies, he'd likely be reprimanded for public drunkenness. Real Paris is not Hollywood Paris, and that is part of what makes it so lovely for most visitors. The city's unbending reverence for tradition keeps its treasures of art, architecture, and classic cuisine alive. But if you're looking for reckless romance or cutting-edge anything, you're likely to be disappointed. The best fashion designers are imported; the restaurant scene (and the food) is much more innovative in San Francisco, New York, and London; the art scene is arguably moribund; and when was the last time you saw a play by a contemporary French playwright? So why come to Paris? Because it is, quite simply, the best place in the Western world to luxuriate in a 19th-century atmosphere.

Is it true that the French hate American culture?... If you ingest a steady diet of Fox News, you probably think the French do hate American culture. When you get here, you'll see to what degree even the open-minded have been manipulated. Lance Armstrong, Richard Gere, Woody Allen, and Jerry Lewis (*still*), among others, are national heroes in France. But, do you really care? It's not as though French people are going to stop you in the street and hold you responsible for past episodes of *Growing Pains* (aptly called in French *Quoi de neuf, docteur*). And if you mistake the upturned nose of Parisian waiters (or underpaid shop clerks) as a specific snub, you're wasting your energy. That whole attitude is merely a pose, and no one knows that better than the French themselves. The truth is, most young French people harbor a passion for American culture—at least the version they've soaked up from movies, TV, the NBA, and pop music. In fact, if you meet up with any Parisians under the age of 25, don't be surprised if they throw themselves at you just because you're American. They dress up in full hip-hop regalia and flock to McDonald's (Burger King no longer exists in France), not to mention the Hard Rock Cafe and Planet Hollywood and other Yankee-inspired insipidness. The wonderful thing is that while decked out in American drag, they still act totally French, kissing their friends on the cheeks upon arrival and departure and observing French table manners to the letter.

Why do people answer me in English when I've spoken to them in French?... For many people a trip to Paris is a chance to go live with the wreckage of once seemingly pointless high-school French classes. So why is it that when you summon up your courage and say, *"Je prends l'omelette au fromage, s'il vous plait,"* the waiter replies, "Do you want it with salad or fries?" This reflexive linguistic upstaging might be helpful if you don't know *"oui"* from *"non,"* but it's really off-putting when you've made the effort to go local. So why do they do it? Partly because your North American accent is just too good a target to resist a putdown, and partly because they're showing off that they're not schnooks either—to wit, "Hey, man, I can speak English, too." More and more French do speak English, and occasionally, an Anglo reply is actually well-intended, but curiously for a country that spends millions propagating its language around the globe and that even has a Ministere de la Francophonie—a cabinet-level post devoted to ensuring the use of French around the world—the locals are pretty bluff when you make the effort. So get used to it, or learn Spanish or Japanese instead.

Why do the French smoke so much?... French cigarettes carry a severe health warning to the tune of "Smoking Kills," and French lungs contract cancer as easily as American ones, but the relaxed attitude toward smoking is part of the ferocious Gallic devotion to the pleasure principal. To their credit, they'll fiercely defend anybody's right to have a good time, even if it includes that most evil of weeds, and there's also an indirect rebuke to what they see as characteristically excessive and draconian American anti-smoking campaigns. Close to 40% of the French smoke, and an astounding 25% of French doctors still smoke. Having said that, there is a growing public that has either quit or finds it less attractive to be inundated with nicotine over a *salade niçoise.* The *zone non-fumeur,* although not religiously respected, does exist in most establishments in Paris today.

Is Disneyland Paris worth a visit?... Only if you're a diehard fan of Mickey or want the experience of a truly weird cultural hybrid. Franco-American has almost never been more Spaghetti-O than it is on the wind-swept plains of Marne-la-Vallée, where the park is located. Other reasons to go might be that you've got the tots in tow, are feeling homesick, hate Florida, or have never been to California, but don't snub *Mona Lisa* to see Donald Duck. More than 11 million folks do journey to Walt's park, making it the most visited attraction in Europe.

Why is that guy staring at me?... The French don't hesitate to stare openly, whether in admiration or condemnation (it's often difficult to tell which is which). You might as well get used to it and stare back. In the Métro, for instance, a woman may study another woman closely, checking out her clothes, hairstyle, makeup, and accessories. This is probably a compliment; she's making mental notes of things to copy. And though French people try not to stand out from the crowd in public, they take great pleasure in seeing someone else do it, and they'll stare unapologetically at anything unusual—an accident, a shouting *clochard* (street person), a man in an ape suit, a woman with purple hair. Go ahead and gawk with them.

No, really, he's hitting on me... A species of French males called *dragueurs* (literally "dredgers") especially like to pick up female American tourists. Some women find this amusing, others find it merely annoying. In either case, *dragueurs* may be persistent, but they're almost never dangerous. Some try to charm you with their French accents, while others get right to the point: "*Bonjour.* Would you like to sleep with me?" If you would, the appropriate answer is, obviously, *"Oui."* If not, the internationally accepted negative response, "No," usually works, especially if you add an evil stare. And don't worry about being slightly rude. (You are, after all, in Paris, where rude is a sport if not an art form.) Try to mildly ignore these people, and keep walking. They'll give up. As in any city, a woman alone is often a target; most French women don't go out by themselves in Paris, not even to dinner. To make sure you'll feel comfortable in restaurants, make reservations in advance; most restaurateurs are solicitous of single female diners. You'll probably have no problems in a café or restaurant during the day.

Why you might as well leave your watch at home... Do not mistake the French for the Swiss. Precision is not a passion in Paris, and time is certainly not of the essence.

Never mind what the T.V guide said; the shows will come on when it is convenient. And if the photo shop says that your prints will be ready at 10am on Tuesday, it means nothing. Maybe they'll be there, maybe they won't, although usually they will, but with a 15- or 20-minute delay. (Don't expect an apology, either. *C'est la vie.*) Many shops, museums, and galleries close at lunchtime (as do some unlikely places such as supermarkets and large electronics stores). And French restaurants have an annoying habit of being closed only when you most want to eat, including Saturday night. Sure, the restaurateurs know they could make more money if they stayed open on Saturday evening, but they don't care. It's more important for them to get out of town on the weekend for rest and relaxation. Are you totally irritated yet? If so, take a deep breath and try to think calm thoughts. After all, isn't it refreshing to be in a place where the dollar (or the euro) isn't worshipped above all else?

How to deal with surly waiters... On the other hand, though you may linger until you are old and gray (especially if you are in a hurry for your check), don't even think about service with a smile. It is simply not part of the French vocabulary. Waiters are rude and that's that. You can try being polite, but it will probably have little or no effect. So do as the French do: Join the attitude war. Unfortunately, in Paris, in-your-face is what works.

How to talk your way into a club... Don't try it. Paris nightclub bouncers are redoubtable. Once a bouncer has refused you, you have to prove you're royalty to get in (and even that might not work—the bouncer's pride might be hurt because he didn't recognize you). Don't show up dowdy or scruffy unless you're famous. The best way to get into the most *branché* (trendy, literally "plugged in") nightclubs is to arrive in some sort of flamboyant costume. Unaccompanied men hardly ever get in because there's always a shortage of women; beautiful women, especially tall American models, are a sure open sesame. On the other hand, many gay bars and nightclubs refuse to admit women at all.

How to talk your way into a fashion show... If you're not a lucky invitation-holder, getting past the gorillas at the gate into Paris's haute couture and *prêt-à-porter* shows is nearly impossible. The key word here is "nearly." Truly dedicated garment groupies have been known to arrive ahead of time at the location of their favorite designer's show and, looking irresistibly pathetic, ask everyone heading inside if they have an extra invitation. This actually works sometimes, but don't count on it for the really hot shows, such as Dior, Givenchy, Dries Van Noten, or Jean-Paul Gaultier. Your best bet, of course, is to have an influential friend who is willing to give you an extra invite. Check with the **Chambre Syndicale de la Couture** (Tel 01-42-66-64-44; www.modeaparis.com) for the location of particular shows.

Where to catch some rays... The moment there's a ray of sunshine (a rarity in this gray city), no matter how chilly it is, Parisian sun worshippers flock to the banks of the Seine, where you'll see nearly naked bodies sprawled on every available stretch of concrete. Okay, so it's not the Riviera, but it isn't Hoboken, either. Feel free to join them. The tips of both the Ile Saint-Louis and the Ile de la Cité are popular, but if you prefer to escape the crowds try the little-known Jardin Tino Rossi, which hugs the Seine on the Left Bank just south of the tip of Ile Saint-Louis.

What is a zebra?... A band of striped pavement across a street is called a zebra crossing, and French law stipulates that a driver must stop for pedestrians who have started to cross in front of them. Yeah, right! When they see you trying to cross the street, French drivers will show no signs of slowing. If you keep going, they may swerve to avoid you, they may stop (unlikely), or they may just run you down. The French don't have the right to bear arms as Americans do, so this is one of the few means available to them to commit homicide. Don't tempt them.

Can't they see I'm walking here?... Even long-time Yankee expats are still amazed that Parisians, unlike American or other northern European city dwellers, wander down the street as if they had it all to themselves. If some sidewalk hog is blocking your path, a stiff, *"Pardon!"* usually does the trick.

w to see the sights without taking a tour bus... The 95 bus passes the Paris Opéra, the Louvre, and the Palais-Royal, then crosses the Seine and goes through Saint-Germain-des-Prés and on to Montparnasse. All it costs is a bus ticket, which you buy from the driver when you board.

How to get a taxi at 2am... That's the witching hour, when many bars close, the Métro is no longer running, the Noctambus provides only infrequent bus service, and many taxi drivers are on their way home to bed after a quick visit to their mistress. The best way to avoid a long walk home is to book a taxi in advance: call **Taxis Bleus** (Tel 01-49-36-10-10; www.taxis-bleus.com), **Taxi G7** (Tel 01-47-39-47-39; www.taxisg7.fr), or **Alpha Taxis** (Tel 01-45-85-85-85). Otherwise, head for a bar or club that stays open all night and grab a taxi discharging new arrivals.

It's Sunday. Where the hell is everybody?... Pressure from still-powerful unions has kept the French "blue laws" in effect. Unless they sell food, stores aren't supposed to open on Sunday, though many small boutiques do anyway. In the Marais, almost all the shops are open on Sunday. Many boutiques around rue des Abbesses in Montmartre are also open on Sunday, and the area also has some wonderful specialty food shops open in the morning. Many museums are open, but they'll be crowded. Instead, visit one of the many atmospheric food markets—the Marché d'Aligre (don't miss Le Baron Rouge wine bar), and the markets on the rue Mouffetard and the rue Montorgueil. Or check out the sprawling flea market at Porte de Clignancourt, skipping the usual cheap leather jackets and cowboy boots and bee-lining for the antique stalls. Have a drink (the food is too bad to contemplate) at Chez Louisette in the Vernaison section of the market and soak up the local color—accordion players, Edith Piaf imitators, and the palm-reading Gypsy lady.

It's August. Where the hell is everybody?... Nearly the entire city goes on vacation for the whole month of August. Many restaurants will be closed—most small-business people would rather close down than trust an outsider to oversee their business. (If your heart is set on eating in a particular restaurant, call ahead to see if it will be open.) The upside of August in Paris is the blissful calm that descends on the city. The streets, normally choked with traffic noise and pollution, become blessedly empty. It doesn't get completely dark until about 11pm, and the larger cafés do stay open. The Eric Rohmer film *Le Rayon Vert* gives a wonderful feeling for Paris in August, when it feels more like a lazy provincial city than a world capital.

Why you shouldn't mind if someone calls you a Bobo... Relax, it has nothing to do with how you get your kit off and with whom. "Bobo" means bohemian-bourgeois, which is what yuppies have morphed into now that the Y-word has become such an embarrassment and so many of them have grown old enough to get editorial jobs, and so defend themselves.

Why you shouldn't spend too much time in Saint-Germain... Paris really has changed, and if you honestly want to discover the city beyond the most seriously shop-worn tourist clichés in the book (not this one, of course), you're not going to do it sitting around in overpriced Left Bank cafés surfing the garbagey conversations of other American college students, British divorcées, Australian backpackers, or, for Parisians that most alarming of all foreign species, honeymooners from Texas. Saint-Germain is all about luxury shopping these days—witness the Louis Vuitton, Chanel, and Cartier boutiques—so if you want to re-enact Audrey Hepburn's role in *Funny Face* (she plays a naïve, intellectually ambitious bookstore clerk)—head for Ménilmontant (it's partly in the 11th arrondissement, partly in the 20th) or Batignolles (17th arrondissement); these places are where the wild things are. And if you really want to immerse yourself in a cool, young French scene, hop the train to Rennes, in Brittany, or Marseilles for the weekend; both are truly happening, in places in a way that Paris isn't anymore but used to be.

ACCOMM

Do Not
Disturb

ODATIONS

1

Map 2: Paris Accommodations—Orientation

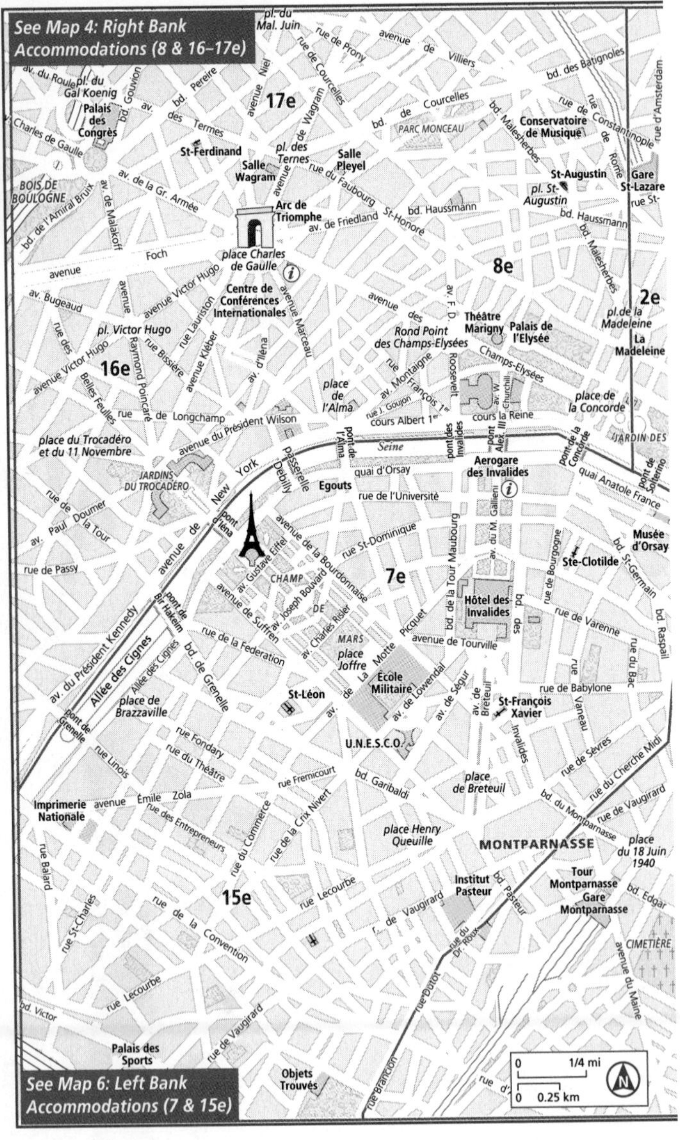

See Map 3: Right Bank Accommodations (1–4, 9–12 & 18e)
See Map 5: Left Bank Accommodations (5–6 & 13–14e)
MONTMARTRE
Moulin Rouge
place Pigalle
Gare du Nord
Gare de l'Est
10e
3e
4e
1er
5e
6e
11e
12e
13e
14e
LE MARAIS
QUARTIER LATIN
ST-GERMAIN-DES-PRÉS
ILE DE LA CITÉ
ILE ST-LOUIS
PARC DES BUTTES-CHAUMONT
Opéra Garnier
place Vendôme
Palais Royal
Musée du Louvre
Bourse des Valeurs
Forum des Halles
Conservatoire des Arts et Métiers
place de la République
Archives Nationales
place des Vosges
place de la Bastille
Opéra Bastille
Hôtel de Ville
Notre-Dame
Sorbonne
Panthéon
Palais du Luxembourg
JARDIN DU LUXEMBOURG
Institut du Monde Arabe
JARDIN DES PLANTES
Gare d'Austerlitz
Gare de Lyon
Observatoire de Paris
place d'Italie
Seine

Basic Stuff

Paris used to be the capital of fantastically hideous floral wallpaper. Almost all of its hundreds of cheap, family-run hotels offered heart-stopping examples, as any veteran of a backpack-and-stale-baguette student trip to Paris knows. Their heating and plumbing systems presented such puzzles as, "How can I wash my face in a 2-inch-deep basin without hitting my head on that beam?"

At the other end of the scale, in *les palaces,* whippet-like men with pencil mustaches once made a life's work out of exponential nastiness, guarding acre-size black-and-white marble lobbies against the blight of your presence. If you got past these guard dogs, your room upstairs invariably had a crystal chandelier, a lot of gilt Louis-something furniture, a very slow-dialing telephone on a short cord, and a flummoxing handheld shower that forced you to bathe on your knees.

The 17€ ($21) triangular room with fluorescent dahlia print wallpaper is gone forever—but Paris still offers a broad choice of comfortable, well-located hotels with lots of local charm for around 65€ to 95€ ($81 to $119) a night. Many of them have been modernized and are run by such chains as the very-good-value Libertel group. Even the palace hotels are enhancing and augmenting their amenities (witness the spectacular underground health club at the glitzy Ritz, of all places). If you are able and willing to veer out slightly from the city's epicenter, you can find inexpensive one-, two-, and even three-star establishments ready to house you. On the other hand, hotels in Saint-Germain-des-Prés and the Marais have caught on to the fact that Americans are used to spending lots for good, city-center hotels. Finally, painful though it may be, many Parisian hoteliers have accepted the inevitable and learned to speak English—and even how to smile.

If stairs are difficult for you, be sure to ask when you book whether the hotel has an elevator. Few Paris hotels are well equipped for travelers with disabilities (even if there is an elevator, there's often a half-flight of stairs that must be mounted). In addition, bathrooms in Paris can be ridiculously tiny and cramped. Be very specific about your needs when booking. There are now some hotels offering nonsmoking rooms and in-room Internet connections. Just ask.

Note that the value-added tax, or TVA, and service are included in all hotel room prices and that tipping is not necessary unless someone has done some very special favor for you. A useful index of hotel listings begins on p. 41.

Winning the Reservations Game

Paris is one of the most popular tourist destinations in the world, so always book a hotel as far in advance as possible, at least 4 to 6 weeks if you can. You may be able to find a room after you arrive, but it probably won't be exactly what you want and may be much more expensive than you'd like. Or you might have to settle for a more modest room or less attractive neighborhood. It's easier to find a room in November, December, July, and August than at other times of the year, when events like fashion shows, trade fairs, conferences, and the Le Bourget air show keep hotels—even modest ones—full. **Ely 12 12,** 182, rue du St. Honoré, 75008 (Tel 01-43-59-12-12, fax 01-42-56-24-31; www.ely1212.com) can usually get a room for you even when the whole town is booked up. The service is free. The **Paris Office du Tourisme,** 25, rue de Pyramides, 75001 (Tel 08-92-68-30-30; www.parisinfo.com) also has a hotel booking service. **Paris Séjour Réservation,** 90, av. Des Champs-Elsées, 75008 (Tel 01-53-89-10-50, fax 01-53-89-10-59; www.psryourhomeinparis.com) can find you an apartment complete with towels, sheets, and maid service for a stay of 7 days or more. A free classified advertising publication called **France–USA Contacts,** or FUSAC, 26, rue Benard, 75014 in Paris (Tel 01-56-53-54-54, fax 01-56-53-54-55), and Box 115, Cooper Station, New York, NY 10276 in the U.S. (Tel 212/777-5553, fax 212/777-5554; www.fusac.fr), carries ads for short-term apartment rentals or apartment exchanges. The popular website **www.paris-anglo.com** also offers links to short and long-term apartment rentals, such as Rentals in Paris (www.rentals-paris.com) and Theo Kilgore's www.paris apartmentsearch.com. If all else fails, and you arrive in Paris without a reservation, the Office du Tourisme has desks at the airports, train stations, and the Eiffel Tower. The pickings might be slim and you might not get a hotel in the area you prefer, but you never know—you might get lucky. And, experience has shown that *if* you find a hotel of your choice, you may even benefit from a same-day, deep discount rate.

When you reserve, ask about special rates, including corporate or weekend packages, which are offered by many large or pricey hotels. Most hotels lower their rates, sometimes considerably, during their low season (July–Aug and Nov–Dec). And, don't forget that many Parisian hotels do offer better rates online, so check the hotel's website for promotional rates.

What the Rating Stars Mean

All French hotels are rated with a star system, ranging from no stars to four, plus four-star deluxe. Though the stars will give you an idea of the relative luxury and price of the hotel, they relate more to technical criteria such as room size and the number of electrical outlets than they do to old-world charm.

It's important to note that the star ratings directly affect the sales and other taxes of a hotel. Some of the most delightful properties have two stars strictly because the owners don't want to raise their property taxes. The French themselves regularly stay in two-stars, where they know they'll get a clean, comfortable room with a private bathroom.

A number of small, inexpensive hotels with no stars or one star don't have toilets or even showers in the rooms, although a sink and a bidet are generally provided. At this level, it's also unlikely that your sheets and towels will be changed daily. If you don't mind scooting down the hall in a bathrobe, you can save a lot of money by staying in these hotels. Some of them are actually comfortable and attractively furnished.

A number of hotels have a range of prices that depend on the size and amenities of different rooms. Rooms with a bathtub rather than just a shower, for example, will cost a bit more, as will rooms with twin beds instead of a double bed. And you may be expected to pay extra for a room with a view or a balcony. Before choosing a terrace, however, remember that street-side rooms are considerably louder than those on the interior, which oftentimes look upon pretty

What to Do with a Bidet

Bidets are—well, were—indispensable to the French. So first off, it's pronounced "bee-day." And it's for washing your private parts after using the toilet or engaging in, ahem, certain other acts. Here's where history figures in. The French had long been an international standing joke for their lack of personal hygiene, but they've fully outgrown that slur and are into the habit of the daily wash-up (although they still use the smallest amount of soap per capita in Europe, which is to their credit because they understand that over-washing and needless shampooing depletes the skin and hair of their natural oils). In retaliation, the French—who consider Americans hypersensitive and at times obsessive in matters of cleanliness and the body in general—get a good laugh out of watching Yankee tourists encountering bidets in their hotel rooms. Some Americans use it to wash out their underwear; others think it's handy for soaking swollen feet after hours of heavy-duty sightseeing. Invent your own use. Note that other than old and bourgeois apartments, Paris private bathrooms do not include bidets anymore.

courtyards. Again, if you have a preference or would rather not pay for extras, say so when you book.

Is There a Right Address?

If you're more interested in hanging out in Algerian Rai clubs or Afro-Cuban salsa joints than in doing the Louvre or the Musée D'Orsay, look for accommodations around the Bastille or Republique. If you want to have plenty of room for your matching Louis Vuitton luggage, need a safe for your jewelry, and need to be close to the couture houses for your fittings, you'll want to pop for a grand hotel. If this is your 12th visit, you might enjoy staying in one of the outlying neighborhoods to sample more of the daily life of the city. First-timers are generally happiest in and around Saint-Germain-des-Prés on the Left Bank or the Marais on the Right Bank, where the local charm veritably screams Paris. Just make sure your hotel is in a district well served by public transportation—when choosing between two similar hotels, go with the one near a Métro stop that's served by several lines instead of just one.

Left Bank or Right Bank? The way Paris is getting gentrified, there's not so much difference anymore. These days the Left Bank is about as bohemian as Betty Crocker, having become more the bastion of the liberal Parisian bourgeoisie than a center of radical thought. But it still looks like the Left Bank, the one part of town that wasn't ruthlessly but brilliantly modernized in the 19th century by Baron Haussmann, master architect and urban planner of the grand boulevard and the style that dominates Paris's apartment buildings today.

Almost all the grande-dame hotels are located on the Right Bank off the **Champs-Elysées** and near the **place de la Concorde** (8th arrondissement). These palaces cost a fortune and a half, but the same area has many of the city's most luxurious boutiques. Heading east along the Seine, you come to **Châtelet** and **Les Halles** (1st arrondissement), two of the city's major pulse points, with lots of car and foot traffic, cafés, bars, restaurants, and clubs. It is a McDonald's–Pizza Hut–KFC-cluttered haven for lounging suburban youth, junkies, and assorted young bloods on shopping sprees, but it's an easy walk to the Centre Pompidou, the Marais, the Ile de la Cité, and the Left Bank. Hotels here run from tiny no-stars on the side streets running off the Les Halles shopping center to big, brassy, commercial chain places.

The maze-like medieval **Marais** (3rd and 4th arrondissements) is home to gorgeous 16th- and 17th-century architecture,

> **Working the Angles**
> *Paris's selection of hotel rooms from 65€ to 140€ ($81–$175) is extensive in almost all areas of the city, although more difficult to attain in the Saint-Germain-des-Prés and Marais areas. Châtelet and Les Halles, la République, parts of the Latin Quarter, and almost all of the close but less central areas such as the Grands Boulevards and the Opera host a number of three-star hotels in this moderate range. The* ***Holiday Inn*** *at place de la République, an elegantly converted 18th-century building, for example, occasionally offers discounts if you book online at www.paris-republique.holiday-inn.com. There is a danger here. You must guarantee your reservation with a credit card, and there are no refunds at this reduced rate if you have to cancel. You forfeit the entire amount you pre-paid. You can also manage to transform a higher-end joint into a moderately priced one by negotiating the rates with the concierge. Yes, you can negotiate, but do so in a serene and tasteful manner if you hope to succeed. For example, say something like, "Could monsieur make a little effort in finding a slightly more reasonable rate?"*

funky little bars and restaurants, and a cosmopolitan character. Here, Hasidic and Sephardic Jews rub shoulders with Paris's vibrant gay community, and chic French *mamans* wheel their NAFNAF- or Gap-clad babies past Asian wholesalers. Hotels tend to be reasonably expensive but romantic, if a bit idiosyncratic, with the odd water-pressure problem or slanting floors. The demand for rooms in the Marais far outstrips availability, so if you have your heart set on this quarter, book extra far in advance.

If you want to indulge a long-nurtured desire to sleep near Mona (Lisa, that is), better known here by its real name *La Jocande,* there are fancy hotels near the **Louvre** and **Palais-Royal** (1st arrondissement) and the **Eiffel Tower** (7th arrondissement). The former is a busy area in the monument-studded but traffic-clogged center of town; the latter, a rather staid residential area. The **Opéra Garnier** (2nd and 9th arrondissements) is another hopping part of town well served by reasonably priced hotels and most of the city's foreign tourist offices and airline ticket offices; this area has been colonized by the resident Japanese population and is popular with Asian visitors, so bet on plenty of good, reasonably priced sushi bars and Korean barbecue restaurants on the busy side streets.

The Left Bank's **Saint-Germain-des-Prés** neighborhood (6th arrondissement) is chic, intelligent, beautiful, and centrally located. There's a large concentration of small hotels overflowing with charm, some very expensive and others surprisingly cheap. A more bohemian choice is the **Latin Quarter** (5th arrondissement), the lively student district that's home to the Jardin du Luxembourg, the Musée de Cluny, and lots of inexpensive restaurants, bookshops, and hotels. The **Montparnasse** area (14th and 15th arrondissements), formerly haunted by writers and artists such as Hemingway, Fitzgerald, Gertrude Stein, and Picasso, is now more sedate, less bohemian, and slightly out of the way for visitors. The famous brasseries are still here and merit a detour.

Hotels continue to pop up in the booming **Bastille** (11th arrondissement) area surrounding the relatively new opera house (opened for the French bicentennial in 1989), where crowds flock to wannabe-trendy eateries, bars, and nightclubs. There's a lot of automobile traffic, but you'll be on line 1 of the Métro, which makes access to other parts of town fairly easy. If you want to be closer to nature than to Notre-Dame, you might choose a hotel in the far end of the swanky 16th arrondissement near the **Bois de Boulogne** or the less swanky and relatively under-exploited areas around the **Bois de Vincennes** (12th arrondissement) on the eastern side of the city. This is a great location for joggers or those seeking tranquillity, but don't expect much in the way of street life or nightlife, aside from the odd mauve-haired baroness promenading a Chanel-swathed Fifi at midnight. **Montmartre,** a quaint village in the 18th arrondissement, still has steep, atmospheric cobbled streets where neither visitors nor trendoids congregate. For those who can sleep through the noise, its Abbesses area features a lively nightlife scene that now reaches down to the crude charm of seedy **Pigalle.**

The Lowdown

Palaces: le top... The biggest, grandest hotels, which the French refer to as *palaces,* are the ultimate in luxury, as only the French know how to do it. And as you'd expect, they fall into the top price bracket. Each room in the **Hôtel le Bristol**—considered by some to be the best hotel in France—is furnished in Louis XIV or Louis XV splendor; the bathrooms are dressed in white Carrara marble, and some of its suites open onto grand terraces. A glass-enclosed swimming pool on the sixth floor was designed by a hotshot naval architect who worked for Onassis, and the hotel's enormous garden, a rarity in the center of Paris, is large enough for meditative strolls. The opulent, old-world **Raphaël,** in the tony 16th arrondissement, is one of the last of the great hotels—after all, how many have a real Turner painting in the lobby? The bedrooms are especially large, and some have hidden alcoves behind the dressing rooms where maids used to iron for their masters and mistresses. If you can afford it, it's the perfect place for an illicit afternoon—the setting is so wonderfully staid and proper that it cries out for naughtiness.

The gallery at the **Plaza Athénée,** with potted palms, crystal chandeliers, and plush furnishings, is the ultimate rendezvous spot, especially for tea in the afternoon or predinner drinks. Perfect too for a classy, understated rendezvous. The rooms and suites are decorated in Louis XV, Louis XVI, and Regency styles, with nary a false detail. The colonnaded **Crillon** attracts modern-day royalty such as Madonna, Meryl Streep, and Tom Cruise, but in earlier times its prime site—looking right out on the place de la Concorde—might have given certain monarchs the heebie-jeebies: Louis XVI and Marie Antoinette were guillotined here during the French Revolution. The **Four Seasons George V** is the most modernized of all the Paris palaces following a makeover so thorough that you might as easily be in Dallas as Paris. Still, the service is efficient and American "Have a Nice Day"–style friendly, the restaurant Le V is superb, and this luxury chain probably serves up the most comfortable beds (special editions Simmons jobs) to be found anywhere in the world, plus there's a sexy little health club with all kinds of massages, sauna, steam room, and pool.

Business travelers also congregate in the 1st arrondissement at the weathered **InterContinental,** between the place Vendôme and the Tuileries Gardens. Its Belle Epoque banquet room, the Salon Impérial, a fantasy in gold leaf and crystal, sets the opulent style for the whole hotel. Starwood's takeover of the **Prince de Galles** was a happy conclusion after a series of ups and downs for this palace near the Champs-Elysées whose Art Deco interior has been refurbished and facilities modernized. The rooms are prettily decorated with toile de Jouy fabric, and some original bathroom mosaics, worthy of a Roman bathhouse, have been preserved.

Palaces: les flops... Right next to the Opéra Garnier is **Le Grand Hotel Paris,** where the eccentric American millionaire James Gordon Bennett once asked Henry Stanley to go off to the wilds of Africa in search of Dr. David Livingstone. Built in 1862, the Grand underwent an unfortunate modernization in the spirit of the Pompidou 1970s. Its owners, InterContinental Hotels, have put a lot of effort into correcting that mistake, and now it's restored to much (but not all) of its former glory. Despite its swell location just on the edge of the place Vendôme, the **Vendôme,** an opulent ultra-luxury boutique hotel, is the right address only for anyone too cheap to travel with his or her bodyguard. The little videophones that let you see who's at the door lead one to suspect it's an ideal setting for shady dealings of various types, and the decor is so studiously Louis-something that only the Beverly Hillbillies would be impressed.

Palaces: over le top... The Ritz, on the place Vendôme, is everything you would expect it to be—and worse. Just like a character from an Inspector Clouseau movie, the uniformed doorman won't let you into the lobby if he doesn't like the way you're dressed. (***Hint:*** Tell him you have a rendezvous in the bar with Anthony Delon, the model and son of actor Alain Delon. This works very well to get past velvet nightclub ropes, too.) After the death of Princess Diana and Ritz-owner Al Fayed's son, security got severely heavy. Some say that every car and pedestrian entering the elegant place Vendôme is videotaped. Do go for a drink at the bar just for the hell of it, and don't forget that Marcel Proust was nourished by take-out beer and frites from the Ritz while writing *Remembrance of Things Past,* or that Marlene Dietrich used to sit on the edge of the bathtub in Hemingway's room there and sing to him while he shaved. Papa Hem actually kept up to 12 hunting rifles in his room here.

Overrated... Since the George V became the Beverly Hills–style Four Seasons George V and the **Plaza Athénée** and the Meurice got multimillion-dollar makeovers, the **Crillon** is starting to look like granny in tattered panties. The restaurants and bar here are great, but rooms need work. Glossy magazines have drooled all over the **Hôtel**

Costes ever since it opened, but the fact is that they pull such nasty attitude that unless you're Gwyneth Paltrow or an internationally famous fashion photographer or magazine editor, you'll get the same small overpriced rooms they fob off on the wannabe fashion buyers who are their real clientele.

Best decor for travelers allergic to gilt and cherubs... If you feel like splashing out on some really classy digs with deep-dish comfort, the **Hotel Lancaster** is an elegant, intimate little gem that was renovated with impeccable town-house decor just off the Champs-Elysées. When she wasn't hanging at the Ritz, Marlene Dietrich lived here for years, and if it was good enough for her, then it's surely good enough for you.

Left Bank hotels often get lost in a bower of cutesy Anglo-French floral prints that should be confined to the nightgowns of adolescent girls, which is why the stately **Hotel d'Aubusson** is a great bet. You can clock a couple of the real namesake tapestries without even leaving the premises, and this place has a sumptuous, vaguely medieval atmosphere that comes from ancient beamed ceilings, silk damask, and real antiques. Also on the Left Bank, the **Montalembert** offers up a perfect mix of contemporary design and Deco, although rooms are a bit small.

Directly across the street from the Bastille opera house is the **Pavillon Bastille,** a town-house hotel with a distinctive bright-yellow and deep-blue decor softened by blond wood and black-and-white floor tiles. Even the flowers in the bathrooms conform to architect Jean-Pierre Heim's color scheme, though each room is unique.

For those who hate surprises... Paris has several chain hotels that provide what are referred to as "international standard" in-room amenities—cable TV, direct-dial phones, minibars, hair dryers—and International Bland decor to match. Some of them, however, have a little extra, including the **Holiday Inn** on the place de la République, which has the advantage of being located in a handsome 19th-century quadrangular building that takes up an entire city block. The glass-sheathed **Hilton Paris** may be right next to the Eiffel Tower, but it's as American as Pop Tarts: Built in 1966, it has everything you were always afraid to

TIP

The four or five hotels around the Gambetta Métro stop in the 20th arrondissement are all reasonable and relatively unknown to North Americans. The advantage in the summer is that from here you're a stone's throw from the back entrance to the Père-Lachaise cemetery, which is cool and breezy and filled with atmosphere and history.

leave home without. (There is one indubitable French touch, though: The hotel accepts cats and dogs in the rooms and coffee shop and even provides food for them.)

The Méridien chain has two hotels in Paris: The **Méridien Etoile,** near Porte Maillot, is ugly as sin but has a very good restaurant, Le Clos Longchamp, plus outstanding live jazz concerts in the lobby every night. The high-rise **Méridien Montparnasse** has lofty views and tiptop business facilities and a particularly copious buffet restaurant. And if you want to stay safe, but go a tiny bit French, the **Ibis** chain is the French equivalent of the Holiday Inn, with about 20 locations around town offering characterless but clean, comfortable rooms at low rates.

Cheap sleeps... It's still possible to get a room for 65€ ($85) or less in Paris, but don't count on luxury. Many include private bathrooms, but some don't (though a private sink is fairly standard). Still, slumming it doesn't mean you have to stay in a slum: Many of the city's most budget-friendly hotels are located in hip areas.

Bouquets of rather dusty fake flowers sum up the decor at the tiny **Hôtel de Lille,** but it's a stone's throw from the Louvre and the Palais-Royal, and thus perfectly situated for anyone planning a lot of heavy-duty museum-going. The carpeting's a bit worn and the Toulouse-Lautrec prints may bring back visions of your teenaged bedroom, but this place is squeaky clean and very inexpensive, so book well in advance. The tiny **Hôtel de Nesle,** snuggled down in the atmospheric Saint-Germain-des-Prés area, has plenty of character and a rather bohemian atmosphere. The main drawback (and it's a biggie) is that no reservations are accepted; you have to call in the morning to see whether a room is available that night, and they don't take credit cards. In the Marais, the **Grand Hôtel Jeanne d'Arc** lies just off the restaurant-lined place du Marché Sainte-Catherine. It's a fabulous deal for this area, so book early. The **Style Hôtel** is off the beaten track, but it's near Montmartre and inexpensive, spacious, clean, and pretty, with a little garden for warm-weather breakfasts. Rooms in the main building have bathrooms.

Cheap sleeps sans *charme*... You might expect to pay through the nostrils to stay in a 400-year-old hotel a few steps away from Notre-Dame, but the **Henri IV** is one of the cheapest around. The rooms are small and basic, with very thin walls, and the shower and toilet are a trek down the hall for most. Still, it's clean, and you may luck into a room with a view. Book far in advance, though—the Henri IV is always full of backpacking Americans and expats from Prague. **Vauvilliers,** located next to Les Halles, Paris's glaringly fluorescent underground shopping mall, is a clean, no-frills, low-cost hotel with a no-nonsense *patronne.* The lobby of the Left Bank's **Rive Gauche** is utterly lacking in taste and the street can be noisy, but the small, serviceable rooms are kind of cozy. Finally, it might be a kick to stay in a hotel on a street named after "bad boys," the rue des Mauvais-Garçons. There's only one hotel that fits the description: the very inexpensive **Grand Hôtel du Loiret.** It's in the Marais, where even charmless rooms are in demand, so reserve in advance.

Where to finally get started on that novel... You can hardly sign a credit card slip in a Paris hotel without feeling a tingle of inspiration from some literary ghost. The early 18th-century building where the great French novelist Stendhal once lived is now a romantic, four-star hotel near the tony place Vendôme. Each chamber at the **Stendhal** is individually decorated with rich fabrics and period furniture, and room 52 pays homage to the author's *The Red and the Black.* Voltaire, Sainte-Beuve, and Victor Hugo used to carouse at the **Relais du Louvre** when it housed the Café Momus, inspiration for the second act of Puccini's *La Bohème.* The venerable Left Bank **Angleterre** has improved greatly since Ernest Hemingway tripped drunkenly up its broken stairs. Formerly the British embassy where American independence was officially recognized, it has also logged less obstreperous author-guests, including Washington Irving and Sherwood Anderson. Expatriate authors have also long been associated with the **Lenox Saint-Germain,** a small Left Bank hotel with snug rooms, a great bar, and names like T.S. Eliot, James Joyce, and Ezra Pound on its guest register. Joyce also stayed at the **Lutétia,** the large Art Deco hotel near Montparnasse, where negative reviews of *Finnegans Wake* threw him into a funk. Other creative types—from Jean Cocteau, Pablo Picasso, Henri Matisse, André Gide, and Josephine Baker to Marcello Mastroianni and Christopher Lambert—have logged time here. Today's government-rated four-star hotel, **Relais-Hotel du Vieux Paris,** started out as the 1480 mansion for the Duc d'O but by the 1950s had become the "Beat Hotel." Poet Allen Ginsberg lived here with his lover Peter Corso, and William Burroughs (author of *Naked Lunch*) was frequently seen doped in the hallways. Fellow beat, Gregory Corso, who also lived with Ginsberg, came back in 1997 to this former flea-bitten dive to discover "where once rats ran from the cellar to the street," a beautifully restored gem.

Where Oscar Wilde slept around... Oscar Wilde died broke and complaining about the wallpaper in a room at **L'Hôtel,** but don't read a description of his last moments or you may not want to spend a night in his painstakingly restored death chamber. Today Mick Jagger stays at this luxurious and eccentrically baroque Left Bank landmark. In Wilde's better days, he rested his head at the **Quai Voltaire,** where he resolutely ignored the views of the Louvre and the Tuileries across the Seine. Despite a past guest roster that also includes Wagner, Baudelaire, and Sibelius (now there's a combination), the rooms here are reasonably priced, not to mention pretty.

Where to paint like Pissarro... At the lavish **Hôtel du Louvre,** a 19th-century luxury hotel located smack in between the Louvre and the Palais-Royal, you can stay in the room where Impressionist painter Camille Pissarro transformed his window view into one of the best-known works of the 19th century.

If I can see the Eiffel Tower, I must be in Paris... The walls of glass that sheathe the 1960s-modern **Hilton Paris** betray an otherwise heroic attempt to make American travelers feel as if they never left the States. If it weren't for the kiss-close view of Gustave Eiffel's engineering wonder, guests tucking into their salads or pizzas at their oh-so-trendy California-style restaurant (an improvement of the former ghastly and embarrassing "Hi, Sheriff"–type Western steakhouse) might think they were in, well, Cleveland. For a real eye-opener, appreciate the Hilton's soaring neighbor from the hotel's rooftop bar.

Across the Seine near the Champs-Elysées, the palatial **Plaza Athénée** has a few rooms with balconies affording views of the tower. Film director Francis Ford Coppola's favorite stop, the large Art Deco **Lutétia,** near Montparnasse, darkly remembered for housing the Gestapo during the War, has some long views of the tower from an unusual Left Bank perspective. In fact, this elegant period piece of a building also has an Eiffel Tower suite from which the tower can be eyed from every window, including the one in front of your sunken bathtub. If you're willing to go for broke, you can also score a view of the Eiffel Tower from rooms or suites on the southern flank of the **Four Seasons George V.**

Other rooms with a view... Oscar Wilde said of his view across the Seine from the **Quai Voltaire:** "Oh, that is altogether immaterial, except to the innkeeper, who of course charges it in the bill." Oscar be damned, it's a heavenly sight. If anything could beat a view across the Seine, it'd be a view from the middle of the Seine, on the ever-so-chic Ile Saint-Louis. The surprisingly homey little **Lutèce** has dynamite views from some rooms, at moderate prices.

The **TimHôtel Montmartre,** a totally affordable hotel on a quiet, tree-lined square in Montmartre, has sweeping views of *tout Paris,* including close-ups of Sacré-Coeur, from its top floors. Terraces on the upper floors of the **Parc Saint-Séverin,** in the Latin Quarter, let you gaze out over Left Bank rooftops and the deliciously creepy gargoyles of Saint-Séverin church—vistas that certainly make up for the hotel's lack of period charm. Also in the Latin Quarter, the restful and renovated **Grands Hommes** offers top-floor perspectives of the Panthéon, where Voltaire and Victor Hugo, among others, were laid to permanent rest.

For somewhat plusher accommodations, try the antique-laden **Left Bank Saint-Germain:** The back rooms offer swoony views of Notre Dame and the rooftops of Paris. If it's outright luxury you want, though, you'll have to pop for the modern **Méridien Montparnasse,** a 25-story high-rise with write-home-about panoramas of the city.

Where the fashion crowd can be found... The famed weeklong Paris shows—biannual events for haute couture, women's ready-to-wear, and men's ready-to-wear—pretty much take over Paris. If you hit town then, almost no decent hotel will be free of fashion victims. Supermodels, celebrities, and the few remaining socialite haute couture buyers deposit their Louis Vuittons at one of the palace hotels like the **Four Seasons George V,** but the quintessential place to see and be seen now is Paris's equivalent of New York City's Royalton: the too-too-trendy **Hôtel Costes** (located around the corner from the snooty place Vendôme), with its Napoléon III decor by Jacques Garcia. Lesser establishments will be full of lesser models, journalists, photographers, fashion students, and other hangers-on.

The fashion crowd particularly favors the Left Bank's trendy **Montalembert,** which ditched its staid, old look for designer decor; the **Prince de Conti,** an intimate Left Bank hotel near the Seine with an interior courtyard and warm, comfy, English-style decor; and the **Lenox Saint-Germain,** also on the Left Bank, where you should definitely ask to be shown your room before signing the register—some are on the small side, but others have dramatic little mezzanines or balconies. Book far in advance if you have to come when the shows are in full swing (in Jan, March, July, and Oct) or you may not get a room at all.

Love in the afternoon... In the film *Love in the Afternoon,* a young Audrey Hepburn and an aging Gary Cooper had a steamy affair at the storied **Ritz,** and you can too if you can afford it—and you have a partner. The romantic and luxurious **Stendhal,** just around the corner, is not much cheaper, but possibly more alluring to those with a literary bent. And what better place for an illicit affair than the staid **Raphaël,** the princely palace near the Arc de Triomphe, where you can make love on a horsehair sofa? The **Istria** has a well-deserved reputation for discretion, having often harbored the illicit trysts of the rich and famous: heiress Nancy Cunard had her secret affairs at this rather out-of-the-way little Montparnasse hotel and Raymond Radiguet cheated on Jean Cocteau here—with a woman, no less.

For those with Merchant-Ivory syndrome, there may be no greater turn-on than a four-poster bed (*lit à baldaquin*), which can be found at certain smaller hotels: the elegant **Pavillon de la Reine,** right on the Marais's splendid place des Vosges; the lovely **Angleterre,** near Saint-Germain-des-Prés, where Hemingway once stayed; the Left Bank's **Hôtel de l'Odéon,** a 16th-century building decked out in tapestries, paintings, skylights, and flower boxes; or the Restoration-style **Elysées** (near the Champs d'), where some rooms have views of Europe's greatest phallic symbol, the Eiffel Tower.

Where to find quirky, funky charm and low rent... For local color, nothing tops **Hotel Eldorado.** We'd give it no stars, and cite its noteworthy features—no TVs, no elevator, no phone. Yet we love it with all its zebra stripes, leopard prints, and unexpected garden patio. Its gracious owner, Anne Gratacos, has stamped her touch on everything from the dyed mud-cloth bedspreads to the colors of solid mustard or royal purple. The fleshpots of seedy place de Clichy are close at hand.

Best courtyard gardens... In the high-end 8th arrondissement, land is at a premium, so it's a distinct perk to have a garden big enough to stroll in, as guests do at the **Hôtel le Bristol,** a palace on the rue du Faubourg Saint-Honoré. The **Prince de Galles,** a luxury 8th-arrondissement hotel now owned by Starwood, has a large flower-filled courtyard garden, too. Then there are the gardens meant to dine in: Near the Tuileries, dinner is served in the flower-filled courtyard of the lavish **InterContinental,** where horse-drawn carriages once deposited visitors, while the handsome exterior of the **Holiday Inn,** on the otherwise undistinguished place de la République, hides a large interior garden where guests dine when the weather's fine. The gourmet restaurant Le Jardin is cradled under a glass bubble in the center of the lush courtyard garden of the **Royal Monceau,** off the Champs-Elysées.

Gardens are even more of a find over on the Left Bank. Most of the rooms in the refined 17th-century **Hôtel des Saints-Pères** overlook courtyard greenery. The individually decorated rooms of the **Relais Christine,** located in a former 16th-century convent on a quiet side street, look onto either a flower-strewn courtyard or a garden (breakfast here is served in one of the vaulted rooms of the cloister). The tiny courtyard of the delightful little **Hotel de la Tulipe,** near the first-rate rue Clerc market in the 7th arrondissement, is also an idyllic place to get a breath of fresh air over breakfast alfresco or a coffee in the afternoon.

Taking care of business... There's no central financial district in Paris; business travelers should choose a hotel near their clients or near the center of town. The big, modern hotels are the best for getting business done, but the decor is generally bland. The **Méridien Montparnasse** has modular conference and exhibition spaces with a capacity of up to 2,000 and a variety of services. The modern **Hilton Paris** has 15 meeting rooms, conference rooms with views over Paris, and two executive floors with a private lounge. The **Holiday Inn** on the place de la République is a classified historical monument, but the cookie-cutter rooms could be found in Kansas.

Those with hefty expense accounts can afford the rich atmosphere at the 8th-arrondissement palaces, though the business facilities may not be as extensive. The discreet Belle Epoque **Royal Monceau** in the same arrondissement is a fair runner-up for meetings. Near the place Vendôme, the **Ritz** goes only for smaller meetings (no riffraff, you know)—it can host up to 300 in its lavish meeting rooms. Businesspeople looking for a more intimate meeting venue can stay on the lovely Ile Saint-Louis; the quaint **Jeu de Paume,** constructed as a 17th-century tennis court by Louis XIII, has a seminar room for 25.

Family values... Most hotels in Paris have rooms that can accommodate three people (sometimes with a proper bed, sometimes with a cot), for hardly more than the cost of a double. But if you've got too many kids to squeeze into that configuration, or if you want a wall between you and other family members, you'll have to search for rare American-style connecting rooms. You will find a few connecting rooms at the friendly **Hotel des Grandes Ecoles** on a quiet cobbled side street; they also have good value triples and quads if you want to keep everyone under one roof and plan on a completely celibate vacation. **Relais du Louvre** also offers connecting rooms, as well as an apartment-size suite on the top floor, complete with kitchen and washer and dryer. An even better deal might be the nearby **Hôtel de l'Abbaye,** which has four duplex suites with terraces, or, one notch further up the price scale, the duplex suite at the **Relais Christine** (also on the Left Bank), with its warm, wood-paneled lobby and attractive rooms. As for kids' programs, kids' menus, game rooms, room service milk 'n' cookies, and all those other family-friendly perks that chain hotels lay on in America...forget about it.

For joggers... The **Hilton Paris,** located right next to the Eiffel Tower, has a jogging path, if running around the Champs de Mars in the 15th arrondissement is your idea of exercise. Those staying at the **Quai Voltaire** have the entire length of the Seine to run along, where you can suck up exhaust fumes to your heart's content. The **Pergolèse** is near the vast Bois de Boulogne, where you can amuse yourself while running by watching customers solicit the transvestite Brazilian prostitutes in the park. To be near the hottest jogging spot in Paris, the Jardin du Luxembourg, stay at the inexpensive **Cluny Sorbonne.** One favorite path for joggers is the Promenade Plantée starting just east of the Bastille and continuing all the way to the Bois de Vincennes on the converted and now green rooftop of an old train-trestle route. Staying anywhere along the Promenade may be blissful for joggers.

Totally Left Bank... This is still the hangout for the *gauche caviar* (limousine lefties), and the Sorbonne still dominates the cityscape as you mount the boulevard Saint Michel. If exposed beams spell charm for you, you'll love the Left Bank.

The **Académie,** on the fashionable rue des Saints-Pères, has been renovated to let its wooden beams and stone walls show through; bright fabrics, Oriental rugs, and 18th-century-style furniture carry through the decor. The **Odéon Hôtel,** on a side street off the boulevard Saint-Germain, not only has the exposed-beam thing going for it, it even has some romantic little rooms tucked up under the eaves. **Bersoly's Saint-Germain,** a gem of a hotel in a renovated town house, has small but pretty rooms, a vaulted basement breakfast room, and exposed beams. The **Angleterre** on the rue Jacob, with its individually decorated rooms, also has exposed beams, some four-poster beds, and a private garden. The lobby of the **Left Bank Saint-Germain,** with its 18th-century Aubusson tapestry, wood paneling, antique baby carriage, porcelain lamps, and Oriental carpets, sets the tone for the rest of the hotel. All hotels in this *très chic* area should be booked way, way, way ahead.

Over in the upscale residential areas near the Musée d'Orsay and the Seine, the **Bellechasse** is refreshingly down-to-earth, with bright, livable rooms and an upbeat staff (for Paris, they're downright chummy). Near the Jardin des Plantes, the **Libertel Maxim's** rooms are overdecorated in toile de Jouy fabric (walls, beds, drapes—*everything*), printed with scenes of life in old France. It hardly fits the Latin Quarter image, but has its own bizarre kind of charm.

Totally Right Bank... Here we're talking money: First and foremost is the stratospheric **Ritz** and other high-end places like the **Castille,** a fantasia on Venice that seems out of place until you realize that its sense of elegance is pure Paris. The **Hotel Saint-Honoré** is an oasis of 1930s-style elegance with the added advantage of having a restaurant whose chef, Eric Lecerf, is supervised by the supposedly retired master of French cuisine, Joël Robuchon. Around the corner on the rue des Capucines lies the modestly priced **Mansart,** its tasteful, modern decor an homage to Louis XIV's architect Mansart, who laid out the place Vendôme. Glitzy palaces may dominate the 8th arrondissement, but off the Champs-Elysées are the more affordable **Galileo,** a small, well-run hotel whose lounge boasts an 18th-century mantelpiece and an Aubusson tapestry, and the **Majestic,** near the Arc de Triomphe, where the ample rooms have Oriental rugs and period furniture. Near the ultra-posh avenue Montaigne is the **Marignan,** somewhat pricier digs with an uncluttered modern look; a collection of original paintings by contemporary artists decorates its walls.

The **Gaillon Opéra** is a small, moderately priced hotel near the Opéra Garnier, the Louvre, and the Palais Royal, with the kind of character you'd expect on the Left Bank. Also near the opera house and the major department stores is the midsize, mid-priced **Lafayette,** with a wood-paneled lobby that resembles a gentlemen's club. Across the street from the Louvre and Saint-Germain-l'Auxerrois, the church of the kings of France, the tiny **Place du Louvre** is a real budget-saving find: The attractive guest rooms are modern, but breakfast is served in a vaulted stone basement dating from the 14th century. Another find is the nearby **Ducs de Bourgogne,** where little touches like a hat rack with three antique *châpeaux* hanging on it show that attention is paid to detail.

Map 3: Right Bank Accommodations (1–4, 9–12 & 18e)

Castille **7**
Crillon **9**
Ducs de Bourgogne **16**
Eldorado **1**
Gaillon Opéra **4**
Grand Hôtel du Loiret **21**
Grand Hôtel Jeanne d'Arc **24**
Henri IV **19**
Holiday Inn Paris–République **20**
Hôtel Costes **10**
Hôtel de Lille **14**
Hôtel du Louvre **13**
InterContinental **11**
Jeu de Paume **23**
Lafayette **2**
Le Grand Hotel Paris **3**

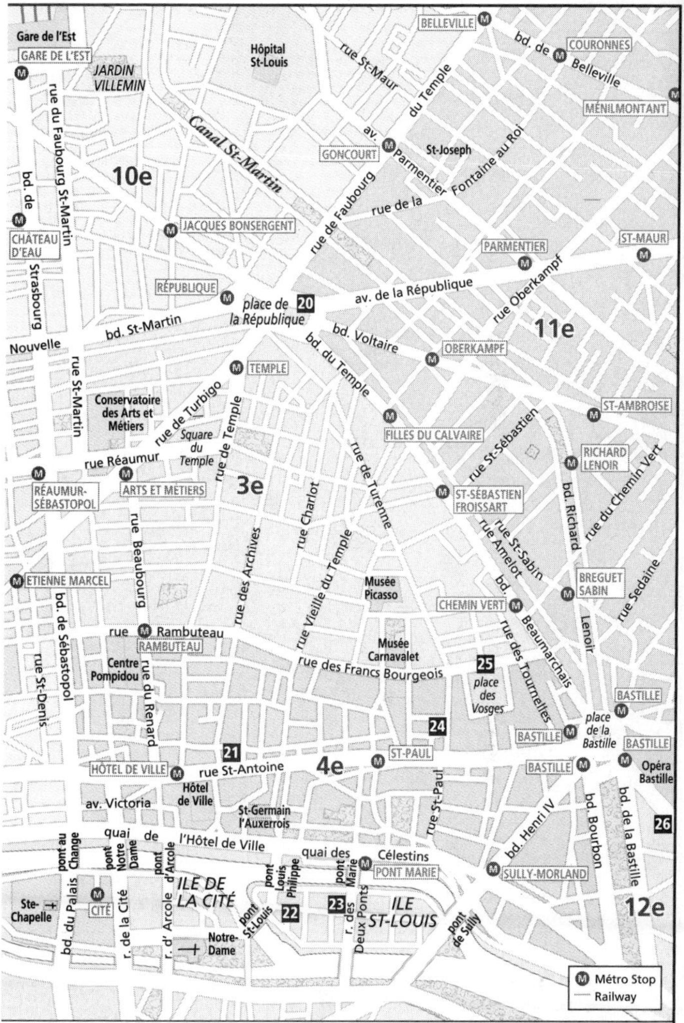

Gare de l'Est
GARE DE L'EST
JARDIN VILLEMIN
Hôpital St-Louis
BELLEVILLE
bd. de Belleville
COURONNES
MÉNILMONTANT
rue St-Maur
du Temple
av. Parmentier
GONCOURT
St-Joseph
rue de la Fontaine au Roi
Canal St-Martin
rue du Faubourg St-Martin
10e
bd. de Strasbourg
CHÂTEAU D'EAU
JACQUES BONSERGENT
rue de Faubourg
PARMENTIER
ST-MAUR
rue Oberkampf
RÉPUBLIQUE
place de la République
20
av. de la République
bd. St-Martin
bd. Voltaire
11e
Nouvelle
OBERKAMPF
bd. du Temple
TEMPLE
rue St-Martin
Conservatoire des Arts et Métiers
rue de Turbigo
rue de Temple
Square du Temple
ST-AMBROISE
FILLES DU CALVAIRE
rue St-Sébastien
RICHARD LENOIR
rue Réaumur
RÉAUMUR-SÉBASTOPOL
ARTS ET MÉTIERS
3e
rue de Turenne
ST-SÉBASTIEN FROISSART
bd. Richard Lenoir
rue du Chemin Vert
rue Charlot
rue St-Sabin
rue Amelot
rue des Archives
rue Vieille du Temple
ETIENNE MARCEL
rue Beaubourg
Musée Picasso
BREGUET SABIN
CHEMIN VERT
bd. Beaumarchais
rue Sedaine
bd. de Sébastopol
rue Rambuteau
RAMBUTEAU
Musée Carnavalet
rue St-Denis
Centre Pompidou
rue du Renard
rue des Francs Bourgeois
25
place des Vosges
rue des Tournelles
BASTILLE
place de la Bastille
24
21
HÔTEL DE VILLE
rue St-Antoine
4e
ST-PAUL
Opéra Bastille
Hôtel de Ville
av. Victoria
St-Germain l'Auxerrois
rue St-Paul
bd. Henri IV
bd. Bourbon
bd. de la Bastille
26
quai de l'Hôtel de Ville
quai des Célestins
pont au Change
pont Notre Dame
pont d'Arcole
pont Louis Philippe
pont Marie
PONT MARIE
SULLY-MORLAND
Ste-Chapelle
CITÉ
bd. du Palais
r. de la Cité
r. d' Arcole
ILE DE LA CITÉ
pont St-Louis
22
23
r. des Deux Ponts
ILE ST-LOUIS
pont de Sully
12e
Notre-Dame
Métro Stop
Railway

Lutèce **22**
Mansart **6**
Pavillon Bastille **26**
Pavillon de la Reine **25**
Place du Louvre **17**
Relais du Louvre **18**
Ritz **8**
Stendhal **5**
Style Hôtel **1**
TimHôtel Montmartre **1**
Vauvilliers **15**
Vendôme **12**

18e
17e
19e
9e
10e
8e
2e
3e
1er
20e
11e
16e
7e
4e
6e
5e
15e
12e
14e
13e

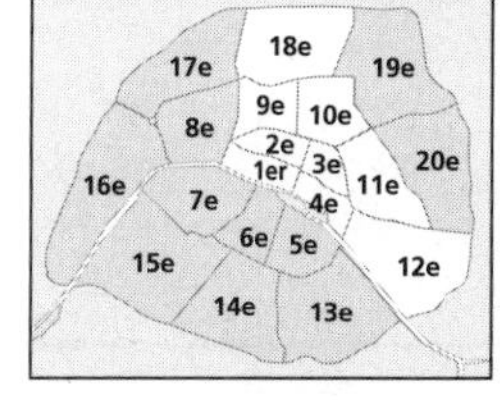

Map 4: Right Bank Accommodations (8 & 16–17e)

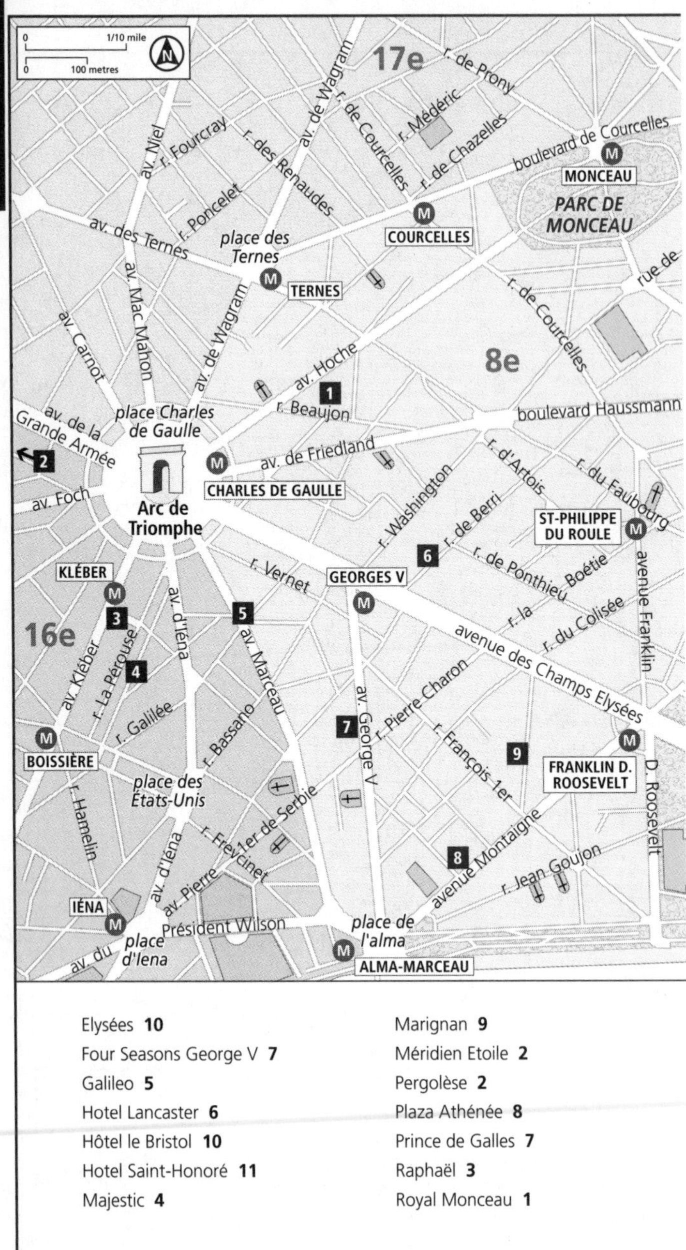

Elysées **10**
Four Seasons George V **7**
Galileo **5**
Hotel Lancaster **6**
Hôtel le Bristol **10**
Hotel Saint-Honoré **11**
Majestic **4**
Marignan **9**
Méridien Etoile **2**
Pergolèse **2**
Plaza Athénée **8**
Prince de Galles **7**
Raphaël **3**
Royal Monceau **1**

av. de Villiers
ROME
VILLIERS
r. de Constantinople
r. de Rome
r. Clapeyron
r. de St. Petersbourg
rue d'Amsterdam
rue de Clichy
r. Ballu
r. Moncey
LIÈGE
9e
place de l'Europe
r. de Londres
r. d'Athènes
r. Blanche
Monceau
bd. Malesherbes
r. du Gal. Foy
r. de Madrid
r. de Lisbonne
r. du Rocher
r. de Rome
Gare St-Lazare
r. de Miromesnil
r. de la Bienfaisance
av. de Messine
ST-LAZARE
TRINITÉ
rue St-lazare
place St-Augustin
r. de la Pépinière
r. Joubert
boulevard Haussmann
HAVRE CAUMARTIN
MIROMESNIL
r. la Boétie
ST-AUGUSTIN
r. des Mathurins
r. de Penthièvre
11
bd. Malesherbes
r. Auber
r. Scribe
St-Honoré
r. Tronchet
r. godot de Mauroy
Opéra Garnier
10
r. de Surène
L'OPÉRA
av. Matignon
place de la Madeleine
bd. des Capuchines
place de l'Opéra
2e
av. de Marigny
MADELEINE
r. du Faubourg St-Honoré
place Vendôme
CHAMPS-ÉLYSÉES CLEMENCEAU
r. Royale
CONCORDE
r. Casiglione
1er
place de la Concorde
r. de Rivoli
Cours la Reine
JARDIN DES TUILERIES
Seine
Métro
17e
18e
19e
8e
9e
10e
2e
1er
3e
20e
16e
7e
11e
4e
6e
5e
15e
12e
14e
13e

Map 5: Left Bank Accommodations (5–6 & 13–14e)

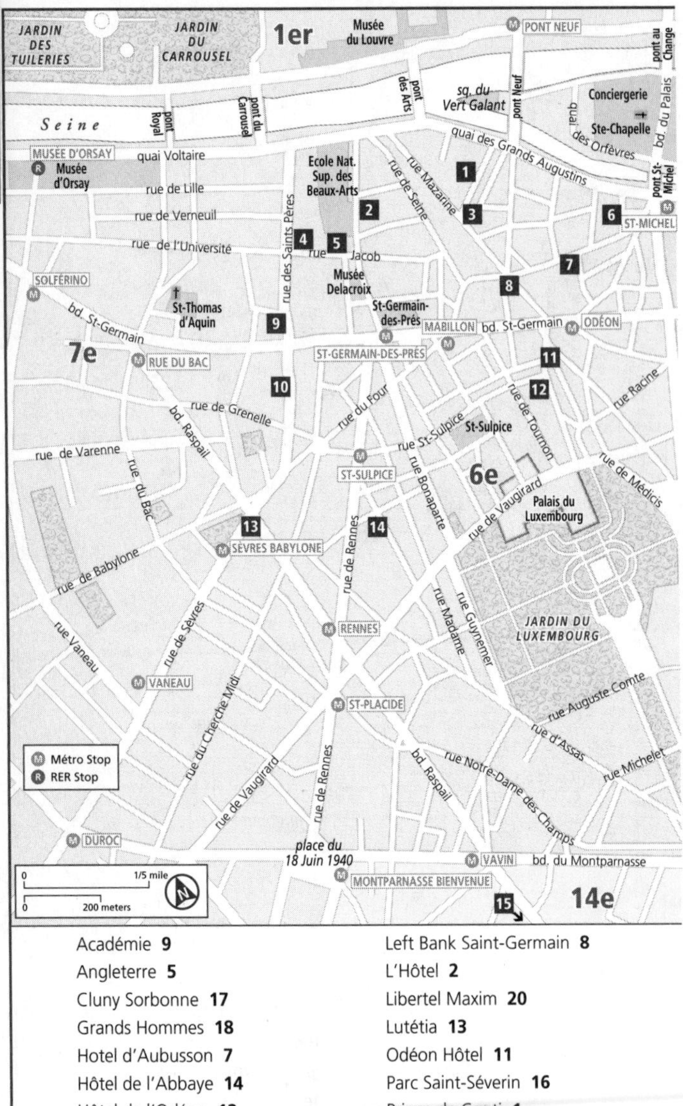

Académie **9**
Angleterre **5**
Cluny Sorbonne **17**
Grands Hommes **18**
Hotel d'Aubusson **7**
Hôtel de l'Abbaye **14**
Hôtel de l'Odéon **12**
Hôtel de Nesle **3**
Hotel des Grandes Ecoles **19**
Hôtel des Saints-Pères **10**
Istria **15**
Left Bank Saint-Germain **8**
L'Hôtel **2**
Libertel Maxim **20**
Lutétia **13**
Odéon Hôtel **11**
Parc Saint-Séverin **16**
Prince de Conti **1**
Relais Christine **7**
Relais Hotel du Vieux Paris **6**
Rive Gauche **4**

SULLY MORLAND
PONT MARIE
4e
pont Notre-Dame
pont d'Arcole
pont Louis Philippe
pont Marie
quai de Bourbon
quai d'Anjou
CITÉ
ILE DE LA CITÉ
rue St-Louis en l'Ile
ILE ST-LOUIS
St-Louis en l'Ile
r. de la Cité
rue de Cloître N.Dame
pont St-Louis
quai d'Orléans
quai de Béthune
Notre-Dame
pont de Sully
Petit Pont
pont au Double
pont de la Tournelle
Seine
ST-MICHEL/ NOTRE-DAME
quai de la Tournelle
Institut du Monde Arabe
16
St-Nicolas
rue Monge
quai St-Bernard
bd. St-Germain
CLUNY–LA SORBONNE
Musée de Cluny
Lemoine
Universités ParisVI-Paris VII
rue Cuvier
rue des Ecoles
rue Jussieu
MAUBERT MUTUALITÉ
Sorbonne
JUSSIEU
JARDIN DES PLANTES
rue St-Jacques
rue Valette
CARDINAL LEMOINE
St-Etienne du Mont
rue Linné
Arènes de Lutèce
17
rue Cujas
rue du Cardinal
19
Panthéon
rue Monge
Museum National d'Histoire Naturelle
rue Soufflot
18
rue St-Hilaire
rue Mouffetard
LUXEMBOURG
5e
PLACE MONGE
bd. St-Michel
rue Lhomond
rue d'Ulm
rue Gay Lussac
CENSIER DAUBENTON
rue Brossolette
20
LUXEMBOURG
Ecole Normale Superieure
rue Monge
rue Bernard
bd. St-Marcel
rue du Val de Grâce
rue Nicole
rue St-Jacques
rue Berthollet
Val-de-Grâce
LES GOBELINS
PORT ROYAL
bd. de Port Royal
bd. de Port Royal
13e
bd. Arago

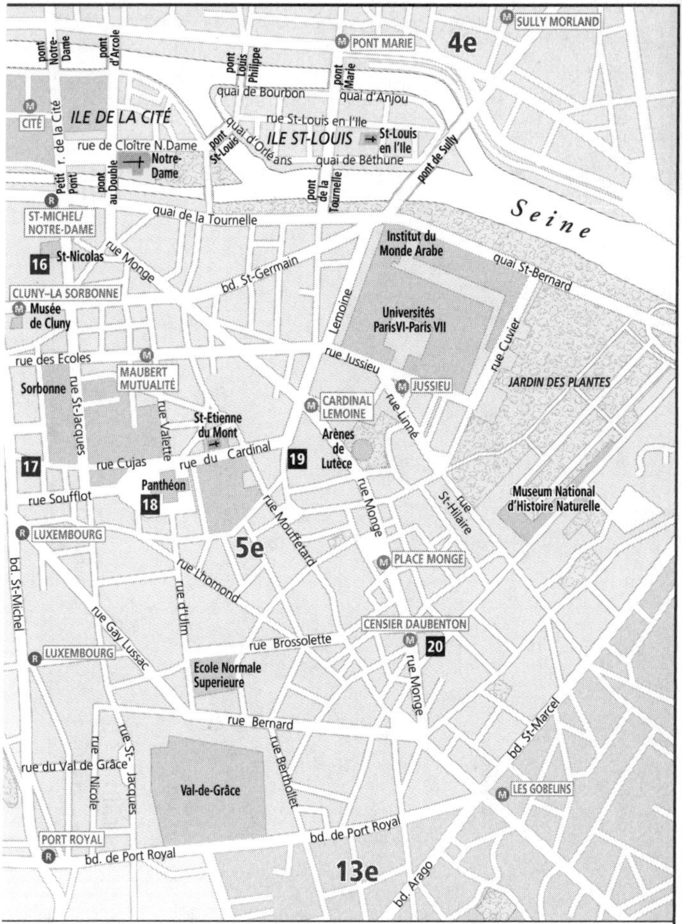

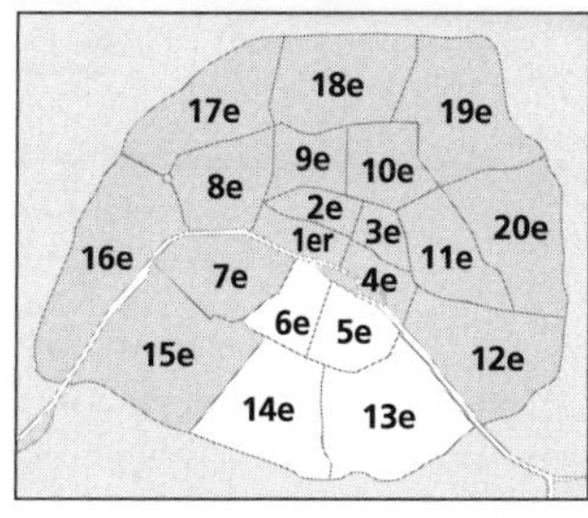

18e
17e
19e
9e
10e
8e
2e
1er
3e
20e
16e
7e
4e
11e
6e
5e
15e
12e
14e
13e

Map 6: Left Bank Accommodations (7 & 15e)

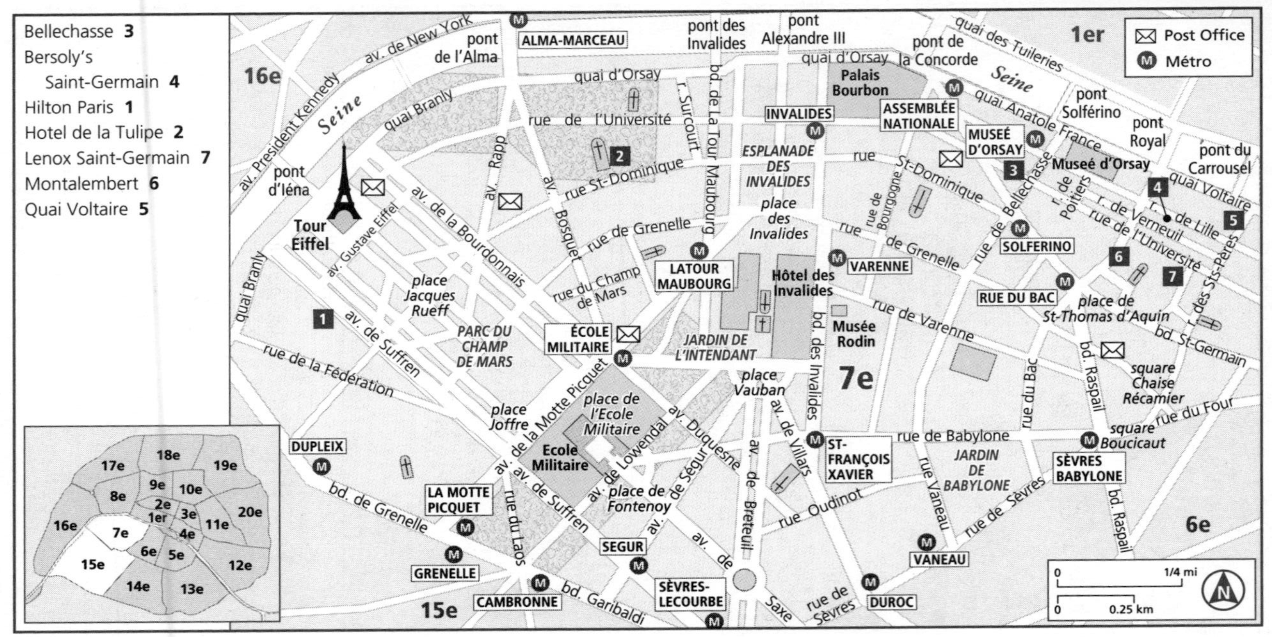

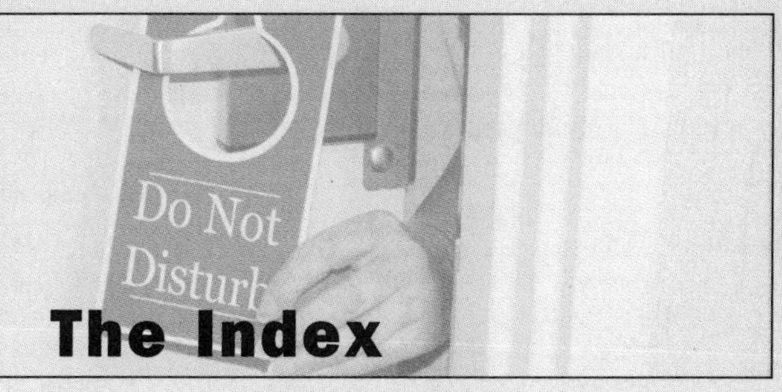

The Index

Note:	1€ = $1.25 U.S.
$$$$$	more than 300€ ($390)
$$$$	205€–300€ ($267–$390)
$$$	140€–205€ ($182–$267)
$$	75€–140€ ($98–$182)
$	less than 75€ ($98)

Price ratings are based on the lowest price quoted for a standard double room in high season, including taxes and charges.

The following abbreviations are used for credit cards:

AE	American Express
DC	Diners Club
DISC	Discover
MC	MasterCard
V	Visa

The word "Hôtel" is often omitted here if it's the first word in the name of the hotel. The arrondissement number is the last two digits of the postal code.

Hotel websites change frequently; if you have trouble with the ones given below, look up the hotel at www.pagesjaunes.fr (France's Yellow Pages), which will provide the most current Web address. And, you can call up a detailed street map and print it.

Académie (p. 32) EIFFEL TOWER Just a block away from dueling cafés the Deux Magots and the Flore, this hotel boasts wooden beams, stone walls, bright fabrics, Oriental rugs, and 18th-century-style furniture in a 17th-century building.... *Tel 800/246-0041 in U.S., or 01-45-48-36-22. Fax 800/246-0041 in U.S. or 01-45-44-75-24. www.academiehotel.com. 32, rue des Saints-Pères, 75007. Métro St-Germain-des-Prés. 34 rooms. MC, V. $$$*

See Map 5 on p. 38.

Angleterre (p. 26) ST-GERMAIN-DES-PRES Each room in this Left Bank hotel has its own charm, whether it be a four-poster bed, exposed beams, or a view of the garden. Halfway between the boulevard Saint-Germain and the Seine.... *Tel 01-42-60-34-72. Fax 01-42-60-16-93. 44, rue Jacob, 75006. Métro St-Germain-des-Prés. 27 rooms. AE, DC, MC, V. $$$–$$$$*

See Map 5 on p. 38.

Bellechasse (p. 33) EIFFEL TOWER Comfortable, cheerfully decorated rooms. Great location near the Musée d'Orsay and the Seine.... *Tel 01-45-50-22-31. Fax 01-45-51-52-36. www.mercure.com. 8, rue Bellechasse, 75007. Métro Solférino. 41 rooms. DC, MC, V. $$$*

See Map 6 on p. 40.

Bersoly's Saint-Germain (p. 32) EIFFEL TOWER A tiny, quiet hotel in a wonderful renovated Left Bank town house.... *Tel 01-42-60-73-79. Fax 01-49-27-05-55. www.bersolyshotel.com. 28, rue de Lille, 75007. Métro St-Germain-des-Prés or Rue du Bac. 16 rooms. Closed second half of Aug. AE, MC, V. $$*

See Map 6 on p. 40.

Castille (p. 33) LOUVRE/LES HALLES An elegant Venetian-style hotel near the exclusive place Vendôme.... *Tel 800/763-4835 in the U.S., or 01-44-58-44-58. Fax 01-44-58-44-00. 37, rue Cambon, 75001. www.sofitel.com. Métro Concorde. 111 rooms and duplex suites. AE, DC, MC, V. $$$$$*

See Map 3 on p. 34.

Cluny Sorbonne (p. 32) LATIN QUARTER Across the street from the Sorbonne and a short walk (or jog) to the Jardin de Luxembourg. The rooms are small and the bathrooms cramped, but the price is right.... *Tel 01-43-54-66-66. Fax 01-43-29-68-07. www.hotel-cluny.fr. 8, rue Victor Cousin, 75005. Métro Luxembourg or St-Michel. 23 rooms. AE, DC, MC, V. $$*

See Map 5 on p. 38.

Crillon (p. 22) CHAMPS-ELYSEES Palace hotel overlooking the place de la Concorde. The salons boast 17th- and 18th-century tapestries, gilt-and-brocade furniture, and Louis XVI chests and chairs. Home of the acclaimed restaurant Les Ambassadeurs, another restaurant called L'Obélisque, and a courtyard garden.... *Tel 800/223-6800 in the U.S., or 01-44-71-15-00. Fax 01-44-71-15-03. www.crillon.com. 10, place de la Concorde, 75008. Métro Concorde. 120 rooms and 43 suites. AE, DC, MC, V. $$$$$*

See Map 3 on p. 34.

Ducs de Bourgogne (p. 33) LOUVRE/LES HALLES The price is right at this hotel, located between the Louvre and Châtelet and directly across the river from the Left Bank via the Pont Neuf.... *Tel 01-42-33-95-64. Fax 01-40-39-01-25. www.hotel-paris-bourgogne.com. 19, rue du Pont-Neuf, 75001. Métro Louvre Rivoli or Châtelet. 50 rooms. AE, DC, MC, V. $$$*

See Map 3 on p. 34.

Eldorado (p. 30) MONTMARTRE This cheap sleep oozes a personal, funky charm and is a most desirable place to stay. Located in a corner of Montmartre, it evokes a Paris of yesterday. From its crooked, wooden stairs to its bizarre color scheme, it exudes atmosphere. It's not everyone's cuppa, but a hell of a lot of fun.... *Tel 01-45-22-35-21. Fax 01-43-87-25-95. www.eldoradohotel.fr. 18, rue des Dames, 70017. Métro Place de Clichy. 33 rooms. AE, DC, MC, V. $*

See Map 3 on p. 34.

Elysées (p. 30) CHAMPS-ELYSEES This Restoration-style hotel has some top-floor Eiffel Tower views.... *Tel 01-42-65-29-25. Fax 01-42-65-64-28. 12, rue des Saussaies, 75008. Métro Champs Elysées Clemenceau. 32 rooms. AE, DC, MC, V. $$*

See Map 4 on p. 36.

Four Seasons George V (p. 22) CHAMPS-ELYSEES This legendary pile has been totally overhauled to make it into the first high-tech palace hotel in Paris. Great health club with pool.... *Tel 800/332-3442 in the U.S., or 01-49-52-70-00. Fax 01-49-52-70-20. www.fourseasons.com. 31, av. George V, 75008. Métro George V. 245 rooms, including 61 suites, 47 with private terraces. AE, DC, MC, V. $$$$$*

See Map 4 on p. 36.

Gaillon Opéra (p. 33) OPERA GARNIER A small hotel near the Opéra Garnier, the Louvre, and the Palais Royal with rustic touches to its decor.... *Tel 01-47-42-47-74. Fax 01-47-42-01-23. www.hotel-paris-gaillon-opera.com. 9, rue Gaillon, 75002. Métro Opéra. 26 rooms. AE, DC, MC, V. $$$*

See Map 3 on p. 34.

Galileo (p. 33) CHAMPS-ELYSEES Small hotel with handsome lounge and small, well-equipped rooms.... *Tel 01-47-20-66-06. Fax 01-47-20-67-17. www.galileohotel.com. 54, rue Galiliée, 75008. Métro George V. 27 rooms. AE, DC, MC, V. $$$*

See Map 4 on p. 36.

Grand Hôtel du Loiret (p. 26) MARAIS Small, basic Marais hotel.... *Tel 01-48-87-77-00. Fax 01-48-04-96-56. 8, rue des Mauvais-Garçons, 75004. Métro Hôtel de Ville. 29 rooms. MC, V. $–$$*

See Map 3 on p. 34.

Grand Hôtel Jeanne d'Arc (p. 25) MARAIS An attractive hotel on a quiet street not far from the Bastille. A very good deal. Reserve in advance.... *Tel 01-48-87-62-11. Fax 01-48-87-37-31. www.hoteljeannedarc.com. 3, rue de Jarente, 75004. Métro St-Paul. 36 rooms. V. $$*

See Map 3 on p. 34.

Grands Hommes (p. 28) LATIN QUARTER The "great men" referred to in the name of this comfortable renovated hotel are buried in the Panthéon across the road.... *Tel 01-46-34-19-60. Fax 01-43-26-67-32. www.hoteldesgrandshommes.com. 17, place du Panthéon, 75005. Métro Luxembourg. 36 rooms. AE, DC, MC, V. $$$*

See Map 5 on p. 38.

Henri IV (p. 26) ILE DE LA CITE Very inexpensive hotel near the Louvre. Rooms are small and very basic, with the shower and toilet down the hall for most, but the place is clean. Book far in advance.... *Tel 01-43-54-44-53. 25, place Dauphine, 75001. Métro Pont Neuf or Cité. 22 rooms. MC, V. $*

See Map 3 on p. 34.

Hilton Paris (p. 24) EIFFEL TOWER Next to the Eiffel Tower, the Hilton is 1960s modern; the rooms are spacious, comfortable, and well-equipped.... *Tel 01-44-38-56-00. Fax 01-44-38-56-10. www.hilton.com. 18, av. Suffren, 75015. Métro Bir-Hakeim. 462 rooms and suites. AE, DC, MC, V. $$$$*

See Map 6 on p. 40.

Holiday Inn Paris–République (p. 24) BASTILLE Typical Holiday Inn–style rooms on the place de la République. Restaurant, bar, garden.... *Tel 01-43-55-44-34. Fax 01-47-00-32-34. www.paris-republique.holiday-inn.com. 10, place de la République, 75011. Métro République. 318 rooms. AE, DC, MC, V. $$$$*

See Map 3 on p. 34.

Hôtel Costes (p. 23) LOUVRE/LES HALLES Fashion victims fill the lobby of what is now the trendiest hotel in town, around the corner from the place Vendôme. The elaborate neoclassical decor is rich and comfy.... *Tel 01-42-44-50-00. Fax 01-42-44-50-01. 239, rue St-Honoré, 75001. Métro Tuileries. 82 rooms. AE, DC, MC, V. $$$$$*

See Map 3 on p. 34.

Hotel d'Aubusson (p. 24) ST-GERMAIN-DES-PRES This classy boutique hotel, just a few steps from the Odéon, has a lot of seigniorial medieval charm with parquet floors, beamed ceilings, and antiques. Ask for one of the rooms with a canopied bed to really get in the mood.... *Tel 01-43-29-43-43. Fax 01-43-29-12-62. www.aubusson-paris-hotel.com. 33, rue Dauphine, 75006. Métro Odéon. 49 rooms. AE, DC, MC, V. $$$$*

See Map 5 on p. 38.

Hôtel de l'Abbaye (p. 31) ST-GERMAIN-DES-PRES Lovely 18th-century hotel, on a quiet Left Bank side street, with 4 duplex suites.... *Tel 01-45-44-38-11. Fax 01-45-48-07-86. www.hotel-abbaye.com. 10, rue Cassette, 75006. Métro St-Sulpice. 46 rooms and suites. AE, MC, V. $$$*

See Map 5 on p. 38.

Hotel de la Tulipe (p. 30) EIFFEL TOWER A real gem tucked away in a pleasant neighborhood with a great market and surprisingly cheap cafés to hang out in; about a 10-minute walk from the Eiffel Tower. The friendly owners are a font of local information.... *Tel 01-45-51-67-21. Fax 01-47-53-96-37. www.paris-hotel-tulipe.com. 33, rue Malar, 75007. Métro La Tour-Maubourg or Invalides, RER Pont de l'Alma or Aerogare des Invalides. 21 rooms and 1 suite. AE, MC, V. $$$*

See Map 6 on p. 40.

Hôtel de Lille (p. 25) LOUVRE/LES HALLES This is a serious budget address, so don't expect phones, minibars, or even a shower in your room unless you ask for one. On the other hand, this place is clean, friendly, and well-located. Book well in advance.... *Tel 01-42-33-33-42. www.hotel-paris-lille.com. 8, rue du Pelican, 75001. Métro Odéon. 13 rooms. AE, DC, MC, V. $–$$*

See Map 3 on p. 34.

Hôtel de l'Odéon (p. 30) ST-GERMAIN-DES-PRES Beautifully furnished, this 16th-century building has the added advantage of a Saint-Germain-des-Prés location. Small garden.... *Tel 01-43-25-70-11. Fax 01-43-29-97-34. www.paris-hotel-odeon.com. 13, rue St-Sulpice, 75006. Métro Odéon. 29 rooms. AE, DC, MC, V. $$$*

See Map 5 on p. 38.

Hôtel de Nesle (p. 25) ST-GERMAIN-DES-PRES A low-priced Left Bank hotel with plenty of character. No reservations accepted; call around 9am the day of arrival.... *Tel 01-43-54-62-41. Fax 01-43-54-31-88. 7, rue de Nesle, 75006. Métro Odéon. 20 rooms. MC, V. $–$$*

See Map 5 on p. 38.

Hotel des Grandes Ecoles (p. 31) LATIN QUARTER There's something winsomely winning about this rather rustic hotel, which is actually a complex of 3 old buildings joined together around a shaded garden. Accommodations range from snug, cozy doubles to more spacious chambers.... *Tel 01-43-26-79-23. Fax 01-43-25-28-15. www.hotel-grandes-ecoles.com. 75, rue du Cardinal Lemoine, 75005. Métro Cardinal Lemoine. 51 rooms. MC, V. $$*

See Map 5 on p. 38.

Hôtel des Saints-Pères (p. 30) ST-GERMAIN-DES-PRES Most rooms in this 17th-century hotel overlook the courtyard garden. The good-size rooms are tastefully decorated.... *Tel 01-45-44-50-00. Fax 01-45-44-90-83. www.esprit-de-france.com. 65, rue des Saints-Pères, 75006, Métro St-Germain-des-Prés. 39 rooms. AE, MC, V. $$*

See Map 5 on p. 38.

Hôtel du Louvre (p. 27) LOUVRE/LES HALLES Lavish 19th-century hotel; Impressionist painter Camille Pissarro immortalized the view from his room here. In-house restaurant and café.... *Tel 800/888-4747 in the U.S., or 01-44-58-38-38. Fax 01-44-58-38-01. www.hoteldulouvre.com. 1, place André Malraux, 75001. Métro Palais Royal. 197 rooms and suites. AE, DC, MC, V. $$$$$*

See Map 3 on p. 34.

Hotel Lancaster (p. 24) CHAMPS-ELYSEES Now that the Champs-Elysées is on the up and up, this venerable vest-pocket luxury hotel is a truly fine address if you want a calm, elegant, clubby luxury pad in a good location.... *Tel 800/223-6800 in the U.S., or*

01-40-76-40-76. Fax 01-40-76-40-00. www.hotel-lancaster.fr. 7, rue de Berri, 75008. Métro George V. 50 rooms and 7 suites. AE, DC, MC, V. $$$$$

See Map 4 on p. 36.

Hôtel le Bristol (p. 21) CHAMPS-ELYSEES A palace hotel on a famed designer shopping street, with spacious ornate rooms, swimming pool, enormous garden, fitness center, and sauna. Saturdays in the bar, guests can preview the latest styles from Parisian fashion houses.... *Tel 01-53-43-43-00. Fax 01-53-43-43-26. www.lebristolparis.com. 112, rue du Faubourg-St-Honoré, 75008. Métro St-Philippe-du-Roule or Miromesnil. 157 rooms and 23 suites. AE, DC, MC, V. $$$$$*

See Map 4 on p. 36.

Hotel Saint-Honoré (p. 33) CHAMPS-ELYSEES In the heart of Proust country and near the high-fashion shopping drag, the Rue du Faubourg-Saint-Honoré, this is a discreet hideaway.... *Tel 01-53-05-05-05. Fax 01-53-05-05-30. 11, rue d'Astorg, 75008. Métro Champs-Elysées Clemenceau. 134 rooms. AE, DC, MC, V. $$$$$*

See Map 4 on p. 36.

Ibis (p. 25) CITYWIDE There are about 20 of these functional, cheap, clean hotels for low-budget business travelers scattered around Paris.... *Tel 800/221–4542 in the U.S., or 01-43-22-00-09. Fax 01-43-20-21-78. www.ibishotel.com. 160, rue du Chateau, 75014. Métro Pernety. 60 rooms. AE, DC, MC, V. $$*

InterContinental (p. 22) LOUVRE/LES HALLES More than a century old, this hotel now attracts many business travelers and has been completely renovated.... *Tel 01-44-77-11-11. Fax 01-44-77-14-60. www.interconti.com. 3, rue Castiglione, 75001. Métro Concorde. 450 rooms and suites. AE, DC, MC, V. $$$$$*

See Map 3 on p. 34.

Istria (p. 29) MONTPARNASSE This comfortable small hotel has hosted Nancy Cunard, Rainer Maria Rilke, Marcel Duchamp, and Man Ray, among others.... *Tel 01-43-20-91-82. Fax 01-43-22-48-45. 29, rue Campagne-Première, 75014. Métro Raspail. 26 rooms. AE, DC, MC, V. $$*

See Map 5 on p. 38.

Jeu de Paume (p. 31) ILE ST-LOUIS Louis XIII's tennis court is now a hotel with a handsomely decorated, rustic interior. Private garden.... *Tel 01-43-26-14-18. Fax 01-40-46-02-76. www.jeudepaumehotel.com. 54, rue St-Louis-en-l'Ile, 75004. Métro Pont Marie. 30 rooms. AE, DC, MC, V. $$$$*

See Map 3 on p. 34.

Lafayette (p. 33) OPERA GARNIER A bit off the beaten track, but within walking distance of the Opéra Garnier and the major department stores.... *Tel 01-42-85-05-44. Fax 01-49-95-06-60.*

www.accorhotels.com. 49, rue Lafayette, 75009. Métro Le Peletier. 105 rooms. AE, DC, MC, V. $$$

See Map 3 on p. 34.

Left Bank Saint-Germain (p. 28) ST-GERMAIN-DES-PRES Rooms have exposed beams, antiques, marble bathrooms, air-conditioning, and soundproofing. In the heart of the Left Bank.... *Tel 01-43-54-01-70. Fax 01-43-26-17-14. 9, rue de l'Ancienne Comédie, 75006. Métro Odéon. 31 rooms. AE, DC, MC, V. $$$*

See Map 5 on p. 38.

Le Grand Hotel Paris (p. 23) OPERA GARNIER After some ups and downs, this hotel has been restored to its grand old self, though rooms are modernized. Fitness center, the famous Café de la Paix, and 2 restaurants.... *Tel 01-40-07-32-32. Fax 01-42-66-12-51. http://paris-le-grand.intercontinental.com. 2, rue Scribe, 75009. Métro Opéra. 578 rooms, including 60 suites. AE, DC, MC, V. $$$$$*

See Map 3 on p. 34.

Lenox Saint-Germain (p. 26) ST-GERMAIN-DES-PRES This Left Bank hotel has been attracting a literary clientele for decades, but now guests are more likely to be in the fashion business.... *Tel 01-42-96-10-95. Fax 01-42-61-52-83. www.lenox saintgermain.com. 9, rue de l'Université, 75007. Métro Rue du Bac or St-Germain-des-Prés. 34 rooms. AE, DC, MC, V. $$*

See Map 6 on p. 40.

L'Hôtel (p. 27) ST-GERMAIN-DES-PRES This eccentric baroque Left Banker is much-coveted as a place to stay.... *Tel 01-44-41-99-00. Fax 01-43-25-64-81. www.l-hotel.com. 13, rue des Beaux-Arts, 75006. Métro St-Germain-des-Prés. 20 rooms. AE, DC, MC, V. $$$$*

See Map 5 on p. 38.

Libertel Maxim (p. 33) LATIN QUARTER Little hotel near the Jardin des Plantes.... *Tel 01-43-31-16-15. Fax 01-43-31-93-87. www.mercure.com. 28, rue Censier, 75005. Métro Censier Daubenton. 36 rooms. AE, DC, MC, V. $$$*

See Map 5 on p. 38.

Lutèce (p. 28) ILE ST-LOUIS One of a few hotels on pretty little Ile Saint-Louis, this one is cozy and attractive; some rooms have views.... *Tel 01-43-26-23-52. Fax 01-43-29-60-25. www.hotel delutece.com. 65, rue St-Louis-en-l'Ile, 75004. Métro Pont Marie. 23 rooms. AE, MC, V. $$$*

See Map 3 on p. 34.

Lutétia (p. 27) ST-GERMAIN-DES-PRES A large Art Deco hotel near Montparnasse with many great names in the guest books.... *Tel 01-49-54-46-46. Fax 01-49-54-46-00. www.lutetia-paris.com. 45, bd. Raspail, 75006. Métro Sèvres Babylone. 200 rooms and 10 suites. AE, DC, MC, V. $$$$$*

See Map 5 on p. 38.

Majestic (p. 33) CHAMPS-ELYSEES Solid comfort near the Arc de Triomphe and the Champs-Elysées; good-size rooms.... *Tel 01-45-00-83-70. Fax 01-45-00-29-48. www.majestic-hotel.com. 29, rue Dumont d'Urville, 75016. Métro Etoile. 31 rooms, including 2 apartments and 1 penthouse. AE, DC, MC, V. $$$$*

See Map 4 on p. 36.

Mansart (p. 33) LOUVRE/LES HALLES An attractive modern decor designed as an homage to Louis XIV's architect Mansart.... *Tel 01-42-61-50-28. Fax 01-49-27-97-44. www.esprit-de-france.com. 5, rue des Capucines, 75001. Métro Opéra. 57 rooms. AE, DC, MC, V. $$$*

See Map 3 on p. 34.

Marignan (p. 33) CHAMPS-ELYSEES A clean, modern decor and a collection of original paintings by contemporary artists. In-house restaurant and tearoom.... *Tel 01-40-76-34-56. Fax 01-40-76-34-34. www.sofitel.com. 12, rue Marignan, 75008. Métro Franklin D Roosevelt. 57 rooms and 16 duplex suites. AE, DC, MC, V. $$$$$*

See Map 4 on p. 36.

Méridien Etoile (p. 25) PARC MONCEAU A 1972 chain hotel with live jazz nightly in the Lionel Hampton Jazz Club in the lobby and 3 restaurants... *Tel 01-40-68-34-34. Fax 01-40-68-31-31. www.lemeridien.com. 81, bd. Gouvion-St.-Cyr, 75017. Métro Porte Maillot. 1,025 rooms. AE, DC, MC, V. $$$$$*

See Map 4 on p. 36.

Méridien Montparnasse (p. 25) MONTPARNASSE The modern business high-rise par excellence. Near Montparnasse train station. 2 restaurants.... *Tel 01-44-36-44-36. Fax 01-40-55-47-00. www.lemeridien.com. 19, rue de Commandant Mouchotte, 75014. Métro Montparnasse Bienvenüe. 953 rooms and suites. AE, DC, MC, V. $$$$$*

Montalembert (p. 24) EIFFEL TOWER A once-staid hotel that has gone trendy. All rooms have marble bathrooms. Portable phones available to guests (no rental fee, charged by the call).... *Tel 800/786-6397 in the U.S., or 01-45-49-68-68. Fax 01-45-49-69-49. www.montalembert.com. 3, rue Montalembert, 75007. Métro Rue du Bac. 51 rooms and 5 suites. AE, DC, MC, V. $$$$$*

See Map 6 on p. 40.

Odéon Hôtel (p. 32) ST-GERMAIN-DES-PRES A small Left Bank hotel with modern amenities (air-conditioning, hair dryers, etc.) and the charm of individually decorated rooms and exposed beams. Reminiscent of a contemporary Norman country inn.... *Tel 01-43-25-90-67. Fax 01-43-25-55-98. www.odeonhotel.fr. 3, rue de l'Odéon, 75006. Métro Odéon. 33 rooms. AE, DC, MC, V. $$$*

See Map 5 on p. 38.

Parc Saint-Séverin (p. 28) LATIN QUARTER This find has simple, attractive modern decor with scattered period furniture. Some rooms have large terraces with views.... *Tel 01-43-54-32-17.*

Fax 01-43-54-70-71. www.esprit-de-france.com. 22, rue de la Parcheminerie, 75005. Métro St-Michel or Cluny. 27 rooms. AE, DC, MC, V. $$

See Map 5 on p. 38.

Pavillon Bastille (p. 24) BASTILLE Designer decor in bright yellow and deep blue. For opera lovers, the hotel has special arrangements for obtaining tickets (often hard to get) for the Opéra Bastille; ask when you reserve.... *Tel 01-43-43-65-65. Fax 01-43-43-96-52. www.pavillon-bastille.com. 65, rue de Lyon, 75012. Métro Bastille. 24 rooms and 1 suite. AE, DC, MC, V. $$$*

See Map 3 on p. 34.

Pavillon de la Reine (p. 29) MARAIS This hotel on the beautiful place des Vosges has lovely gardens. It looks old, but only part of it dates from the 17th century.... *Tel 01-40-29-19-19. Fax 01-40-29-19-20. www.pavillon-de-la-reine.com. 28, place des Vosges, 75003. Métro St-Paul. 45 rooms and 10 suites. AE, DC, MC, V. $$$$$*

See Map 3 on p. 34.

Pergolèse (p. 32) BOIS DE BOULOGNE Spacious and modern, with splashes of warm color. One beautiful room under the eaves has a view of the neighboring rooftops.... *Tel 01-53-64-04-04. Fax 01-53-64-04-40. www.hotelpergolese.com. 3, rue Pergolèse, 75016. Métro Argentine. 40 rooms. AE, DC, MC, V. $$$$*

See Map 4 on p. 36.

Place du Louvre (p. 33) LOUVRE/LES HALLES A tiny hotel near the Louvre with attractively furnished modern rooms and a breakfast room in a 14th-century vaulted stone basement.... *Tel 01-42-33-78-68. Fax 01-42-33-09-95. www.esprit-de-france.com. 21, rue des Prêtres-St-Germain-l'Auxerrois, 75001. Métro Louvre Rivoli or Pont-Neuf. 20 rooms. AE, DC, MC, V. $$*

See Map 3 on p. 34.

Plaza Athénée (p. 22) CHAMPS-ELYSEES Elegant palace hotel. Rooms and suites are decorated in Louis XV, Louis XVI, and Regency styles. Home of the gourmet restaurant Le Régence, the more casual Le Relais, and an English-style bar.... *Tel 01-53-67-66-65. Fax 01-53-67-66-66. www.plaza-athenee-paris.com. 25, av. Montaigne, 75008. Métro Franklin D Roosevelt. 205 rooms and suites. AE, DC, MC, V. $$$$$*

See Map 4 on p. 36.

Prince de Conti (p. 29) ST-GERMAIN-DES-PRES English-style comfort in a small, handsome, 18th-century building near the Seine, surrounded by art galleries, antique shops, and boutiques. All rooms are air-conditioned and soundproofed.... *Tel 01-44-07-30-40. Fax 01-44-07-36-34. 8, rue Guénégaud, 75006. Métro Odéon. 26 rooms, plus 6 in annex. AE, DC, MC, V. $$$*

See Map 5 on p. 38.

Prince de Galles (p. 22) CHAMPS-ELYSEES Art Deco palace with flower-filled courtyard garden and rooms decorated in yellow or blue toile de Jouy fabric. Some rooms have balconies. In-house restaurant, Le Jardin des Cygnes.... *Tel 01-53-23-77-77. Fax 01-53-23-78-78. www.starwood.com. 33, av. George-V, 75008. Métro Odéon. 168 rooms and suites. AE, DC, MC, V. $$$$$*

See Map 4 on p. 36.

Quai Voltaire (p. 27) EIFFEL TOWER Left Bank hotel with great views over the Seine toward the Louvre and the Tuileries Garden. Insist on one of the 29 rooms in the front of the hotel.... *Tel 01-42-61-50-91. Fax 01-42-61-62-26. www.quaivoltaire.fr. 19, quai Voltaire, 75007. Métro Rue du Bac. 33 rooms. AE, DC, MC, V. $$*

See Map 6 on p. 40.

Raphaël (p. 22) BOIS DE BOULOGNE Old-world opulence at one of the palace hotels. The wood-paneled, English-style bar is a popular celebrity meeting place.... *Tel 01-53-64-32-00. Fax 01-53-64-32-01. www.raphael-hotel.com. 17, av. Kléber, 75016. Métro Kléber. 90 rooms and suites. AE, DC, MC, V. $$$$$*

See Map 4 on p. 36.

Relais Christine (p. 30) ST-GERMAIN-DES-PRES A former 16th-century convent located on a quiet Left Bank side street.... *Tel 01-40-51-60-80. Fax 01-40-51-60-81. www.relais-christine.com. 3, rue Christine, 75006. Métro St-Michel or Odéon. 51 rooms. AE, DC, MC, V. $$$$*

See Map 5 on p. 38.

Relais du Louvre (p. 26) LOUVRE/LES HALLES A small hotel near the Louvre that inspired the setting for Puccini's opera *La Bohème*. An apartment-size room on the 6th floor can accommodate 6 people.... *Tel 01-40-41-96-42. Fax 01-40-41-96-44. www.relaisdulouvre.com. 19, rue des Prêtres-St-Germain-l'Auxerrois, 75001. Métro Louvre Rivoli or Pont Neuf. 21 rooms. AE, DC, MC, V. $$$*

See Map 3 on p. 34.

Relais-Hotel du Vieux Paris (p. 27) LATIN QUARTER The memory of the Beat poets who once lived here is still honored, but in the restoration all the furnishings associated with these artists and junkies were burned. A bright, new, renovated jewel awaits you today, but the memories linger on.... *Tel 01-43-26-00-15. Fax 01-43-26-00-15. www.vieux-paris.com. 9 rue Git-le-Coeur, 75006. Métro St-Michel. 20 rooms. AE, DC, MC, V. $$$$*

See Map 5 on p. 38.

Ritz (p. 23) LOUVRE/LES HALLES Nothing beats the fabled Ritz for overdone luxury and snobbery. Houses the gourmet restaurant Espadon, as well as a swimming pool and health spa.... *Tel 800/223-6800 in the U.S., or 01-43-16-30-30. Fax 01-43-16-31-78. www.ritzparis.com. 15, place Vendôme, 75001. Métro Concorde. 178 rooms and suites. AE, DC, MC, V. $$$$$*

See Map 3 on p. 34.

Rive Gauche (p. 26) ST-GERMAIN-DES-PRES A good deal, especially considering its location in the heart of Saint-Germain-des-Prés. The rooms are small but serviceable.... *Tel 01-42-60-34-68. Fax 01-42-61-29-78. 25, rue des Saints-Pères, 75006. Métro St-Germain-des-Prés. 21 rooms. AE, DC, MC, V. $$*

See Map 5 on p. 38.

Royal Monceau (p. 30) CHAMPS-ELYSEES Spacious rooms in a palace hotel. The Michelin one-star restaurant Le Jardin is located in the courtyard garden, and there's also an Italian restaurant, Carpaccio. Fully equipped beauty spa, fitness center, and swimming pool.... *Tel 01-42-99-88-00. Fax 01-42-99-89-90. www.royalmonceau.com. 37, av. Hoche, 75008. Métro Etoile. 202 rooms and suites. AE, DC, MC, V. $$$$$*

See Map 4 on p. 36.

Stendhal (p. 26) OPERA GARNIER Small, luxurious hotel that was once home to the French author. Cozy bar with fireplace.... *Tel 01-44-58-52-52. Fax 01-44-58-52-00. 22, rue Danielle Casanova, 75002. Métro Pyramides. 20 rooms. AE, DC, MC, V. $$$$*

See Map 3 on p. 34.

Style Hôtel (p. 26) MONTMARTRE Clean, attractive, inexpensive hotel with a small courtyard garden. Rooms in the 2nd building share bathrooms.... *Tel 01-45-22-37-59. Fax 01-45-22-81-03. 8, rue Ganneron, 75018. Métro Place de Clichy. 35 rooms. MC, V. $*

See Map 3 on p. 34.

TimHôtel Montmartre (p. 28) MONTMARTRE Exceptional for its quiet location on a little square in Montmartre, its panoramic views from the upper floors, and reasonable prices.... *Tel 01-42-55-74-79. Fax 01-42-55-71-01. www.timhotel.com. 11, rue Ravignan (place Emile-Goudeau), 75018. Métro Abbesses. 63 rooms. AE, DC, MC, V. $$–$$$*

See Map 3 on p. 34.

Vauvilliers (p. 26) LOUVRE/LES HALLES A simple, cheap hotel near Les Halles and the Louvre. Not all rooms have showers. Reserve ahead.... *Tel 01-42-36-89-08. 6, rue Vauvilliers, 75001. Métro Les Halles. 14 rooms. No credit cards. $*

See Map 3 on p. 34.

Vendôme (p. 23) LOUVRE/LES HALLES Ultra-luxury on the place Vendôme. Plush rooms decked with ornate shades, lamps, and flowers.... *Tel 01-55-04-55-00. Fax 01-49-27-97-89. www.hoteldevendome.com. 1, place Vendôme, 75001. Métro Concorde. 30 rooms and suites. AE, DC, MC, V. $$$$$*

See Map 3 on p. 34.

D I N

I N G

2

Map 7: Paris Dining—Orientation

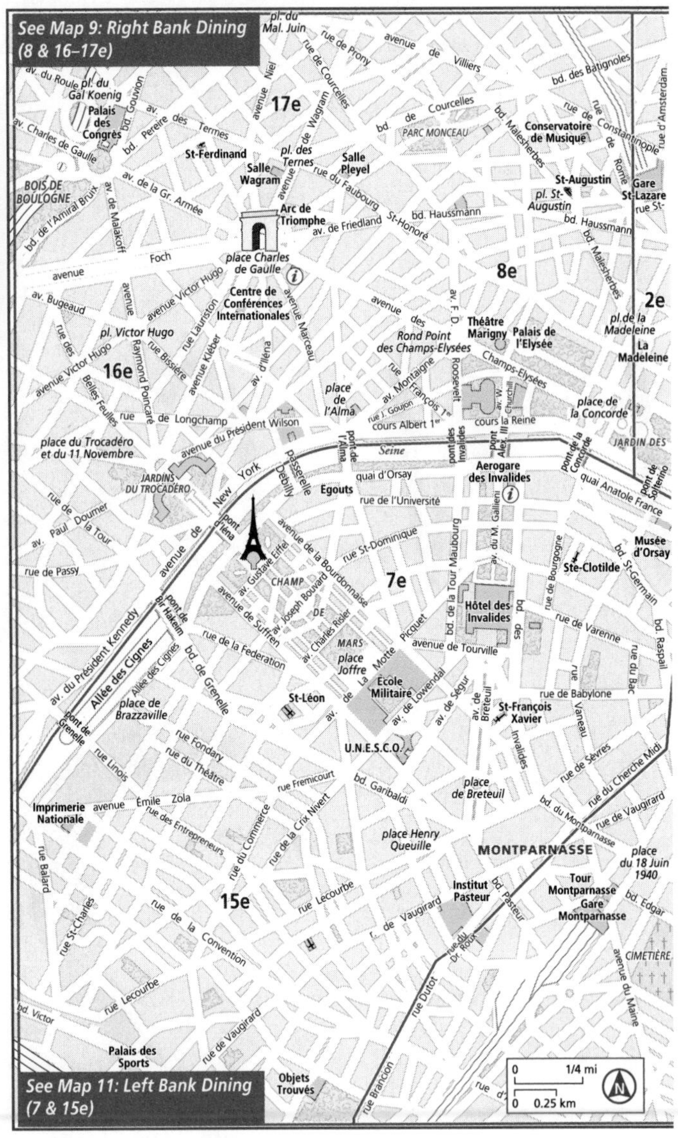

See Map 8: Right Bank Dining (1–4, 9–12 & 18e)
See Map 10: Left Bank Dining (5–6 & 13–14e)
MONTMARTRE
Moulin Rouge
Gare du Nord
Gare de l'Est
Casino de Paris
Ste-Trinité
Notre-Dame de Lorette
Folies Bergère
St-Vincent de Paul
St-Laurent
St-Joseph
St-Georges
place du Colonel Fabien
PARC DES BUTTES-CHAUMONT
10e
Opéra Garnier
place de l'Opéra
Bourse des Valeurs
place Vendôme
St-Roch
Palais Royal
place A. Malraux
TUILERIES
1er
Musée du Louvre
Bourse du Commerce
Forum des Halles
Conservatoire des Arts et Métiers
place de la République
11e
3e
LE MARAIS
Archives Nationales
St-Denis
St-Ambroise
Théâtre du Châtelet
St-Merri
4e
Ecole Nationale des Beaux-Arts
ST-GERMAIN-DES-PRÉS
Hôtel de Ville
St-Gervais
St-Paul
place des Vosges
Théâtre de la Bastille
ILE DE LA CITÉ
Notre-Dame
ILE ST-LOUIS
St-Louis
place de la Bastille
Opéra Bastille
12e
6e
Palais du Luxembourg
Sorbonne
QUARTIER LATIN
Institut du Monde Arabe
JARDIN DU LUXEMBOURG
Panthéon
Université Paris VII
5e
JARDIN DES PLANTES
Gare de Lyon
Université Paris V
Gare d'Austerlitz
St-Médard
Université Paris III
DU MONTPARNASSE
Observatoire de Paris
14e
13e
place d'Italie
Seine

DINING

Basic Stuff

The cherished idea that it's impossible to have a bad meal in Paris is just plain wrong. If you're looking for a cutting-edge dining scene, you'll do just as well in New York, San Francisco, Sydney, or London as you will in Paris, where "fusion" cooking has finally arrived, and then only because foreigners or expatriate chefs like Jean-Georges Vongerichten, whose restaurant **Market** became a hit, set up shop.

Furthermore, if Paris still remains the ultimate global culinary reference, the capital's restaurants are besieged by the introduction of an obligatory 35-hour work week, a make-work scheme—designed to make room for more employees—which some say has gone wrong. The idea of asking more people to work less isn't a bad one, but on the restaurant scene where long hours are part of the tradition, some owners have responded by paring down their menus and cutting back opening hours. That, with steeply rising costs and a hefty sales tax, means that many innovators are operating on a razor's edge of profitability. Not surprisingly, this has caused many to resort to short-cut industrial ingredients and to increased use of that great nemesis to real cuisine, microwave ovens.

In fact, to eat well in Paris requires as much research and planning as it does in any other city. Many restaurants that survive French recessions, which seem to come and go frequently, do so by either catering to an expense-account clientele or throwing in the towel and becoming tourist traps. A number of restaurants and cafés on the city's most heavily traveled boulevards are relatively awful. Most of the restaurants near the city's main sights have become completely mediocre by catering to a never-to-be-seen-again and don't-speak-French-so-can't-really-complain foreign clientele, who may not know that gristly steaks, frozen frites, and industrial salads aren't typical French food.

As prices in restaurants rose higher and higher in the '80s and '90s, restaurant owners confronted a price-resistant public at the millennium. Patrons merely stayed away from these grand citadels of overpriced cuisine. To cope with that, restaurant owners opened annex restaurants, lower-priced offshoots of their big-ticket dining rooms. Chef Michel Rostang led the way with **Le Bistrot d'à Côté** in 1987 and was soon followed by many other chefs, most notably Guy Savoy, who now has four satellites—Les Bouquinistes, La Butte Chaillot, **Le Cap Vernet,** and Le Bistro de l'Etoile—around town. **Le Bofinger** opened a less-ornate sister site right across the street from its Art Deco landmark brasserie.

As the big-time chefs opened annexes, the younger generation, led by chef Yves Camdeborde of the still-fabulous **La Régalade,** decided that the best way to launch themselves after the requisite years of pirouetting through various famous kitchens was by opening a bistro. Yup, a bistro: not a fancy place with fresh flowers and silver candelabra on linen tablecloths—classic bait for Michelin inspectors—but a good-value spot offering market menus (menus that change regularly to follow not only the best prices in produce, but the best of the season), where luxury produce, haute-cuisine techniques, and foreign seasonings were used to create intriguingly and very appetizingly modern versions of old-fashioned bistro dishes and regional specialties. Best of all, this young crowd, including Thierry Breton of **Chez Michel,** committed themselves to offering a truly memorable but affordable feed.

Higher up the food chain, there's been a spectacular renaissance of regional cooking with the arrival in Paris of chefs from the provinces like southwesterner **Hélène Darroze** of the eponymous one-star restaurant on the Left Bank, or Provençal maestro Alain Solivérès at **Taillevent.** All of these chefs have brilliantly updated one of the many regional kitchens that together form the true glory of French cooking. And up on the Mount Olympus of gastronomy that is the rarified world of three-star dining, chef Alain Passard created a stir when he converted his eminent restaurant **Arpège**

You Are What You Drink

In France, un café is like an Italian espresso (but not quite as good). If you prefer it more diluted, ask for a café allongé. A coffee with a splash of milk is a noisette, while café au lait or café crème are about half coffee and half steamed milk (the French usually drink coffee with milk only at breakfast time, but most waiters are pretty used to North Americans asking for this at all hours). If you like really high-octane coffee, simply ask for your café serré, which means less water.

When you order water with your meal, the waiter may assume you want bottled mineral water, which of course you have to pay for. But however much Gallic attitude he pulls, don't let the waiter pressure you into getting mineral water if you don't want it; restaurants are required to give you a pitcher of tap water with your meal if you request it. Ask clearly for une carafe d'eau, which is understood to be tap water (eau du robinet). It's perfectly drinkable. If you do opt for mineral water, you'll have to decide if it'll be eau plate (still) or eau gazeuse (sparkling). Note that the main gazeuses are Badoit and the popular Italian San Pellegrino, which is fine, but less fine than Badoit. Perrier is bubblier and is usually ordered as an aperitif.

to an almost all-vegetarian menu. Mad cow disease didn't scare him into it, either—he said he just wanted a challenge.

In another development, free-spending bobo (bohemian bourgeois) couples have—to the scorn and dismay of many locals who care about good food—fueled a fashion-restaurant boom. If you live in New York, L.A., Miami, London, or any other glamour-puss major city, you know these places. They're all about seeing and being seen, ditzy wannabe-model waiters and waitresses, furtive and usually futile star-spotting, a sexy "major-statement" decor where it's always hard to find the toilets, attitude so bad it warrants Alcatraz, and somewhere way out past Pluto, oh yeah, food. For most people a trip to Paris remains a precious chance to get at some mind-blowingly good food, so only several of these spots make the grade here. One is **Georges,** for its fabulous view from the top of the Centre Pompidou, great terrace during the good weather, decent snacky little meals for a lunch in a museum, and, well, 'cuz even if the food's forgettable there's no doubt it's a happening spot. Others are **Le Buddha Bar** and **Man Ray,** both for their decor. However, anyone who'd choose a meal at any of these three, over, say, **Les Elysées du Vernet** or even **Le Train Bleu,** should be shot, no, guillotined—you've been warned.

Only in Paris

A few tips to help you negotiate your way through a meal: Every restaurant is required to post its menu outside, so you should not have any surprises when the bill (*l'addition*) arrives. In cafés, the lowest prices are at the zinc bar, where customers stand for a quick coffee or drink; if you sit at a table, you pay more, and if you sit on the terrace, you pay more still. This is all legal, as is charging higher prices after 10pm or if there is live music. Check the board headed TARIFS DES CONSOMMATIONS carefully—it lists all the different prices. Service is always included, so make sure that you never, ever, ever leave 15% or 20% more than the bill shows. You can and should leave a euro or two in the dish as a tip or token of appreciation. This is not for the service.

Vegetarianism is a concept that is not likely ever to take France by storm. The French are too proud of their traditional cuisine, with all its meats and innards. Even salads commonly contain ham or chicken livers or sliced duck breast. If asked politely, most restaurants will make an effort to put together some sort of meat-free platter for you, but be careful—their idea of meat-free may not be the same as yours. Having said this, you should note that more and more French people are eating lighter and lighter meals, more salads and less cheese after long and calorie-heavy meals.

Eating places are classified as **cafés,** which serve drinks, snacks, and sometimes meals; **bistros,** small restaurants, usually with limited or simple menus; **brasseries,** which traditionally offer Alsatian specialties like *choucroute* and beer, oysters and other shellfish (usually banked on ice on the sidewalk), fish, and grilled meats; and lastly "proper" and more formal **restaurants** with full menus, which usually serve only at traditional mealtimes and are less amenable to substitutions and variations of the structure of the French meal. Here, you do not split appetizers or desserts unless you are very charming or obviously in love. The French will make exceptions for romantic love, but are not too keen on accommodating calorie-conscious couples.

When to Eat

French people like to do things at specific times, and they flock to lunch spots at precisely 1pm. This means that every decent restaurant in Paris will be jam-packed from 1 to 2pm. The clever visitor will have lunch at noon or even 12:30 (that way you can get a table and still enjoy the uproar of the lunch rush) or at 2. Be careful, though: Many restaurants will not serve lunch after 2:30. If you miss the lunch hour, you might have to settle for a *sandwich jambon-beurre* (sliced ham on a buttered baguette, which can be sublime when made with quality ingredients), a *croque-monsieur* (open-face ham and cheese sandwich with béchamel sauce—try it on *pain Poilâne* if it's available), or an omelette. These snacks are usually served at all times in cafés.

Most restaurants are empty at 8pm and only begin to fill up around 9. It can be difficult to get served after 10:30, however (see "Late-night bites" and "All-nighters," later in this chapter, for suggestions).

Getting the Right Table

Reservations are imperative in Paris, and if you have your heart set on a table with a view or you want to sit outside, make this firmly known when you book. Walk-in customers are given what is available, but if the restaurant is not full, don't be afraid to ask to move if you don't like your table. In chic or expensive restaurants, the best tables are given to the rich and famous, and to regular customers. The best way to assure that you will not be sent to Siberia is to ask the concierge at your hotel to reserve for you. Also note that French waiters do not like to give larger tables to small parties. If you're dining as a duo and you're seated at a charmless two-top in a roomful of empty four-seaters, you have two choices: Ask very, very nicely to be moved and be prepared to lose, or ask for a table of four because the others will be coming a bit later. (But will they *really?*)

French restaurants are supposed to have designated smoking and nonsmoking areas, unless they have sophisticated ventilation systems (very few do). In practice, however, the smoking regulations are generally ignored. Insisting nicely helps—like saying that you're recovering from tuberculosis. More and more places are getting hip to the nonsmoking crowd, but there is still a long way to go before you'll be spared the charms of passive smoke.

Plugged-In Cafés

*The word for "hip" in French is branché, which literally means "plugged in"—though branché and its hipper backward version, chébran, are getting kind of dated. You have to buy a cinema ticket to get into the cybernetic café in the **Cité-Ciné UGC** in the Nouveau Forum des Halles, Forum des Halles Level 4 at 7, place de la Rotonde, 1e (Tel 08-92-70-00-00, ext. 11; Métro Les Halles). **Access Academy,** 60-62, rue Saint-André des Arts, 6e (www.accessacademy.com; Métro St-Michel or St-Germain-des-Prés), is the largest cybercafé in France, with two floors accommodating 400 computer stations with high-speed Internet connections, qwerty keyboards, and Microsoft Office. **Tip:** Don't leave your bag with wallet and passport on the floor under your computer station; things tend to disappear in all large cities.*

Where the Chefs Are

Among the top restaurants in Paris—according to the secretive cult/publisher Michelin—are **Alain Ducasse, Taillevent, Lucas-Carton, Arpège, Pierre Gagnaire,** and **Le Grand Véfour.**

If you want the best food and service that Paris can offer, you should consider Taillevent and Alain Ducasse. The exalted opinion of Michelin notwithstanding, many people are disappointed by the ho-hum decor of Arpège and find Alain Passard's food at once rather too minimalist and intellectual; and while Lucas-Carton is a beautiful restaurant, the service is imperious, especially to foreigners. Le Grand Véfour is one of the most romantic restaurants in Paris, with a jewel-box setting in the Palais Royal and a stunning decor of painted glass ceilings, but while chef Guy Martin is indisputably a talent, many Parisian food critics believe that his third star has been awarded rather prematurely, especially when a really marvelous chef like

Guy Savoy waited years for this ultimate accolade. Of course, there is something to be said for dining at what was Voltaire's table, or where Napoléon looked into the eyes of his darling Josephine.

So assuming that you're unlikely to take in all seven—a meal for two at any of them will run at least $400, depending upon which wine you chose and the exchange rate—which one of them is right for you? Overall, Alain Ducasse is a sublime experience. Located in the plush but edgy—it's a mix of the usual Louis stuff and postmodern cool—dining room of the Hôtel Plaza Athénée, this restaurant gets everything right. Service is as graceful and perfectly timed as any ballet, and Ducasse is a genius at inventing new dishes that tempt—even taunt—the palette without overwhelming it. Come here if you're a serious gourmet who wants to visit the Olympus of Parisian gastronomy without venturing into the realm of the truly experimental or weird.

Taillevent, long the great-aunt of the three-star club, is the talk of the town for having hired Alain Solivérès. Taillevent also has one of the world's great wine lists, and service is nothing less than gallant.

For a really wonderful, sometimes weird experience of the real cutting-edge of French gastronomy, though, the place to go is Pierre Gagnaire. Gagnaire previously had three stars at his restaurant in Saint-Etienne (nondescript south-central industrial city), but went bankrupt and reopened in Paris. The capital has been intrigued by his astonishingly delicious and nuanced cooking, such as a starter of foie gras cooked two ways—au natural and then wrapped in bacon and lacquered like a Chinese duck.

Tradition takes visitors to **La Tour d'Argent.** The view is gorgeous but the food beyond the signature roast duck is forgettable, the service borders on pomposity, and the overall effect is time-warp zone 1958. Ditto **Maxim's,** still legendary despite its ludicrously high prices, cagey waiters, and frequently morbid ambience, although the food here is improving by leaps and bounds, but not enough to justify its shudderingly high prices.

Though they're a rung down from the three stars, you'll still eat splendidly well at the other best-of-the-best chefs in Paris, including **Le Pré Catelan,** where Robuchon-trained chef Frédéric Anton just gets better and better, **Les Elysées** (Eric Briffard), **Guy Savoy,** Philippe Conticini's **Restaurant Petrossian, Ledoyen** (Christophe Le Squer), and **Le Bristol,** which pulled off a real coup by hiring young Turk Eric Frechon to take over its kitchens. Frechon's one of the best of the new generation and previously ran a hugely popular bistro with a prix-fixe menu in the remote reaches of the 19th arrondissement.

The great middle ground of Paris restaurants—tables that run from 65€ to 125€ ($81–$156) a head—is dangerous territory these days. A lot of these places are living off their reputations, so you're far better off assiduously seeking out some of the brilliant new wave of young chefs. Five of the best junior tables are Yves Camdeborde's **La Régalade,** Thierry Breton's **Chez Michel,** Pascal Barbot's **L'Astrance,** ThierryBurlot's **La Cristal Room Baccarat,** and Laurent Delarbre's **Restaurant de l'Astor.**

The Lowdown

Book before you fly... Most Paris three-stars should be booked a solid month ahead of time to avoid disappointment. In the case of particularly modish chefs like **Alain Ducasse** or **Pierre Gagnaire,** a 2-month lead time is often necessary. If you're staying somewhere swanky, you can, of course, try to get your concierge—supposing you have one—to shake down a table for you; otherwise lunch is usually much less busy at the haute-cuisine places than is dinner, especially since many French execs have had their expense accounts slashed as the previously terrarium-like world of French business has opened up to global competition.

Overrated... A diminishing culinary reputation doesn't seem to have hurt the popularity of **La Tour d'Argent.** Customers come despite decent but hardly awesome food, high prices, and a sense that you're lucky to be allowed in. The view is memorable, and you'll be amused to learn that gossip has it that the restaurant paid for the lighting on its side of Notre Dame Cathedral.

Long the favorite haunt of politicians, philosophers, and writers, **Brasserie Lipp** ain't what it used to be. It still has the fabulous decor, but the food's only so-so, and the service is a mixed bag, sometimes awful, sometimes lively and spirited. **Maxim's** is also way past its prime, but tourists still flock here. Although Michelin ranks **Lucas-Carton** as one of Paris's top five restaurants, it loses points in this book for its scattered service and dull menu.

Other well-known tables with inflated reputations include the brasseries **Julien** and **La Coupole**—part of the same chain and suffering from the same really mediocre cooking—and ghastly **Le Buddha Bar,** where you should drink and gaze but definitely not eat. However, after midnight, **La Coupole** still captures the spirit of the literary and artistic haunt it once was; a *plateau* of oysters and a bottle of chilled Sancerre at this landmark still manage to please the heart.

The rest of the best... Now that he has access to one of the most luxurious pantries in the world, Eric Frechon is thriving at **Le Bristol,** where he does original and elegant dishes like veal sweetbreads seasoned with stick cinnamon and served on a bed of spinach and tiny mushrooms, plus killer desserts, including a wild-thyme parfait with chocolate ice cream and a sauce of salted caramel. At **Ledoyen,** Christian Le Squer keeps the bliss meter beeping with herbed risotto topped with lobster, langoustines, scallops, and a thin slice of Spanish Jabugo ham. Shy and intensely dedicated young chef Alain Solivérès serves exquisite food at **Taillevent,** and is considered by Parisian gourmets to be the most prodigious talent of the new generation of chefs. After being seemingly doomed to senility, **L'Espadon,** the restaurant at the Ritz, is back and, under the aegis of chef Michel Roth, who trained here, it's once again one of the ritziest spots in the town for a blow-out feast; dress to the nines before you try superb dishes like lobster salad, veal chop with a crust of polenta, and the best *mille-feuille* in town, and be forewarned of its stunningly expensive wine list.

Baby bistros... The "baby bistro" phenomenon and the ongoing cost squeeze on Paris restaurants have leveled off a bit. It all began when Michel Rostang launched the trend with **Le Bistrot d'à Côté,** still going strong, which has good traditional French food (try the terrine and the roast shoulder of lamb), a winsome old-fashioned bistro decor, and friendly service. Rostang's also operates **Rue Balzac,** which seems to be his attempt to respond to the fusion cooking trend with a modish decor that recalls Le Cirque 2000 in New York and a menu that offers his famous truffle sandwich, risotto with ham, and a superb *mille-feuille.* The other major player in the "baby game" has been Guy Savoy, whose Parisian bistro, **Le Cap Vernet,** serves excellent shellfish and fish. Another baby worth any fish fiend's attention is the **Bistrot du Dôme,** the popular annex of the famous Montparnasse fish house nearby that serves an impeccably fresh catch-of-the-day menu at much gentler prices. The only chef still putting a lot of energy into the bistro concept these days, though, is Alain Ducasse, with his growing chain of **Spoon, Food and Wine** restaurants (the first one opened in Paris, and they now exist in London, Tokyo, Mauritius, Monaco, and Tunisia).

Cutting-edge bistros... If the last wave of change on the Paris restaurant scene was the bistro-annexes of famous chefs, the latest is the brilliant crop of easygoing, comfortably priced new bistros that are being opened by a generation of ambitious, passionate young chefs.

The latest hit in this category is **L'Astrance:** Opened by brilliant young Pascal Barbot, former second chef to Alain Passard at Arpège and private chef to the head of the French Pacific fleet, it has become one of the toughest reservations to snag in Paris. Typical of Barbot's style are his soup of milk and toasted bread crumbs (sounds like hospital food, but really is fabulous) and avocado ravioli stuffed with crabmeat. Though it's way off the beaten track and, like most of this genre, horribly noisy, Christophe Beaufort's L'Avant Goût in the 13th arrondissement is worth the trek. The menu changes daily but might include shellfish bisque as a starter, followed by tomatoes stuffed with oxtail. Over near the Bastille, **Le Repaire de Cartouche** is a fabulous bistro as long as you don't get stuck in the chilly, lost-in-right-field front room. Rodolphe Paquin does hearty, earthy dishes like veal chop in Madeira sauce or a thick steak of grilled bacon. And desserts like caramelized pineapple are moaningly good.

It's worth braving a slightly dreary part of town for the offerings at Thierry Breton's **Chez Michel.** The sophisticated menu is spiked with several old-fashioned and rarely encountered Breton dishes. French food critics have showered **Les Ormes** with deserved acclaim since it opened; chef Stephane Mole trained with retired superstar Joel Robuchon and it shows. Another small place gone big is **La Régalade;** make a reservation here before you even unpack so you'll be able to try dishes such as gratin of potatoes and lobster.

Best brasseries... When you're in the mood for a good meal (not haute cuisine, but solid food) in a jumping atmosphere, try a Parisian brasserie. **Le Bofinger,** near the place de la Bastille, is one of the best examples, with its hustle and bustle and Belle Epoque decor. Unfortunately, most of Paris's brasseries have become part of one of the two local chains, Groupe Flo and Les Frères Blanc, and while these groups are to be grudgingly credited with restoring the authentic decors in some of the city's prettiest and most famous brasseries, the food's often mediocre. The best of the Flo brasseries are **Le Boeuf sur le Toit** (off the Champs-Elysées), **Terminus Nord** (handily across the street from the Gare du Nord), **Le Vaudeville** (next to the Paris Bourse), and **Le Balzar** (right next door to La Sorbonne), which is arguably the chicest brasserie in town, pulling an intriguing crowd of fashion folk, academics, and foreigners. **Au Pied de Cochon** is the star of Les Frères Blanc's stable.

One of the best brasseries in town is **Garnier,** the quiet man in front of the Gare Saint Lazare. Though many local design snobs regret its former decor ('70s-ghastly that had just tipped into being fabulous), the new look—dark wood, wicker chairs, and original Art Deco light fixtures—is comfortable, and the fish, oysters, and other shellfish here are excellent. Note, too, that they run a tiny belly-up-to-the-counter oyster bar that's a brilliant spot for a quick bivalve snack when you're shopping at Printemps and Galeries Lafayette, the big department stores just down the road.

Classiest cafés... The two top cafés are **Café de Flore** for its Art Deco decor, high-quality food, good people-watching terrace, and star-studded clientele; and the **Café Marly,** for its location in the Louvre and its two handsome dining rooms with their completely different ambiences. The first manages to be classic and modern at the same time, while the second is brighter and airier. Then there's the **Café Beaubourg,** with Christian de Portzamparc's original interior design, which includes a bridge that connects the two parts of the mezzanine and comfortable wicker armchairs on the terrace facing the Centre Pompidou. One of Paris's best kept secrets is **Café Panique** which opened in the early '90s and still seems undiscovered by visitors, in spite of its easygoing atmosphere and delectable cuisine. Against a backdrop of a mellow ambience, you're served scrumptious food from the vastly improved kitchen. To enjoy this discovery, you have to journey to the increasingly trendy 10th arrondissement.

You can really eat in the hotel?... The leering-waiter-and-fish-with-white-sauce image of hotel dining in Paris has been banished. In fact, some of the best restaurants in town are in hotels, which compete fiercely for star chefs. Even before it opened its doors, the Four Seasons George V had hired chef Philippe Legendre away from Taillevent to bang the pots and pans at its sumptuous luxury restaurant, **Le Cinq.** Not too surprisingly, Legendre does sublime and very classic luxury cooking rather like what he did at, well, Taillevent, with luscious dishes like a tartare of scallops and oysters with caviar and lobster with chestnuts. Over at the Crillon, chef Dominique Bouchet is keeping the lavish dining room at **Les Ambassadeurs** on course as one of the best tables in Paris, as seen in dishes like a crispy potato pancake topped with smoked salmon, crème fraîche, and caviar.

Dining under a delicate Belle Epoque *verrière* at **Les Elysées du Vernet** only adds to the pleasure of some really brilliant food from young chef Eric Briffard. The service here is impeccable, too, and the cheeky young sommelier loves to tease you to venture beyond the usual burgundies and bordeaux with little-known and very reasonably priced regional vintages. With a glassed-in dining room overlooking the magnolia-planted inner courtyard for summer and an oval-shaped, oak-panelled sanctuary with crystal chandeliers for winter, **Le Bristol** has been extremely popular since the arrival of chef Eric Frechon, who won his reputation with a shrewd prix-fixe bistro in the remote 19th arrondissement. He does sumptuous aristo food like foie gras–stuffed ravioli in chicken broth with truffle shavings. And the latest haute cuisine act to go hotel is **Alain Ducasse,** who moved to the swanky Plaza Athénée hotel several years ago.

Late-night bites... Because many restaurants stop serving at about 10:30pm or even earlier, it can be difficult to find a good après-movie or -theater meal. The **Bistrot Beaubourg** is an inexpensive, upbeat, little restaurant in the center of town with good, simple French food. **Coude de Fou,** a popular, laid-back restaurant in the Marais, offers service until 2am. **Le Boeuf sur le Toit** is an enormous brasserie near the Champs-Elysées with good shellfish and meats. It's part of the Groupe Flo chain, as are the **Terminus Nord** and **Le Vaudeville.** Each has high-quality food; different, old-fashioned brasserie decor that has been carefully restored; a lively atmosphere; good service; and a special, low-priced fixed menu after 11pm (including oysters). The Terminus Nord is especially fun late at night, full of satisfied diners and friendly waiters running from table to table. **Le Bofinger,** a famous Belle Epoque brasserie at Bastille, has a similar ambience and menu. Actors come to **La Cloche d'Or,** near Pigalle, when their working nights are done.

For something hipper, there's the Costes brothers' desperately cool restaurant **Georges** on the sixth floor of the Centre Pompidou. The views are fabulous, as is the decor, with three huge brushed aluminum pods occupying an airy loft space with lit-from-within brushed glass tables. The food's decent, but not cheap, although you can always just order a club sandwich or an omelette. Make sure to book ahead. In the hot new party precincts off the Champs-Elysées in the 8th arrondissement, you can get into a perfect pre-club funk at **Market,** New York star Jean-Georges Vongerichten's slick place in the Christie's headquarters building. With a disco-goes-ethnic decor by Christian Liagre, who did Jean-George's hip Mercer Kitchen in New York, this place is packing major star power for the type of fusion food that tastes best against an aural backdrop of acid-jazz and lounge music.

All-nighters... Most nightclubs in Paris don't open until 11pm or midnight, so by 3 or 4am you may have worked up an appetite. There are several all-night restaurants in the Les Halles area, vestiges of the days when Paris's major wholesale food market was located there. Try **Au Pied de Cochon,** the place to go if you like pig parts, especially at 3am. They actually serve the snout here, cut in two, the tail on the plate along with the trotter. For the squeamish, enormous platters of shellfish, as well as more ordinary fare, are also available 24 hours a day.

Smoky and bawdy, **La Tour de Montlhery** dates back to the days when Les Halles was "the belly of Paris" rather than an ugly mall, and it serves up massive mutton chops and steaks with real frites.

Decor to die for, but skip the food... **Chartier** is a Paris experience that's not to be missed despite all the tourists. This is an enormous *bouillon* (originally, a cheap workers' restaurant that served *pot-au-feu*) that hasn't changed much since the 19th century—some of the waiters look as if they've been there since then as well. The food is cheap and acceptable, the service brusque, and the ambience lively. **Brasserie Lipp** no longer stands out for its food or service, but its enormous mirrors, ceramic panels, and frescoes are as memorable as its ghosts. Since the 1920s, nearly all the political nabobs of France have been regulars here, along with an equally long list of writers and other celebrities. Owner Pierre Cardin, the king of commercialization, has thankfully not messed around with **Maxim's** incredible Art Nouveau decor, though the restaurant has pretty much been ruined.

The Groupe Flo chain has also carefully restored the original decor of its brasseries (see "Best brasseries," above), although food and service often leave much to be desired; if you're an interiors freak and want to clock some of these places, come late, when they're quieter, and order very, very simply. The famous Art Deco **La Coupole** has paintings on the columns by 32 artists who were paid with unlimited free drinks. Saved from destruction in the 1980s when it was declared a national monument, this is one of those places in Paris where the past really seems present. Art Nouveau **Julien** is a work of art in itself. Its carved mahogany bar, glass ceiling with floral motifs, huge mirrors, molded glass panels painted with female allegories of the four seasons, and extravagant moldings are a delight; unfortunately, the same cannot be said for its food and frantic service.

On the more modern side of things, **Man Ray,** a slick *Chinatown*-style mega-seater off the Champs-Elysées, is a gorgeous setting in which to tipple. Ditto the slightly past prime **Le Buddha Bar,** where a gigantic gold-painted polystyrene Buddha remains mum on the mediocre Asian food; or **Barrio Latino,** the latest hipster joint near the Bastille, where the food is feeble but the decor around an open atrium in what was once a furniture showroom is as luxuriant as a honeymoon in Havana.

Decor to die for, and don't miss the food... Opened in 1864, **Le Bofinger** is perhaps the quintessential Paris brasserie, with its stained-glass dome, sweeping staircase, wood paneling, large mirrors, black banquettes, potted palms, and brass coat racks. Waiters bustle about as customers indulge in oysters, *choucroute,* or wild duck. For over-the-top Belle Epoque decor, **Le Train Bleu** wins hands down. It's also classified as a historic monument, and its sumptuous decorations cover every inch of the walls, while the 11m- (36-ft.) high ceilings with gilded moldings and paintings by turn-of-the-20th-century artists provide a voyage around France. A similar atmosphere reigns at **Les Elysées du Vernet** under a superb glass *verrière* (domed ceiling) that was designed by none other than Gustave Eiffel himself. Potted palms, silver candelabras, and waiters in tuxedos complete the counts-traveling-with-steamer-trunks atmosphere here. With its lavish Art Nouveau decor, **Lucas-Carton** is where you should demand that your lover take you if you've just become his frisky mistress or her energetic boy toy. The ceiling squirms with 17th-century plaster cherubim at **Les Ambassadeurs,** the stunning restaurant in the Hôtel Crillon, with its black-and-white marble floors, crystal chandeliers, and drop-dead view of the place de la Concorde; chef Dominique Bouchet's cuisine is a suave study in discreet luxury against this operatic background. Sensitively renovated, **Restaurant Plaza Athénée,** the terribly fashionable brasserie at the Hôtel Plaza Athénée, serves up an Art Deco feast reminiscent of the public rooms in the great ocean liners like *La Normandie,* and the straightforward and simple food is actually pretty good.

Best circus decor... Two cafés located near Paris's Cirque d'Hiver (Winter Circus) have slapped up a few circus posters and named themselves Rendezvous des Clowns and Circus Bar, but there is only one **Clown Bar,** with hand-painted ceramic tiles that date to the 1920s; wood-framed Art Nouveau windows, door, and mirrors; an S-curved zinc bar; and antique clown memorabilia. Add to all this good food, wine, and atmosphere and you've got just about the perfect little bistro.

Historic surroundings... Originally the Café de Chartres in the 18th century, **Le Grand Véfour** was a hangout for plotters of the French Revolution and later of Royalists during the Terror. Famous customers over the decades have included Victor Hugo, Colette, Jean Cocteau, and Greta Garbo. Cocteau designed the menu and the ashtrays.

Peckish near the Centre Pompidou... The **Bistrot Beaubourg** is a small, informal, and inexpensive restaurant with tasty food. **Dame Tartine** has a terrace overlooking the wacky and wonderful Stravinksy fountain and serves creative open-face sandwiches that make for a cheap meal. **Georges,** on the sixth floor of the slickly renovated museum, has a striking modern decor and serves nonstop from 11am to 2am; reservations are essential.

If it's mealtime in the Marais... As popular as it is for hanging out and having a good time, the Marais is not a great restaurant neighborhood. Aside from the excellent falafel stands along the rue de Rosiers, one of the best deals in this neck of the woods is **La Baracane,** which won't ever show up in a decorating magazine with its worn red carpet, framed posters, and plain vanilla walls, but it's a crowd-pleaser with its inexpensive and delicious southwestern French cooking. The *confit de canard,* grilled preserved duck, is splendid, and the wines by the glass are cheap and good drinking. Though it's on the very northern fringes of the neighborhood, **Le Reconfort** is worth some shoe leather. This attractive amber-walled bistro draws the shave-heads and unisex ponytail crowd and, quite surprisingly, the food's very good.

Chow time on the Champs-Elysées... Once a near wasteland of fast-food outlets and dreary, tourist-trap cafés, the Champs-Elysées has been slowly reemerging as a destination for Parisians themselves ever since its makeover a few years ago, and one of the reasons the locals are back is that a variety of good—and trendy but less good—restaurants have opened on and off the avenue. Though it may puzzle North Americans, six-star chef Alain Ducasse's dopily named **Spoon, Food and Wine** is a knockdown hit with the locals. What's on offer here is Ducasse's take on world food, which means a menu that includes everything from a very high-tech BLT to all kinds of pasta, Asian stir-fries, and even cheesecake and donuts (served as a dessert). The food's actually pretty good; it's an ultra-chic scene; and there's a fascinating if pricey wine list, half of which is, to the utter astonishment of the French, from the United States. For a quick feed during a stomp down the avenue, or before or after a movie, **Lo Sushi,** a conveyor-belt sushi place with video screens and a decor by star interior designer Andree Putmann, is convenient and popular with local trendies.

Other places to eat on the tourist beat... Tourists seem intimidated by the crowds and the chic of **Le Fumoir,** the wonderful café that Parisians instantly went wild for. Don't let those pretty faces and I'm-so-cool expressions keep you away. The fact is, the people who work here are very friendly and the food is pretty good. **Polidor,** an old restaurant near Odéon, is looking a bit shabby, but the food is still very good. You may be dubious as you walk in, but you'll be won over by the charming female service, classic French food, and low prices. Not far from the literary haunts of Montparnasse, **Chez Marcel** is a true find—a *trouvaille,* a family-run bistro with popular Lyonnaise cooking.

Where the media types go... Alain Ducasse's **Spoon, Food and Wine** is very popular with French television stars, which may explain why the couple at the table next to you look like a game-show host and a weather girl. On the Left Bank, you'll find book editors and writers at **Hélène Darroze,** the superb southwestern restaurant with a sassy contemporary decor, and **La Table d'Aude,** where the lure is first-rate cassoulet and as much wine as you can guzzle or dare to request as part of a prix-fixe menu. Movie people favor the lush decor at **Man Ray,** Mick Hucknell (you know, of Simply Red) and Johnny Depp's mega-seater off the Champs-Elysées; and **La Maison Blanche,** when you're pretending that you're having a casual, discreet night out on the town, but know that photographers from *Paris-Match* are regularly lurking.

La Ferme Saint-Simon, on the très chic rue de Saint-Simon, attracts media and fashion people, as well as deputies from the nearby Assemblée Nationale, for its classic French cuisine. The modern decor of wood, steel, and glass at the high-priced **Arpège** sets the stage for the cuisine of young chef Alain Passard, whose creations include vegetable couscous and sweet-and-sour lobster.

Where to seal a deal... Café Marly, in the Louvre, is another hot spot at lunchtime and also serves good international cuisine. **Restaurant Plaza Athénée,** in the Hôtel Plaza Athénée, specializes in grilled meats and has its original Art Deco interior. In the old days, Maurice Chevalier, Josephine Baker, and Marlene Dietrich dined here; today, the person sitting next to you might be Jack Nicholson, a Kuwaiti oilman, or a rich, old French lady with her two miniature poodles. Another Left Bank choice is **Le Voltaire,** a Paris classic with its sober wood paneling, reliable French food, and excellent service, but if you want to be grand, book at **L'Espadon.**

Alfresco... The French take to the terrace the moment there's a ray of sunshine. Terraces come in all varieties, from lush, peaceful gardens, to a few tables on the sidewalk with exhaust-spouting Citroëns rushing by. **Le Pré Catelan,** one of the city's better restaurants, is in the first category. On a summer evening, its jazzy modern French cuisine can bring you near to paradise. **La Grande Cascade,** also surrounded by lovely gardens in the Bois de Boulogne, serves classic French cuisine. Between these two wonders and the Citroën exhaust, there are the terraces of the top-notch fish restaurant **La Cagouille;** the très chic **Café Marly,** housed in the Louvre itself, with a view of Pei's pyramid and an international menu; and the **Café Very** for inexpensive meal-size *tartines* (open-face sandwiches) under the trees of the Tuileries. The **Restaurant du Palais-Royal,** isolated from the noise of passing traffic in the tranquil confines of the Palais-Royal, where Colette and Jean Cocteau once lived, serves fine French food at moderate prices. Trendy **La Maison Blanche** has a rooftop terrace with a view of Paris, and the food's on par with the view.

Great wine bars... The old-style wine bars in Paris serve nothing but wine and *tartines.* They usually close at around 9:30pm and are often located near food markets. **La Tartine** is a classic example; nothing much has changed since Trotsky drank here. The walls are stained with decades of tobacco smoke, and it would be easy to believe that the eagle-eyed patron, who's in his 90s but continues to terrify both customers (everyone from yuppies to artsy and intellectual types) and staff, was around when Leon was. It's a great, though intimidating, place for a pre-dinner kir or a glass of wine and a tartine topped with pâté, rillettes, or cantal.

The newer version of the wine bar is a bistro that serves simple meals to complement an extensive wine list. The atmosphere is usually relaxed and informal in these little restaurants. One of the best examples is the **Clown Bar,** a historic monument. It is located next to the Cirque d'Hiver (Winter Circus), hence the name (pronounced "kloon") and the colorful tiles behind the bar depicting clowns.

Two of the city's better wine bars, more chic than those listed above, are actually owned by Englishmen. **Willi's Wine Bar** has become a fashionable institution here, appreciated both for its excellent selection of wines and its creative, nouvelle-ish cuisine. The owner is known in Paris as a connoisseur of wines from the Rhône region. Its baby brother, **Juveniles,** has lower prices, but the food and wine are in the same excellent vein. The atmosphere is informal, and it is worth chatting about wine with the very knowledgeable owner, Tim Johnston.

La vie en rose... There are still a few places around where old-time Paris, à la Edith Piaf, can still be found. For an authentic, old-fashioned Paris bistro, a genus that's almost extinct, try **Chez La Vieille-Adrienne,** one of the worthiest old-fashioned bistros in the city, with superb food, charming service, and taunting wisps of nostalgia. Come here if you want to experience how generous Paris bistros once were (this place has never heard of "portion management") or if you've never heard a rotary phone ring before. Master chef Alain Ducasse pops up everywhere these days, including at **Aux Lyonnais,** which has been known for decades for serving the best Lyonnais food in Paris. Set against an 1890s bistro backdrop of potted palms and etched glass, this is a time-mellowed place given a new lease on life. Down by the Pantheon, **Perraudin** has been around since the 19th century. Today its walls look like they were marinated in tea, and the vaudeville posters have been here forever. Scholars and professors, among other diners, patronize this mellow old favorite that for Marcel Proust might evoke a remembrance of things past.

Isn't it romantic?... Romantic settings in Paris are not limited to candlelit tables—lovers here are not shy about staring deeply into each other's eyes and kissing in any public place. For those who are looking for the appropriate romantic ambience, though, there are intimate restaurants like **Prunier,** with its cozy Art Deco dining room and sexy food with a twist of originality—think caviar, smoked salmon, oysters, and chilled vodka or champagne. If you can afford it, the rosy glow of candlelight at **Les Elysées du Vernet** in the evening can inspire much more than one's appetite. On a balmy night, fill your beloved's eyes with stars by dining under them—book a terrace table at **Le Pré Catelan.** The Palais-Royal at night is one of the most romantic places in the world; a terrace table at the **Restaurant du Palais-Royal** is spellbinding on a summer night.

Victuals with a view... Unlike most restaurants with a view in major cities, **Le Jules Verne** is as famous for what you can eat there as it is for what you can see. Located on the second floor of the Eiffel Tower, its understated gray-and-black interior is designed to not distract attention from the wide-ranging view of Paris, nor from the cuisine of Alain Reix, considered one of Paris's better chefs. **La Maison Blanche** has an unbeatable view of the Eiffel Tower, the Seine, and the Hôtel des Invalides that is especially spectacular at night. The large terrace is an added advantage in summer. Located on the sixth floor of the Théâtre des Champs-Elysées, this lively restaurant serves modern French cuisine to a hip clientele. The super-expensive **La Tour d'Argent** is famous, of course, for its view of the flying buttresses of Notre-Dame, but you also get a pretty spectacular view of Paris from the tip of the Ile de la Cité, where you can picnic in almost the same place that Leslie Caron danced with Gene Kelly in *An American in Paris.* And less expensive but much sassier, **Georges,** on the top floor of the Centre Pompidou, also has killer views.

Cheap eats... Okay, don't expect miracles, but decent, basic French food is served with flourish at the historic **Chartier,** with its perfectly preserved, 19th-century decor. One that's so good it'd be worth traveling across town for even if money weren't an issue: **La Boulangerie,** in so-cool-it's-almost-over Ménilmontant (a nabe that's young, cheap, trendy, and sort of artistic). It offers really good food and house wine for about $22 a head—what your cheeseburger, fries, and beer feast now cost at home—and when you see what you can get for this dough, you'll probably want to eat here more than once. Yo, bro, how's about pears roasted with goat cheese, chicken with spices and grapefruit, and homemade shortbread with apples flamed in Calvados, plus a 9€ ($11) carafe of Chinon?

Near the Centre Pompidou, **Bistrot Beaubourg** is a spot that serves good, French classics at very low prices, so come and relax with surf and turf at this unpretentious neighborhood hangout. Parisians and tourists alike love sitting at the outdoor tables. **Le Petit Keller,** with a fabulous '50s decor, is a great spot for dinner if you're planning to do the lively bar scene in and around the Bastille. Delicious home cooking—the *daube de boeuf* is better here than at many much pricier places—and low tabs will leave you with more euros for after-dinner guzzling.

Lunching out cheaply... In terms of the quality and sophistication of food, **L'Ebauchoir,** near Bastille, rates as the best in this category. In addition to now hard-to-find onion soup, the menu includes escargots, raw sardines stuffed with minced vegetables, and tuna steak with orange sauce. Two restaurants with the same owner have made a success out of converting what has traditionally been a wine-bar snack, the *tartine,* into something more substantial and inventive. One is fittingly called **Dame Tartine** and has a terrace next to the Stravinsky fountain near the Centre Pompidou. The other, the **Café Very,** is located in the Tuileries and is a pleasant spot for an outdoor lunch or dinner on a nice day. The cute little bistro **Chez Nénesse** in the Marais is frequented by neighborhood people, both artsy and working-class. Red-and-white tablecloths, a wood stove, and plants and flowers provide the backdrop at lunchtime for inexpensive French dishes. **Au Babylone,** open for lunch only, is great for a cheap, solid meal in a quintessentially Parisian setting if you're doing a long trek around the Left Bank. This place is almost a Parisian equivalent of a good New York coffee shop.

Luxury lunches at bargain prices... **Le Reminet,** a tiny and friendly bistro on the Left Bank just across from Notre-Dame, offers a fine 32€ ($40) feed from a menu that changes daily but might include such treats as lentil salad with foie gras, smoked duck breast, and a poached egg in a balsamic vinaigrette. **Chantairelle,** a pleasant little Latin Quarter bistro specializing in the hearty food of the central Auvergne region, and **Les Ormes,** a stylish spot with a talented young chef in the 16th arrondissement, both do your wallet a favor with lunch menus at 28€ and 32€ ($35 and $40), respectively. The midday prices at top-flight tables used to be a great way to get a taste of the best for a fraction of the cost, but the prices of the lunch menus have been skyrocketing. Still cheaper than dinner, though. Try **Lucas-Carton** 80€ ($100), **Pierre Gagnaire** 95€ ($119), and, the best of the bunch, the 178€ ($223) menu at **Ledoyen.**

Best brunch... This American habit has now become established in Paris. The **Café Beaubourg** is a designer café in the heart of Paris, inevitably full of too-too-trendy types. Somewhat overpriced, it's still a pleasant café to hang out in for an hour or two, and the American-style brunch is available all day, every day. At **Coffee Parisien,** which does a version of American food, there is no set brunch formula, but all the elements are there on the menu: pancakes and bacon, fried eggs, etc. Reservations are a must in this tiny restaurant full of aspiring models. The tea salon in the gift shop **Marais Plus** is a popular brunch spot on Saturday and Sunday, but for a change of pace, try the Moroccan restaurant **404,** or head out to **Quai Ouest.** Though located in the suburb of St. Cloud, it's accessible by Métro, and the riverside location, loft-chic decor, and lively young crowd make it a good destination when you want to take it easy on a sunny weekend.

Vegging out... Until chef Alain Passard went veggie at his three-star **Arpège,** vegetarian restaurants in Paris were stuck in a 1968 vintage time warp. Now many trendy tables offer good veg options, including **La Maison Blanche.** The **Piccolo Teatro** in the Marais specializes in delicious vegetarian gratins in a friendly *baba-cool* (hippie) atmosphere. Nearby, **Aquarius** offers steamed vegetable plates and vegetable tarts. There's not much in the way of decor, but the food is satisfying and cheap. The 14th arrondissement has another, unrelated restaurant named **Aquarius;** this one boasts a pleasant blond-wood decor and more sophisticated dishes like soybean quenelles and tarragon cannelloni. In Montmartre, the laid-back **Au Grain de Folie,** serving salads, tarts, and vegetable and rice dishes, seems like another throwback to the '60s. Though it's not strictly vegetarian, **Il Baccello,** a stylish Italian restaurant in the 17th arrondissement, serves a lot of first-rate veggie dishes; the chef trained at Joia, the brilliant luxury vegetarian restaurant in Milan.

Something fishy... Paris may be landlocked, but fresh seafood is shipped to restaurants every day from Normandy and

Brittany. **La Cagouille** is airy and modern with a pleasant terrace for summer dining. The seafood is extremely fresh, the desserts sublime, and the service congenial. The second floor dining room and oyster bar at **Garnier** are considered by sophisticated Parisians to be the ideal backdrop to a swanky seafood feast. Run by chef Jean-Pierre Abitane, **Bistrot Côté Mer** is an excellent, reasonably priced fish house on the Left Bank. Try the roasted mussels with mushroom salad and tartare sauce. Cost-conscious diners should try the chain called **Le Bar à Huîtres,** which guarantees the freshness of its oysters, lobsters, and other seafood.

Satisfying your sweet tooth... For the best hot chocolate in Paris, **Angélina** wins hands down for its thick, rich "African chocolate." Or sip *chocolat à l'ancien* in the palm-lined gallery of the Hôtel Plaza Athénée (see the Accommodations chapter).

Ladurée, an elegant tearoom has given rise to people who would do anything for their macaroons—fragile, sugary cookies that have nothing to do with the heap o' coconut jobs by the same name in North America. Ladurée's macaroons come in a variety of sublime flavors, including chocolate, coffee, and raspberry. All of their pastries are bliss, and these two addresses make irresistibly happy pit stops during any day on the town.

The best indigenous ice cream is found at **Berthillon,** which must be the only ice-cream shop that allows itself the luxury of shutting down during the summer. The pear sorbet tastes like a frozen pear (and even has the right texture), and the chocolate and coffee ice creams are sublime.

Where to go when you're sick of French cooking... **Fogon St-Julien** serves superb paella with great Spanish wines and has a lively atmosphere. **Il Baccello,** one of the most authentic Italian restaurants in Paris, is tucked away in the remote reaches of the 17th arrondissement; it's a great spot for vegetarians because it does succulent pastas and risottos. **Coffee Parisien** serves credible versions of American favorites, including hamburgers and salads. For good couscous try **Chez Omar,** and for some really delicious Indonesian cuisine, head for **Djakarta Bali**. The brother/sister team who run the restaurant are delightful, and there are occasional live performances of Indonesian music and dance.

Map 8: Right Bank Dining (1–4, 9–12 & 18e)

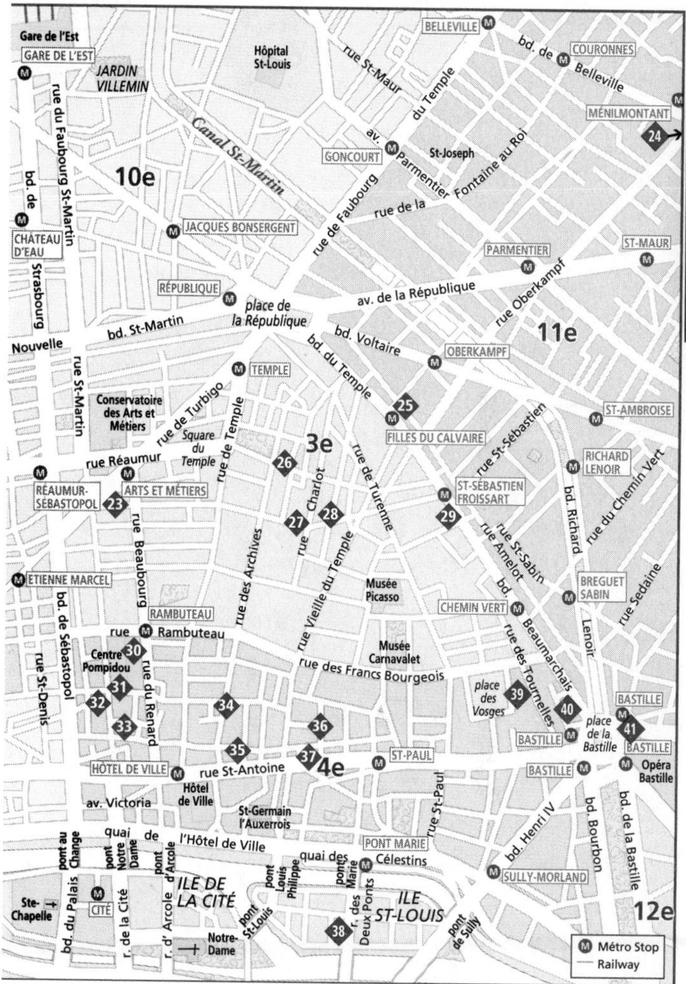

Le Repaire de Cartouche **29**
Le Vaudeville **9**
Piccolo Teatro **36**
Restaurant du Palais-Royal **16**
Terminus Nord **4**
Willi's Wine Bar **14**

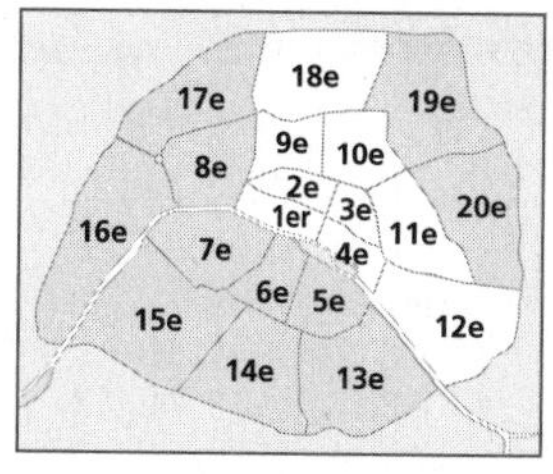

Map 9: Right Bank Dining (8 & 16–17e)

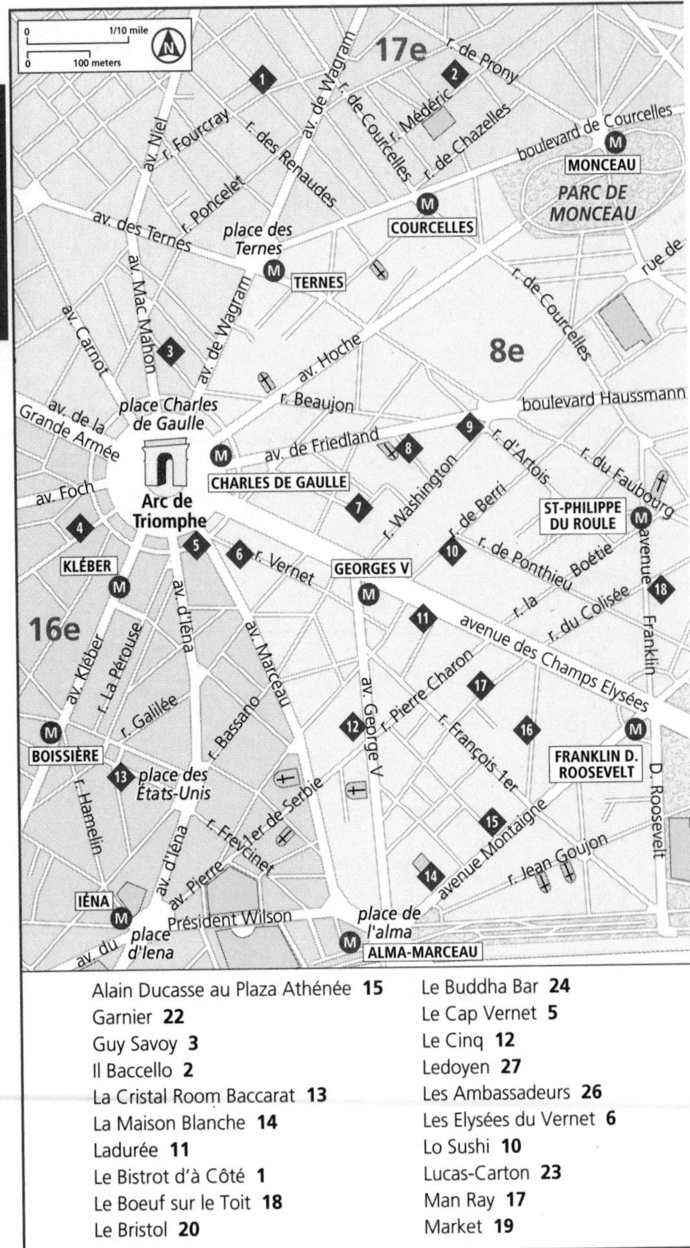

Maxim's **25**
Pierre Gagnaire **7**
Prunier **4**
Restaurant de'l Astor **21**
Restaurant Plaza Athénée **15**
Rue Balzac **8**
Spoon, Food and Wine **16**
Taillevent **9**

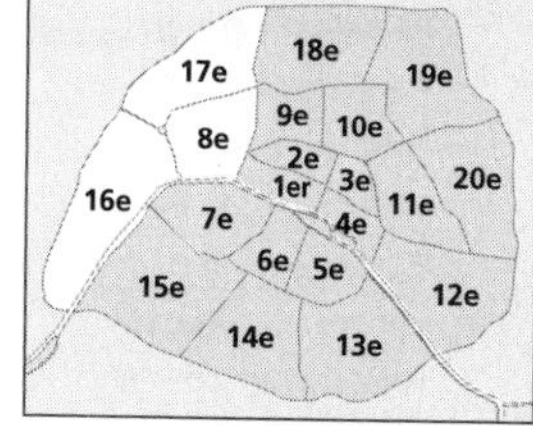

Map 10: Left Bank Dining (5–6 & 13–14e)

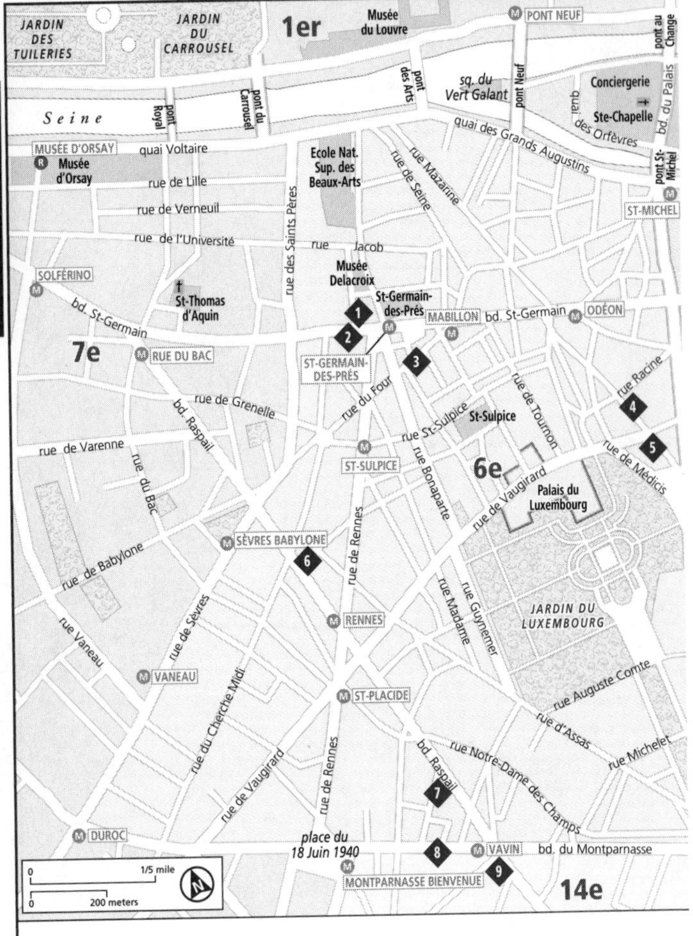

Bistrot Côté Mer **13**
Bistrot du Dôme **9**
Brasserie Lipp **2**
Café de Flore **1**
Chantairelle **16**
Chez Marcel **7**
Coffee Parisien **3**
Fogon St-Julien **10**
Hélène Darroze **6**
La Coupole **8**
La Table d'Aude **5**
La Tour d'Argent **11**
Le Balzar **15**
Le Bar à Huîtres **14**
Le Reminet **12**
Perraudin **17**
Polidor **4**

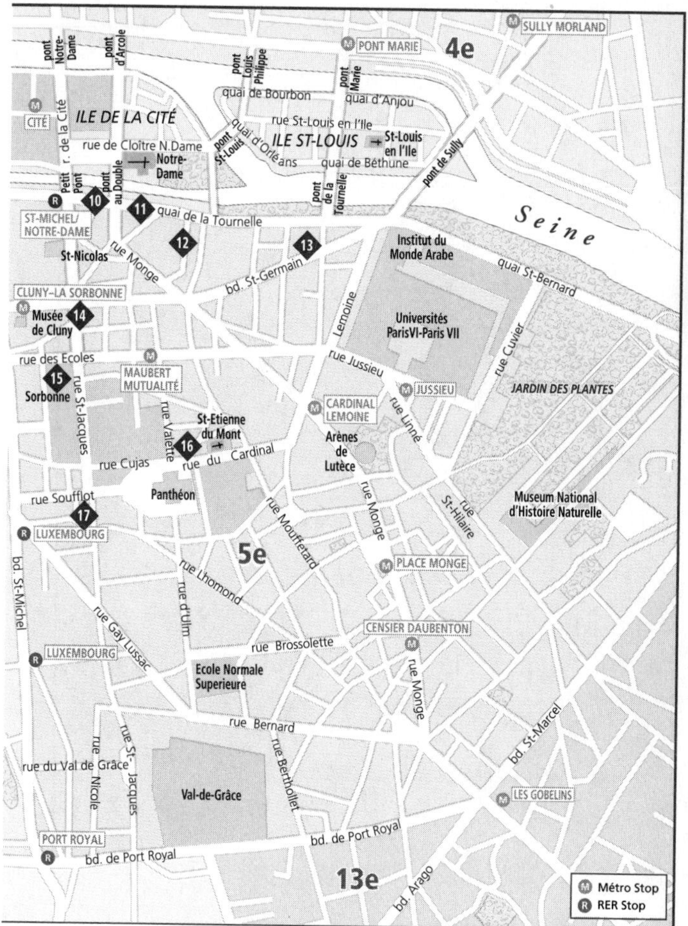

4e
SULLY MORLAND
PONT MARIE
pont Notre-Dame
pont d'Arcole
pont Louis Philippe
pont Marie
quai de Bourbon
quai d'Anjou
CITÉ
ILE DE LA CITÉ
r. de la Cité
rue St-Louis en l'Ile
ILE ST-LOUIS
St-Louis en l'Ile
rue de Cloître N.Dame
Notre-Dame
pont St-Louis
quai d'Orléans
quai de Béthune
pont de Sully
Petit Pont
pont au Double
pont de la Tournelle
10
11
quai de la Tournelle
Seine
ST-MICHEL/ NOTRE-DAME
12
13
Institut du Monde Arabe
St-Nicolas
rue Monge
bd. St-Germain
quai St-Bernard
CLUNY-LA SORBONNE
Musée de Cluny
14
Lemoine
Universités ParisVI-Paris VII
rue Cuvier
rue des Ecoles
rue Jussieu
MAUBERT MUTUALITÉ
15
Sorbonne
rue St-Jacques
JUSSIEU
JARDIN DES PLANTES
CARDINAL LEMOINE
rue Valette
St-Etienne du Mont
rue Linné
Arènes de Lutèce
16
rue du Cardinal
rue Cujas
rue Soufflot
Panthéon
rue Monge
rue St-Hilaire
Museum National d'Histoire Naturelle
17
LUXEMBOURG
rue Mouffetard
5e
PLACE MONGE
bd. St-Michel
rue Lhomond
rue d'Ulm
rue Gay Lussac
CENSIER DAUBENTON
LUXEMBOURG
rue Brossolette
Ecole Normale Superieure
rue Monge
rue Bernard
bd. St-Marcel
rue du Val de Grâce
rue Nicole
rue St-Jacques
rue Berthollet
Val-de-Grâce
LES GOBELINS
PORT ROYAL
bd. de Port Royal
bd. de Port Royal
13e
bd. Arago
Métro Stop
RER Stop

18e
17e
19e
9e
10e
8e
2e
20e
1er
3e
16e
11e
7e
4e
6e
5e
15e
12e
14e
13e

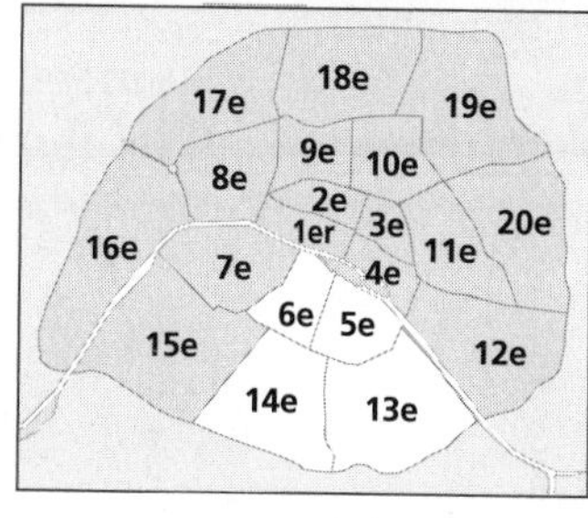

Map 11: Left Bank Dining (7 & 15e)

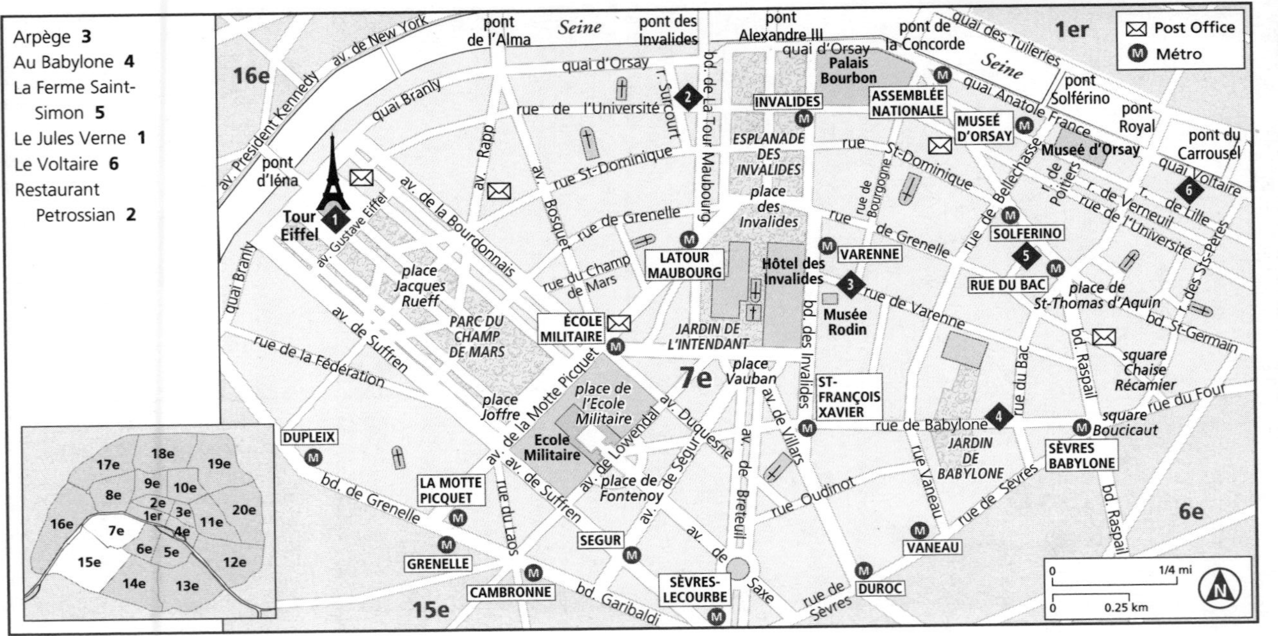

The Index

Note:	1€ = $1.25 U.S.
$$$$$	more than 175€ ($219)
$$$$	125€–175€ ($156–$219)
$$$	75€–125€ ($94–$156)
$$	35€–75€ ($44–$94)
$	35€ ($44)

Prices given are per person for entrees only.
As a rule, try to make reservations.

The following abbreviations are used for credit cards:

AE	American Express
DC	Diners Club
DISC	Discover
MC	MasterCard
V	Visa

Many restaurants (especially those with the priciest menus or youngest *proprietaires*) have websites with their current menu and sometimes an online reservation service. France's excellent online Yellow Pages, www.pagesjaunes.fr, is the best way to find a restaurant's most current Web address. If you can read a bit of French, www.paris.planresto.fr allows you to search by several criteria, such as main dish, neighborhood, price, special diet, and cuisine by country. Access to the search engine is free, but it can be awfully slow.

Alain Ducasse au Plaza Athénée **(p. 60)** CHAMPS-ELYSEES *CLASSIC FRENCH* Ducasse moved from his former town-house setting in the 16th arrondissement, and this slickly decorated hotel dining room—think crystal chandeliers hidden inside of giant gray moiré shades, a mix of modern art and Louis something, and unctuous waiters—suits him to a T. The maestro's rarely in the kitchen (he's more of an exec than a chef these days), but the team he trains turns out smashingly good food like langoustines topped with caviar and cream, plus seasonal specials like an earthy, elegant tart of crepes with crayfish or a perfect duckling roasted in fig leaves with a sauce of aged vinegar and pan drippings.... *Tel 01-53-67-65-00. Hôtel Plaza Athénée, 25, av. Montaigne, 8e. Métro Franklin D Roosevelt. Reservations required. Thurs–Fri 12:45–2pm, Mon–Fri 7:45–10pm. AE, DC, MC, V. $$$$$*

See Map 9 on p. 80.

Angélina (p. 77) LOUVRE/LES HALLES *FRENCH/TEA* A chic, Viennese-style, Belle Epoque tearoom that serves fabulously rich hot chocolate, refined lunches, and decadent desserts.... *Tel 01-42-60-82-00. 226, rue de Rivoli, 1er. Métro Tuileries. Daily 9am–7pm; closed Tues in Aug. AE, MC, V. $*

See Map 8 on p. 78.

Aquarius (p. 76) MARAIS *VEGETARIAN* A satisfying, cheap, and basic vegetarian restaurant.... *Tel 01-48-87-48-71. 54, rue Sainte-Croix-de-la-Bretonnerie, 4e. Métro Hôtel de Ville. Mon–Sat 11am–11pm; closed 2 weeks in Aug. MC, V. $*

See Map 8 on p. 78.

Aquarius (p. 76) MONTPARNASSE *VEGETARIAN* This restaurant serves generous helpings of inventive, flavorful dishes, including tofu croquettes, soybean quenelles, mushroom tarts, and mushroom lasagna. Organic wines available.... *Tel 01-45-41-36-88. 40, rue de Gergovie, 14e. Métro Pernety. Reservations recommended on weekends. Mon–Sat 11:45am–2:30pm and 7–10pm. AE, MC, V. $*

Arpège (p. 57) EIFFEL TOWER *MODERN FRENCH* Elegant "designer" decor sets the stage for the cuisine of chef Alain Passard, who stunned the food world by converting his three-star to an almost entirely vegetarian menu. Try the vegetable couscous and sweet-and-sour lobster.... *Tel 01-45-51-47-33. 84, rue de Varenne, 7e. Métro Varenne. Reservations required. Mon–Fri 12:30–2pm and daily 8–9:30pm. AE, DC, DISC, MC, V. $$$$$*

See Map 11 on p. 84.

Au Babylone (p. 75) EIFFEL TOWER *FRENCH* Ideal for a cheap atmospheric lunch on the Left Bank. The amiable waitresses fly through the room with plates of grated carrot salad, lamb stew, and runny wedges of Camembert, and most of the crowd drinks the house red by the carafe.... *Tel 01-45-48-72-13. 13, rue de Babylone, 7e. Métro Sèvres Babylone. Mon–Sat 11:30am–2:30pm; closed Aug. No credit cards. $*

See Map 11 on p. 84.

Au Grain de Folie (p. 76) MONTMARTRE *VEGETARIAN* Salads, tarts, and vegetable and rice dishes are served here in a *baba-cool* atmosphere.... *Tel 01-42-58-15-57. 24, rue La Vieuville, 18e. Métro Abbesses. Daily 12:30–2:30pm and 7:30–11:30pm. No credit cards. $*

See Map 8 on p. 78.

Au Pied de Cochon (p. 65) LOUVRE/LES HALLES *TRADITIONAL FRENCH* This 24-hour spot specializes in body parts of the pig, from the foot to the snout, as well as shellfish platters and more ordinary fare. Lively atmosphere. Reservations are taken only until 8:30pm.... *Tel 01-40-13-77-00. 6, rue Coquillière, 1er. Métro Louvre or Les Halles. Open 24 hrs a day. AE, DC, MC, V. $$*

See Map 8 on p. 78.

Aux Lyonnais (p. 73) LA BOURSE/LYONNAIS *TRADITIONAL FRENCH* A meal of Lyonnais specialties here will convince you why the city of Lyon is called the gastronomic capital of France. Pig out on pike dumplings (the best in Paris), skate meunière, and a peppery coq au vin. Start with foie gras and end your bliss with a heaven-sent Cointreau soufflé.... *Tel 01-42-96-65-04. 32, rue St-Marc, 2e. Métro Grands-Boulevards. Reservations required. Tues–Sat noon–2pm and 7:30–11:30pm. AE, DC, MC, V. $$$*

See Map 8 on p. 78.

Barrio Latino (p. 68) BASTILLE *INTERNATIONAL* The plush decor here, with a central atrium and a Moorish-style back bar, is more clearly aimed at gilded suburban youth than would-be revolutionaries. The menu runs to fashion food like salmon tartare and carpaccio more than to any of the earthy grub you find in Latin America.... *Tel 01-55-78-84-75. 46/48, rue du Faubourg St-Antoine, 12e. Métro Bastille. Reservations recommended. Mon–Sat noon–1:30am. AE, DC, MC, V. $$*

See Map 8 on p. 78.

Berthillon (p. 77) ILE ST-LOUIS *DESSERTS* The best ice cream in Paris is made on the Ile Saint-Louis and sold almost exclusively in the shop itself, in cafés, and from take-out windows. Expect to wait in line.... *Tel 01-43-54-31-61. 31, rue St-Louis-en-l'Ile, 4e. Métro Pont-Marie. Take-out window Wed–Sun 10am–8pm; café Wed–Fri 1–8pm and Sat–Sun 2–8pm; closed during school vacations except Christmas. No credit cards. $*

See Map 8 on p. 78.

Bistrot Beaubourg (p. 66) MARAIS *CAFE* An unpretentious, non-touristy, inexpensive little restaurant near the Centre Pompidou. Neighborhood residents enjoy simple dishes like beef with carrots or perch with shrimp sauce. Outdoor dining in the summertime.... *Tel 01-42-77-48-02. 25, rue Quincampoix, 4e. Métro Rambuteau or Châtelet Les Halles. Daily noon–midnight. MC, V. $*

See Map 8 on p. 78.

Bistrot Côté Mer (p. 77) LATIN QUARTER *SEAFOOD* Jean-Pierre Abitane runs this popular and reasonably priced fish house with a trendy Breton atmosphere. Start with oysters, followed by the catch of the day, and a killer cocoa soufflé for dessert....

Tel 01-43-54-59-10. 16, bd. St-Germain, 5e. Métro Maubert Mutualité. Reservations recommended. Daily noon–2pm and 7:30–10:30pm. AE, MC. $$

See Map 10 on p. 82.

Bistrot du Dôme (p. 64) MONTPARNASSE *TRADITIONAL FRENCH* The lower-priced bistro of the famous Dôme in Montparnasse also specializes in seafood.... *Tel 01-43-35-32-00. 1, rue Delambre, 14e. Métro Vavin. Reservations recommended. Daily 12:15–2pm and 7:30–11pm. AE, MC, V. $$*

See Map 10 on p. 82.

Brasserie Lipp (p. 62) ST-GERMAIN-DES-PRES *TRADITIONAL FRENCH* One of the haunts of former president François Mitterrand and a long list of writers and other celebrities. The classic French food and service, however, are not what they used to be.... *Tel 01-45-48-53-91. 151, bd. St-Germain, 6e. Métro St-Germain-des-Prés. Reservations recommended. Daily noon–1am; closed 3 weeks in Aug. AE, DC, MC, V. $$*

See Map 10 on p. 82.

Café Beaubourg (p. 65) MARAIS *CAFE* This chic café facing the Centre Pompidou serves drinks and slightly upscale café fare (*croques-monsieurs,* salads). American-style brunch is served at all times.... *Tel 01-48-87-63-96. 43, rue St. Merri, 4e. Métro Rambuteau or Hôtel de Ville. Daily 8am–1am. AE, MC, V. $*

See Map 8 on p. 78.

Café de Flore (p. 65) ST-GERMAIN-DES-PRES *CAFE* A classic café with an Art Deco interior, ridiculously high prices, high-quality café fare, and great people-watching possibilities.... *Tel 01-45-48-55-26. 172, bd. St-Germain, 6e. Métro St-Germain-des-Prés. Daily 7:30am–1:30am. AE, DC, MC, V. $*

See Map 10 on p. 82.

Café Marly (p. 65) LOUVRE/LES HALLES *ECLECTIC* The "in" place for lunch, dinner, or in-between drinks, located in a wing of the Louvre. The menu includes gazpacho, Caesar salad, poached haddock, and even a cheeseburger (in the Louvre!).... *Tel 01-49-26-06-60. Cour Napoléon, 93, rue de Rivoli, 1er. Métro Palais Royal. Daily 8am–2am. AE, MC, V. $$*

See Map 8 on p. 78.

Café Panique (p. 65) GARE DU NORD *TRADITIONAL FRENCH* With its improved cuisine, this café has landed on the culinary map of serious Parisian foodies. Feast on such delights as *magret de canard* (duckling) or melt-in-the-mouth ravioli of foie gras.... *Tel 01-47-70-06-84. 12, rue des messagerie, 10e. Métro Poissonière. Reservations recommended. Mon–Fri 12:15–2:15pm and Mon–Sat 9–11:15pm. AE, MC, V. $$$*

See Map 8 on p. 78.

Café Very (p. 72) LOUVRE/LES HALLES *CAFE* A café in the Tuileries serving tasty open-face sandwiches and crêpes under the chestnut trees or in the woodsy interior.... *Tel 01-47-03-94-84. Jardin des Tuileries, 1er. Métro Concorde or Tuileries. Daily until 10:30pm. MC, V. $*

See Map 8 on p. 78.

Chantairelle (p. 75) LATIN QUARTER *REGIONAL FRENCH* Relaxed and admirably devoted to its regional calling, which is promoting the food and charms of the Auvergne, this little spot in the Latin Quarter is fine for a tasty filling of dishes like stuffed cabbage and bilberry tart.... *Tel 01-46-33-18-59. 17, rue Laplace, 5e. Métro Maubert Mutualité. Reservations recommended. Mon–Sat noon–2pm and 7–10pm; Nov–May closed Sat lunch. MC, V. $*

See Map 10 on p. 82.

Chartier (p. 67) OPERA GARNIER *TRADITIONAL FRENCH* An enormous *bouillon* (originally, a cheap workers' restaurant that served *pot-au-feu*) that has not changed much since the 19th century. Cheap, acceptable food, brusque service, and tons of atmosphere.... *Tel 01-47-70-86-29. 7, rue du Faubourg-Montmartre, 9e. Métro Grands Boulevards or Rue Montmartre. Daily 11:30am–3pm and 7–9:30pm. V. $*

See Map 8 on p. 78.

Chez La Vieille-Adrienne (p. 73) LOUVRE/LES HALLES *TRADITIONAL FRENCH* Come to this preciously fusty old bistro for a deep dose of Paris, the eternal capital of Gaul, which comes from the non-descript cobbled-together decor, the waitresses who continuously baby you, and delicious and abundant old-fashioned French cooking. The assorted hors d'oeuvres alone are a meal, including help-yourself terrines of duck, head-cheese, lentils, veal-stuffed courgettes, avocado and tomato salad with hard-cooked egg wedges, marinated leeks, and a sublime celery remoulade. Follow with a steak, roast chicken, veal braised with green olives, and ewe's-milk-cheese–stuffed cannelloni, and wash it down with a bottle of Alzipratu, a fine Corsican red.... *Tel 01-42-60-15-78. 1, rue Bailleul/37, rue de l'Arbre Sec, 1er. Métro Louvre Rivoli. Mon–Fri noon–2pm and Thurs 7–10pm. AE, MC, V. $$*

See Map 8 on p. 78.

Chez Marcel (p. 71) ST-GERMAIN-DES-PRES *TRADITIONAL FRENCH* For coq au vin or *canard a l'orange,* dip into this little bistro near Montparnasse. Romantic and intimate setting with an excellent wine list. Order what your *serveur* (the boss) recommends.... *Tel 01-45-48-29-94. 7, rue Stanislas, 6e. Métro Notre-Dame-des-Champs. Reservations recommended. Mon–Sat noon–2pm and 7:30–10pm. MC, V. $$*

See Map 10 on p. 82.

Chez Michel (p. 57) GARE DU NORD *MODERN FRENCH* Chef Thierry Breton's scallops in cider and *kouign aman,* a sugared puff pastry served with apple sorbet, make a journey to this slightly dreary part of town worth the effort.... *Tel 01-44-53-06-20. 10, rue de Belzunce, 10e. Métro Gare du Nord. Reservations required for dinner. Tues–Fri noon–2pm, Mon–Sat 7pm–midnight. V. $$*

See Map 8 on p. 78.

Chez Nénesse (p. 75) MARAIS *TRADITIONAL FRENCH* A little neighborhood bistro that serves inexpensive lunches like roast lamb shoulder with white beans or pork ribs with lentils. In the evening, the menu becomes more sophisticated and the prices somewhat higher.... *Tel 01-42-78-46-49. 17, rue de Saintonge, 3e. Métro Arts et Métiers. Mon–Fri noon–2:15pm and 8–10:30pm; closed Aug. MC, V. $–$$*

See Map 8 on p. 78.

Chez Omar (p. 77) MARAIS *NORTH AFRICAN* A trendy restaurant with marvelous old bistro decor that needs a coat of paint. The couscous and grilled meats are very good and bargain-priced.... *Tel 01-42-72-36-26. 47, rue de Bretagne, 3e. Métro Arts et Métiers. Mon–Sat noon–2:30pm, daily 7–10:30pm. No credit cards. $*

See Map 8 on p. 78.

Clown Bar (p. 69) BASTILLE *TRADITIONAL FRENCH* One of the best wine bars in the city. Circus decor, excellent, market-fresh French food, and well-chosen wine list. Reserve.... *Tel 01-43-55-87-35. 114, rue Amelot, 11e. Métro Filles du Calvaire. Mon–Sat noon–3pm and 7pm–1am; closed part of Aug. No credit cards. $*

See Map 8 on p. 78.

Coffee Parisien (p. 76) ST-GERMAIN-DES-PRES *AMERICAN* A hip, young crowd heavy on aspiring models comes to this little restaurant to sample the perfectly prepared American fare, including hamburgers, eggs Benedict, and cheesecake.... *Tel 01-43-54-18-18. 4, rue Princess, 6e. Métro Mabillon. Daily noon–11:30pm. AE, MC, V. $*

See Map 10 on p. 82.

Coude de Fou (p. 66) MARAIS *MODERN FRENCH* A popular restaurant. Daily specials might include *salade de boudin frit* (salad with fried blood sausage) or an entrecôte steak with blue-cheese sauce.... *Tel 01-42-77-15-16. 12, rue du Bourg-Tibourg, 4e. Métro Hôtel de Ville. Mon–Sat noon–3pm, daily 7:30pm–2am. AE, MC, V. $*

See Map 8 on p. 78.

Dame Tartine (p. 70) MARAIS *LIGHT BITES* A restaurant in the heart of town serving creative *tartines* (open-face sandwiches) with toppings like smoked duck with wilted lettuce, chicken with almonds and cinnamon, or beef with artichoke and hazelnut cream.... *Tel 01-42-77-32-22. 2, rue Brisemiche, 4e. Métro Hôtel de Ville. Daily 11am–11:30pm. DC, MC, V. $*

See Map 8 on p. 78.

Djakarta Bali (p. 77) LOUVRE/LES HALLES *INDONESIAN* Tucked away in a side street near Les Halles, this superb restaurant, with its pretty decor and gracious service, provides a great opportunity to discover the delicious and relatively little-known cuisine of Indonesia. Start with the *soto ayam,* a delicate soup of chicken broth, rice noodles and vegetables, and *lumpia,* fried homemade spring rolls served with a fresh peanut sauce, and then try *rendang daging,* beef in coconut milk seasoned with Indonesian herbs and *ayam jahe,* carmelized chicken in ginger sauce.... *Tel 01-45-08-83-11. 9, rue Vauvilliers, 1er. Métro Louvre Rivoli or Les Halles. Tues–Sun 7–11pm. V. $–$$*

See Map 8 on p. 78.

Fogon St-Julien (p. 77) LATIN QUARTER *SPANISH* This little vest-pocket place with stone walls serves delicious paella in several different variations. Friendly service and a laid-back crowd make it a fun night out.... *Tel 01-43-54-31-33. 10, rue St-Julien-le-Pauvre, 5e. Métro St-Michel. Tues–Sun 7pm–midnight and Sat–Sun noon–2:30pm. MC, V. $$*

See Map 10 on p. 82.

404 (p. 76) MARAIS *MOROCCAN* One of the best Moroccan restaurants in town. Ask for a seat on the tiny mezzanine, reached via a treacherous, winding staircase. The *pastilla* (pigeon in a flaky pastry crust dusted with cinnamon) is fantastic, as are the couscous and tagines. Brunch on weekends.... *Tel 01-42-74-57-81. 69, rue des Gravilliers, 3e. Métro Arts et Métiers. Reservations required. Daily noon–2:30pm and 8pm–2am; closed for 1 week in Aug. AE, DC, DISC, MC, V. $$*

See Map 8 on p. 78.

Garnier (p. 65) CHAMPS-ELYSEES *SEAFOOD* As the city's remaining independent brasseries become an increasingly scarcer breed, Garnier soldiers on, and having recently been renovated with a decor that's a slightly flashy mix of modern and Art Deco, it's better than ever. This place specializes in seafood—note the charming little oyster bar just inside the front door.... *Tel 01-43-87-50-40. 111, rue St-Lazare, 8e. Métro St-Lazare. Daily noon–11pm. AE, DC, MC, V. $$*

See Map 9 on p. 80.

Georges (p. 58) MARAIS *INTERNATIONAL* One of the hippest restaurants in town, with a gorgeous crowd of posers who come to nibble at dishes like shrimp tempura, monkfish with tandoori spices, and smoked salmon. This place really rocks at night.... *Tel 01-44-78-47-99. Centre Pompidou, rue Rambuteau and rue St-Merri, 4e. Métro Rambuteau or Hôtel de Ville. Reservations required. Daily 11am–2am. AE, MC, V. $$*

See Map 8 on p. 78.

Guy Savoy (p. 61) PARC MONCEAU *HAUTE CUISINE* Blond wood and modern paintings and sculptures brighten the dining room of Guy Savoy, who some call the best chef in Paris. His desserts, especially the crème brûlée with apples, are heavenly.... *Tel 01-43-80-40-61. www.guysavoy.com. 18, rue Troyon, 17e. Métro Etoile. Reservations required. Mon–Fri noon–2pm, Mon–Sat 7–9:30pm. AE, DC, DISC, MC, V. $$$$*

See Map 9 on p. 80.

Hélène Darroze (p. 57) ST-GERMAIN-DES-PRES *MODERN FRENCH* The short menu changes regularly, but leads off with three different preparations of foie gras, and runs to dishes like roasted free-range chicken from Les Landes and red mullet with a tomato risotto in beef juice with black olives. The bistro on the main floor is cheaper and more casual than the pricey, stylish main table upstairs.... *Tel 01-42-22-00-11. 88, rue Rennes, 6e. Métro Sévres Babylone or St-Sulpice. Reservations required. Tues–Sat noon–2:30pm, daily 7:30–10:30pm. AE, DISC, MC, V. $$$$*

See Map 10 on p. 82.

Il Baccello (p. 76) PARC MONCEAU *ITALIAN* Young chef Raphael Bembaron is a real talent who trained at Joia, the superb gourmet vegetarian restaurant in Milan. Standout specials like a chick pea soup garnished with pancetta-wrapped langoustines.... *Tel 01-43-80-63-60. 33, rue Cardinet, 17e. Métro Wagram. Tues–Sat noon–2:30pm and 7:30–11pm. MC, V. $$*

See Map 9 on p. 80.

Julien (p. 63) GARE DU NORD *FRENCH* A gorgeous Art Nouveau restaurant with quality brasserie fare.... *Tel 01-47-70-12-06. 16, rue du Faubourg-Saint-Denis, 10e. Métro Strasbourg-St-Denis. Daily noon–3pm and 7pm–1am. AE, DC, MC, V. $$*

See Map 8 on p. 78.

Juveniles (p. 73) LOUVRE/LES HALLES *FUSION* An English-owned wine bar. The sausage and mashed potatoes with chutney is an example of a classic French dish (*saucisson avec purée de pommes de terre*) with a twist. Wines can be purchased to go.... *Tel 01-42-97-46-49. 47, rue de Richelieu, 1er. Métro Palais Royal. Mon–Sat noon–11pm. AE, MC, V. $*

See Map 8 on p. 78.

La Baracane (p. 70) MARAIS *REGIONAL FRENCH* Ignore the drab decor for some really good southwestern French cooking. This place is the bistro annex of Marcel Baudis, a talented chef whose main table is lost in space near Bercy. The prix-fixe menus here are an excellent buy.... *Tel 01-42-71-43-33. 38, rue des Tournelles, 4e. Métro Bastille or Chemin Vert. Tues–Sat noon–2pm, Mon–Sat 7–11pm. MC, V. $*

See Map 8 on p. 78.

La Boulangerie (p. 74) MENILMONTANT *FRENCH* This quiet corner of the trendy Ménilmontant district is the setting for some of the finest cheap bistro food in eastern Paris. The three-course prix fixe is the way to go, too. Typical dishes run to a croustade of wild mushrooms, remoulade of mussels, salmon in sherry-spiked onion cream sauce, and yellow plum and caramel *mille-feuille*. The wine list (nothing over 25€/$31) offers good drinking, including St-Emilion and other faves.... *Tel 01-43-58-45-45. 13, rue Victor Letalle, 20e. Métro Ménilmontant. Daily noon–2:30pm, Mon–Sat 7:30–11pm (until midnight Fri–Sat). DC, MC, V. $*

See Map 8 on p. 78.

La Cagouille (p. 72) MONTPARNASSE *SEAFOOD* Excellent seafood restaurant. The meal starts with a complimentary dish of sublime cockles in melted butter and continues with generous portions of fresh fish, perfectly prepared.... *Tel 01-43-22-09-01. http://la-cagouille.fr. 10, place Constantin Brancusi, 14e. Métro Gaité. Reservations required. Daily noon–2:30pm and 7:30–10:30pm. MC, V. $$*

La Cloche d'Or (p. 67) PIGALLE *FRENCH* A late-night restaurant frequented by actors. Relaxed atmosphere and simple food like onion soup, sole meunière, and mussels (*moules*).... *Tel 01-48-74-48-88. 3, rue Mansart, 9e. Métro Blanche. Daily noon–2:30pm and 7:30pm–4am (until 1am Sun). MC, V. $$*

See Map 8 on p. 78.

La Coupole (p. 63) MONTPARNASSE *CAFE* The famous hangout of everyone from Ernest Hemingway to Fernand Léger still merits a visit for its ambience.... *Tel 01-43-20-14-20. 102, bd. Montparnasse, 14e. Métro Vavin. Reservations recommended. Daily 8am–1am; closed Dec 24. AE, DC, MC, V. $$*

See Map 10 on p. 82.

La Cristal Room Baccarat (p. 62) BOIS DE BOULOGNE *MODERN FRENCH* The famous Taittinger family has opened this Baccarat-laden room in the former townhouse of Marie-Laure de Noailles, who was a famous patroness of such artists as Man Ray and Salvador Dalí. Philippe Starck designed the stunning minimalist decor. The brilliant chef, Thierry Burlot, is a true original, creating his own version of such classics as oyster ravioli or even a caramel soufflé.... *Tel 01-40-22-11-10. 11, Place des Etats-Unis,*

16e. Metro d'Iena or Boissière. Reservations required. Open Mon-Sat 8:30-10:30am, noon-2pm, 8-10pm. AE, DC, MC, V. $$$$

See Map 9 on p. 80.

Ladurée (p. 77) CHAMPS-ELYSEES *TEA/TRADITIONAL FRENCH* This elegant 1862 vintage tearoom in the heart of town not only serves weepingly good pastries but is a fine way to skip out on a lousy hotel breakfast, since its coffee and croissants are wonderful, too. The newer branch at 75, av. des Champs-Elysées, 8e (Tel 01-40-75-08-75; Métro Franklin D Roosevelt) pulls a trendy crowd, while the original pulls grandes dames on a shopping spree.... *Tel 01-42-60-21-79. www.laduree.fr. 16, rue Royale, 8e. Métro Concorde or Madeleine. Daily 7am–midnight. AE, DC, MC, V. $$*

See Map 9 on p. 80.

La Ferme Saint-Simon (p. 71) EIFFEL TOWER *FRENCH* Media types and politicians indulge in such delicacies as warm pigeon salad with fois gras vinaigrette.... *Tel 01-45-48-35-74. 6, rue St-Simon, 7e. Métro Rue du Bac. Reservations recommended. Mon–Fri 12:30–2pm, Mon–Sat 7:30–10pm. AE, DC, MC, V. $$$*

See Map 11 on p. 84.

La Grande Cascade (p. 72) BOIS DE BOULOGNE *TRADITIONAL FRENCH* Restored Belle Epoque restaurant at the foot of a waterfall in the Bois de Boulogne. Classic menu features specialties like duckling with sweet-and-sour sauce and ginger and crab ravioli with chervil.... *Tel 01-45-27-33-51. Bois de Boulogne, Allée de Longchamp, 16e. Métro Porte Maillot, then bus 244 (until 8pm; taxi necessary thereafter). Reservations required. Daily 12:30–2pm and 7:30–9:30pm; closed Dec 20–Jan 20 and a few weeks in Feb. AE, DC, MC, V. $$$$$*

La Maison Blanche (p. 71) CHAMPS-ELYSEES *MODERN FRENCH* Located on the sixth floor of the Théâtre des Champs-Elysées, this trendy modern restaurant, now run by the Pourcel brothers, the three-star culinary duo from Montpelier, serves dishes like roast kidneys with macaroni gratin and bass tartare made with olive oil and served with sun-dried tomatoes. Great views of Paris and a large terrace.... *Tel 01-47-23-55-99. 15, av. Montaigne, 8e. Métro Alma Marceau. Reservations recommended. Mon–Fri noon–2pm and daily 8–10pm; Aug closed Sun–Mon. AE, DC, MC, V. $$$$*

See Map 9 on p. 80.

La Régalade (p. 57) MONTPARNASSE *TRADITIONAL FRENCH* This hugely successful place has evolved from delighting neighborhood locals to attracting an international mink-coat crowd. Chef Yves Camdeborde is a veteran of the Crillon, and his credentials shine in dishes like his gratin of potatoes and lobster.... *Tel 01-45-45-68-58. 49, av. Jean-Moulin, 14e. Métro Alésia or Porte* *d'Orléans. Reservations required. Tues–Fri and Sun noon–2pm, Tues–Sun 7–10pm. MC, V. $$*

L'Astrance (p. 62) BOIS DE BOULOGNE *FUSION* Occupying a surprisingly edgy space in a part of town that's anything but, this is a real discovery. Chef Pascal Barbot formerly worked at Arpège in Paris and Ampersand in Sydney, and this experience shows in shrewd, chic, minimalist, and absolutely delicious dishes like baked mussels with a Moroccan-style salad of grated carrots; scallops in peanut cream sauce; red mullet cooked in a banana leaf and served with a superb tamarind sauce and a gratin of bananas. For dessert, try the deconstructed apple crumble and milk ice cream with *pain perdu.* Book well in advance.... *Tel 01-40-50-84-40. 4, rue Beethoven, 16e. Métro Passy or Rue de la Pompe. Reservations required. Mon–Fri 12:30–3:30pm and 8–9:30pm. AE, DC, MC, V. $$–$$$*

La Table d'Aude (p. 71) ST-GERMAIN-DES-PRES *REGIONAL FRENCH* Charming owner Bernard Patou and his wife Veronique take a contagious pleasure in serving up the best of their home turf, the Aude, a long narrow department in the Languedoc-Roussillon that includes Carcassonne, Castelnaudry—famed for its cassoulet and some of the most rapidly ascending vineyards in France, including Minervois and Corbieres.... *Tel 01-43-26-36-36. 8, rue de Vaugirard, 6e. Métro Odéon or RER Luxembourg. Reservations recommended. Mon–Sat noon–2pm and 7–10pm. MC, V. $*

See Map 10 on p. 82.

La Tartine (p. 72) MARAIS *LIGHT BITES* An ancient wine bar with an ancient owner. A great place for an aperitif and a *tartine* topped with pâté, rillettes, or cantal.... *Tel 01-42-72-76-85. 24, rue de Rivoli, 4e. Métro Hôtel de Ville or St-Paul. Wed–Mon noon–10pm; closed 2 weeks in Aug. No credit cards. $*

See Map 8 on p. 78.

La Tour d'Argent (p. 61) LATIN QUARTER *TRADITIONAL FRENCH* Everyone knows about the fabulous views of Notre-Dame, the famous duckling, and the charming owner, Claude Terrail. They don't always know about the pretentious atmosphere, the ho-hum food, and the fact that a plate of gussied-up scrambled eggs goes for a bundle of euros.... *Tel 01-43-54-23-31. www.latourdargent.com. 15, quai Tournelle, 5e. Métro Maubert Mutualité. Reservations required. Wed–Sun noon–1:30pm, Tues–Sun 7:30–10pm. AE, DC, MC, V. $$$$$*

See Map 10 on p. 82.

La Tour de Montlhery (p. 67) LOUVRE/LES HALLES *TRADITIONAL FRENCH* If you agree that feasting on country pâté and juicy lamb chops in the dead of night is a particularly Parisian pleasure, this 24-hour place is for you. This old market bistro has loads of scruffy charm and is just as pleasant during regular dining hours.... *Tel 01-42-36-21-82. 5, rue des Prouvaires, 1er. Métro Châtelet. Reservations required. Mon–Fri 24 hrs; closed mid-July through mid-Aug. MC, V. $$*

See Map 8 on p. 78.

Le Balzar (p. 65) LATIN QUARTER *TRADITIONAL FRENCH* There's always a great buzz in this vest-pocket Left Bank brasserie, which, in spite of tourist popularity, remains much beloved by a frisky and diverse crowd of Parisians. Everybody from academics to fashion designers loves this place for its friendly, aproned waiters, reliable cooking, and über-Parisian atmosphere. Strategically placed ceiling mirrors allow you to scan the whole room, which gives the place an amusing edge. Fab *choucroute garni* (sauerkraut and pork), onion soup, and roast chicken.... *Tel 01-43-54-13-67. 49, rue des Ecoles, 5e. Métro Cluny-La Sorbonne. Reservations recommended. Daily noon–11:30pm. AE, MC, V. $$*

See Map 10 on p. 82.

Le Bar à Huîtres (p. 77) LATIN QUARTER *SEAFOOD* A chain restaurant that serves good, fresh seafood, including oysters and lobster, at reasonable prices.... *Tel 01-44-07-27-37. www.lebarahuitres.com. 33, rue St-Jacques, 5e. Métro St-Michel. Daily noon–midnight. AE, DC, MC, V. $$*

See Map 10 on p. 82.

L'Ebauchoir (p. 75) BASTILLE *TRADITIONAL FRENCH* Simple decor and French cuisine with a touch of creativity: onion soup, escargots, raw sardines stuffed with minced vegetables, and tuna steak with orange sauce. Lively ambience and friendly service. Can get very noisy in the evening. Inexpensive, fixed-price lunch menu.... *Tel 01-43-42-49-31. 43–45, rue de Citeaux, 12e. Métro Faidherbe-Chaligny. Mon–Sat noon–2:30pm and 8–11pm. DC, MC, V. $*

Le Bistrot d'à Côté (p. 56) PARC MONCEAU *TRADITIONAL FRENCH* One of the three baby bistros created by big-time chef Michel Rostang. It has a very reasonable, fixed-priced lunch menu, but even in the evening you won't break the bank.... *Rue Gustave-Flaubert: Tel 01-42-67-05-81; 10, rue Gustave-Flaubert, 17e; Métro Courcelles; daily 12:30–2:30pm and 7–11pm, closed Sat lunch and Sun in summer only. Av. Villiers: Tel 01-47-63-25-61; 16, av. Villiers, 17e; Métro Villiers; Mon–Fri noon–2:15pm, Mon–Sat 7:45–10:30pm. Reservations recommended at both locations. AE, MC, V. $$*

See Map 9 on p. 80.

Le Boeuf sur le Toit (p. 65) CHAMPS-ELYSEES *TRADITIONAL FRENCH* This busy Art Deco restaurant serves classic brasserie fare of good quality, as do all the restaurants that are part of the

Groupe Flo chain.... *Tel 01-53-93-65-55. 34, rue du Colisée, 8e. Métro St-Philippe-du-Roule. Reservations recommended on weekends. Daily noon–3pm and 7pm–midnight; closed Dec 24. AE, DC, MC, V. $$*

See Map 9 on p. 80.

Le Bofinger (p. 56) MARAIS *TRADITIONAL FRENCH/ALSATIAN* One of the best Paris brasseries, with its stained-glass dome, sweeping staircase, wood paneling, large mirrors, black banquettes, and potted palms. Specialties include oysters, *choucroute*, and wild duck. Reserve, or arrive before 8pm or after 10pm.... *Tel 01-42-72-87-82. 3, rue de la Bastille, 4e. Métro Bastille. Daily noon–3pm and 7:30pm–1am. AE, DC, DISC, MC, V. $$*

See Map 8 on p. 78.

Le Bristol (p. 61) CHAMPS-ELYSEES *HAUTE CUISINE* This grande dame is a shrewd player in the local gastronomic sweepstakes since it hired culinary wunderkind Eric Frechon. The food's sublime, and it plays a real full house of luxury by having a summer dining room in its inner courtyard and a winter one with stunning Hungarian oak paneling and crystal chandeliers.... *Tel 01-53-43-43-00. www.lebristolparis.com. Hôtel Bristol, 112, rue Faubourg St-Honoré, 8e. Métro Miromesnil. Daily 6:30–10:30am, noon–2:30pm, and 7:30–10:30pm. AE, DC, DISC, MC, V. $$$$*

See Map 9 on p. 80.

Le Buddha Bar (p. 58) CHAMPS-ELYSEES *LIGHT BITES* Buddha himself surely never suspected that he'd be at the heart of a busy singles scene. Better for drinks than dinner, but the bar snacks are fine.... *Tel 01-53-05-90-00. 8, rue Boissy d'Anglas, 8e. Métro Concorde. Mon–Fri noon–3pm, daily 6pm–dawn. AE, MC, V. $$*

See Map 9 on p. 80.

Le Cap Vernet (p. 56) CHAMPS-ELYSEES *FRENCH/SEAFOOD* Guy Savoy's baby bistro offers a variety of starters and main courses as well as salads, shellfish platters, and great fish.... *Tel 01-47-20-20-40. 82, av. Marceau, 8e. Métro Etoile. Reservations recommended. Daily noon–2:30pm and 9–11pm. AE, DC, MC, V. $$*

See Map 9 on p. 80.

Le Cinq (p. 66) CHAMPS-ELYSEES *HAUTE CUISINE* Chef Philippe Legendre, formerly at Taillevent, has apparently been given *carte blanche* with luxury ingredients like caviar, lobster, and foie gras. Typical grub here is a delicious lasagna of langoustines between two gossamer sheets of pasta accented with Parmesan and lime zest. Service is friendly and earnest but often slow.... *Tel 01-49-52-70-00. www.fourseasons.com. 31, av. George V, 8e. Métro George V. Reservations required for dinner. Daily noon–2:30pm and 6:30–10:30pm. AE, DC, DISC, MC, V. $$$$$*

See Map 9 on p. 80.

Ledoyen (p. 61) CHAMPS-ELYSEES *FRENCH* Talented young chef Christophe Le Squer runs this restaurant set among the chestnut trees of the Champs-Elysées. Specialties include grilled wild salmon with red pepper mousse, carmelized roast duck, and, for dessert, passion-fruit soufflé.... *Tel 01-53-05-10-01. 1, av. Dutuit, 8e. Métro Champs Elysées Clemenceau. Reservations required. Tues–Fri 12:30–2:30pm, Mon–Fri 8–10pm. AE, MC, V. $$$$*

See Map 9 on p. 80.

Le Fumoir (p. 71) LOUVRE/LES HALLES *CAFE* An intriguing mix of hip Parisians and Euro-lounger types comes to linger over coffee or eat relatively good food in a setting of book-lined walls that recalls the great cafés of Mitteleuropa, French colonial Indochina, and the American '30s.... *Tel 01-42-92-00-24. Place du Louvre, 6, rue de l'Amiral-Coligny, 1er. Métro Louvre. Daily noon–2am. AE, DC, MC, V. $$*

See Map 8 on p. 78.

Le Grand Véfour (p. 60) LOUVRE/LES HALLES *HAUTE CUISINE* Michelin jacked this grande dame up to three stars, but while chef Guy Martin's cooking is great, it's not that great. Gorgeous decor, though.... *Tel 01-42-96-56-27. 17, rue Beaujolais, 1er. Métro Palais Royal. Reservations required. Mon–Fri 12:30–3pm, Mon–Thurs 8–10pm; closed July 25–Aug 25. $$$$$*

See Map 8 on p. 78.

Le Jules Verne (p. 74) EIFFEL TOWER *TRADITIONAL FRENCH* Stunning views of the city from the second floor of the Eiffel Tower. Chef Alain Reix's dishes include rockfish ravioli with mushrooms and artichokes, and new baby vegetables in puff pastry with morel butter. Reservations are a must.... *Tel 01-45-55-61-44. 2nd floor, Eiffel Tower, 7e. Métro Trocadéro. Reservations required. Daily 12:30–2:30pm and 7:30–11pm. AE, DC, MC, V. $$$$$*

See Map 11 on p. 84.

Le Petit Keller (p. 75) BASTILLE *TRADITIONAL FRENCH* This vintage 1950s spot with friendly tongue-in-cheek waiters and delicious home-cooked dishes like roast guinea hen and duck breast with honey is constantly packed with locals. An added bonus is the reasonable prices.... *Tel 01-47-00-12-97. 13, rue Keller, 11e. Métro Ledru-Rollin. Reservations recommended. Mon–Sat 7–11pm. MC, V. $*

Le Pré Catelan (p. 61) BOIS DE BOULOGNE *FUSION* The regulars tend to eat inside, but there is little that can match the pleasure of eating outside here amid the emerald green grass and flowers on a balmy summer evening. Chef Frédéric Anton brings a modern touch to dishes like roast duck with tamarind or black risotto with scampi, flavored with Thai basil and citronella. The service is faultless.... *Tel 01-44-14-41-14. Route de Suresnes, 16e. Métro Porte Maillot, then bus 144 (until 8pm; taxi necessary thereafter). Reservations recommended. Tues–Sun noon–3:30pm, Tues–Sat 7:30–9:30pm; closed during Feb school vacation. AE, DC, MC, V. $$$$$*

Le Reconfort (p. 70) MARAIS *FRENCH* An international fashion crowd loves this friendly, attractive place on the northern fringes of trendy Marais.... *Tel 01-49-96-09-60. 37, rue de Poitou, 3e. Métro St-Sebastian-Froissart. Reservations recommended. Daily noon–2pm and 8–11pm. MC. $$*

See Map 8 on p. 78.

Le Repaire de Cartouche (p. 64) BASTILLE *FRENCH* Tucked away between the Place de la République and the Bastille, this cozy bistro is popular for the sensational cooking of young chef Rodolphe Paquin, and its easy prices and friendly service.... *Tel 01-47-00-25-86. 8, bd. des Filles-du-Calvaire, 11e. Métro St. Sebastien-Froissart. Open Tues–Sat noon–2:30pm and 7:30–10pm. No credit cards. $$*

See Map 8 on p. 78

Le Reminet (p. 75) LATIN QUARTER *FRENCH* Chandeliers and mirrors accent the old stone walls of this cozy bistro with a friendly young staff. The prix-fixe menus at both lunch and dinner are very good value and include dishes like a salt-cod filet on a bed of braised endive in a sauce of honey and lemon.... *Tel 01-44-07-04-24. 3, rue des Grands Degrés, 5e. Métro Maubert Mutualité. Thurs–Mon noon–2:30pm and 7–10pm. MC, V. $$*

See Map 10 on p. 82.

Les Ambassadeurs (p. 66) CHAMPS-ELYSEES *MODERN FRENCH* The elegant marble-lined restaurant in the Hôtel Crillon offers the acclaimed cuisine of Dominique Bouchet—traditional dishes with a modern touch. Specialties include crispy bass with sesame seeds and mullet roasted in fennel oil served with a tomato-mozzarella tart.... *Tel 01-44-71-15-00. www.crillon.com. Hôtel Crillon, 10, place de la Concorde, 8e. Métro Concorde. Reservations recommended. Daily noon–2pm and 7:30–10pm. AE, DC, DISC, MC, V. $$$$*

See Map 9 on p. 80.

Les Elysées du Vernet (p. 58) CHAMPS-ELYSEES *TRADITIONAL FRENCH* In addition to chef Eric Briffard's splendid cooking, this handsome hotel dining room not only has a restful far-from-the-maddening-crowd feel—even though it's just a few steps off the Champs-Elysées—but superlative service, right down to the parting gift of a long-stemmed rose for ladies and a sachet of carmelized nuts for gents.... *Tel 01-44-31-98-00. Hôtel Vernet, 25, rue Vernet, 8e. Métro George V. Reservations required.*

Mon–Fri 12:30–2pm and 7:30–10pm; closed July 25–Aug 25. AE, MC, V. $$$$

See Map 9 on p. 80.

Les Ormes (p. 64) BOIS DE BOULOGNE *MODERN FRENCH* It's worth the trip to a remote part of the 16th arrondissement to discover the cooking of talented young chef Stephane Mole, who trained with Joel Robuchon—and it shows. His lusty and refined cooking runs to dishes like John Dory with wild mushrooms and artichoke hearts.... *Tel 01-46-47-83-98. 8, rue Chapu, 16e. Métro Exelmans. Reservations recommended. Tues–Sat 12:30–2pm and 7:45–10pm. AE, MC, V. $$*

L'Espadon (p. 63) LOUVRE/LES HALLES *TRADITIONAL FRENCH* With the arrival of chef Michel Roth, one of the most sumptuous dining rooms anywhere in the world is yet again one of the best restaurants in Paris, with service so precise and graceful that it's sort of a cross between a classical ballet and a Prussian artillery troop drill. Most importantly, the food's so good that it obviously warrants a second star. Don't miss the lobster salad, veal chop with a crust of polenta, and the best *mille-feuille* in town.... *Tel 01-43-16-30-80. The Ritz, 15, place Vendome, 1er. Métro Madeleine or Concorde. Reservations required on weekends. Daily noon–2:30pm and 7–10:30pm. AE, DC, MC, V. $$$$–$$$$$*

See Map 8 on p. 78.

Le Train Bleu (p. 58) GARE DE LYON *TRADITIONAL FRENCH* Though this landmarked dining room has always been one of the most romantic restaurants in Paris, for years the food was so drab that it was only worth coming for a drink. Now, under new management, they're serving delicious traditional French grub like a veal chop with a cap of melted cheese and lobster salad on a bed of walnut-oil–dressed mixed leaves.... *Tel 01-43-43-09-06. www.le-train-bleu.com. Gare de Lyon, 20, bd. Diderot, 12e. Métro Gare de Lyon. Reservations required. Daily 11:30am–3pm and 7–11pm. AE, MC, V. $$*

Le Vaudeville (p. 65) LA BOURSE *TRADITIONAL FRENCH* The wonderful Art Deco decor, the reflections in the mirrors, the huge bright flower arrangements, the speedy but cheerful waiters, and the general hustle and bustle make eating here a nearly total Paris experience.... *Tel 01-40-20-04-62. 29, rue Vivienne, 2e. Métro Bourse. Reservations recommended. Daily noon–3pm and 7pm–1am. AE, MC, V. $$*

See Map 8 on p. 78.

Le Voltaire (p. 72) EIFFEL TOWER *TRADITIONAL FRENCH* This meeting place for Left Bank publishers has a clubby, old-world atmosphere. The food is not out of the ordinary, but good and reliable.... *Tel 01-42-61-17-49. 27, quai Voltaire, 7e. Métro*

Solferino. Reservations recommended. Tues–Sat 12:30–2:30pm and 7:30–10:15pm. V. $$$

See Map 11 on p. 84.

Lo Sushi (p. 70) CHAMPS-ELYSEES *SUSHI* This cool self-service sushi bar is a fast alternative to another boring café salad, and the quality of the sushi, sashimi, California rolls, makis, and tekka-makis is pretty decent. Prepare to wait in line.... *Tel 01-45-62-01-00. 8, rue de Berri, 8e. Métro George V. Daily noon–12:30am. AE, MC, V. $–$$*

See Map 9 on p. 80.

Lucas-Carton (p. 60) CHAMPS-ELYSEES *HAUTE CUISINE* Art Nouveau decor, a helpful staff and some of the finest cuisine in the city. Specialties include wild rice risotto with chanterelles, *homard à la vanille,* and foie gras with cabbage, and for dessert, *gâteau au chocolat croustillant.* Reserve at least 3 weeks in advance.... *Tel 01-42-65-22-90. 9, place de la Madeleine, 8e. Métro Madeleine. Reservations required. Tues–Fri noon–2pm, Tues–Sat 8–10:30pm; closed July and 3 weeks in Aug. AE, DC, MC, V. $$$$$*

See Map 9 on p. 80.

Man Ray (p. 58) CHAMPS-ELYSEES *FUSION/ASIAN* The decor here at this vast sunken space is tastier than the food, but that doesn't stop a dressed-in-black crowd from settling in on the low arm chairs and banquettes for dishes like duck with lychees or sushi.... *Tel 01-56-88-36-36. www.manray.info. 34, rue Marbeuf, 8e. Métro Franklin D Roosevelt. Reservations recommended. Bar daily from 6pm; kitchen 7:30–10pm. MC, V. $$*

See Map 9 on p. 80.

Marais Plus (p. 76) See the Shopping chapter for a complete rundown.

See Map 25 on p. 178.

Market (p. 56) CHAMPS-ELYSEES *FUSION* Jean-Georges Vongerichten stars at this furiously popular Euro-Asian fusion spot in the glamorous Christie's building just off the Champs-Elysées. If you've been to any of his other restaurants, from Hong Kong to London or Las Vegas, you know the Franco-Asian gig.... *Tel 01-56-43-40-90. www.jean-georges.com. 15, av. Matignon, 8e. Métro Champs Elysées Clemenceau. Reservations required. Daily 8–11am, noon–3pm, and 8pm–1am. AE, DC, MC, V. $$*

See Map 9 on p. 80.

Maxim's (p. 61) CHAMPS-ELYSEES *TRADITIONAL FRENCH* Mediocre brasserie-style food at extreme prices in an authentic Art Nouveau setting.... *Tel 01-42-65-27-94. 3, rue Royale, 8e. Métro Concorde. Sun and Tues–Fri noon–2pm, Tues–Sun 8–11pm. AE, MC, V. $$$$$*

See Map 9 on p. 80.

Perraudin (p. 73) PANTHEON *TRADITIONAL FRENCH* You expect Emile Zola to walk through the door at any moment (he's buried nearby). Have a glass of kir at the zinc bar before digging into all those old favorites such as onion tart, pumpkin soup, rich terrines, and, of course, boeuf bourguignon. Expect to wait in line unless you arrive before 8pm.... *Tel 01-46-33-15-75. 157, rue St-Jacques, 5e. Métro Cluny-La Sorbonne. Reservations accepted only 7–8pm. Mon–Fri noon–2:15pm and 7–10pm. DC, MC, V. $$$*

See Map 10 on p. 82.

Piccolo Teatro (p. 76) MARAIS *VEGETARIAN* Tasty vegetarian gratins are served in a pleasant, slightly hippie-ish atmosphere.... *Tel 01-42-72-17-79. 6, rue des Ecouffes, 4e. Métro St-Paul. Reservations recommended. Daily noon–3pm and 7–11pm; closed Aug. AE, V. $*

See Map 8 on p. 78.

Pierre Gagnaire (p. 60) CHAMPS-ELYSEES *MODERN FRENCH* Pierre Gagnaire is an extraordinary cook. Go to his cobalt-blue dining room for veal sweetbreads roasted with cardamom and coffee, served with a fondue of endives and cigarette-like rolls of toasted eggplant.... *Tel 01-58-36-12-50. 6, rue Balzac, 8e. Métro George V. Reservations required. Mon–Fri noon–3:30pm, Mon–Fri and Sun 7:30–10pm; closed July 19–Aug 3. AE, MC, V. $$$$$*

See Map 9 on p. 80.

Polidor (p. 71) ST-GERMAIN-DES-PRES *TRADITIONAL FRENCH* A shabby, old restaurant with good, cheap food, and charming service. Try the escargots, the duck, the blanquette de veau, or the boeuf bourguignon.... *Tel 01-43-26-95-34. 41, rue Monsieur-le-Prince, 6e. Métro Odéon. Daily noon–2:30pm and 7:30–11pm. No credit cards. $–$$*

See Map 10 on p. 82.

Prunier (p. 73) BOIS DE BOULOGNE *CAVIAR* The lavish Art Deco mosaics add glamour to a meal at this luxury restaurant near the Arc de Triomphe, where caviar stars. French caviar from the Gironde River near Bordeaux is excellent and less expensive than anything Russian or Iranian. The smoked salmon and baked potato with caviar are heaven, too, and there's an array of vodkas served iced in carafes.... *Tel 01-44-17-35-85. 16, av. Victor Hugo, 16e. Métro Charles de Gaulle Etoile. Reservations recommended. Mon–Sat 12:30–2:30pm and 7:30–10:30pm; closed Aug. MC, V. $$$$–$$$$$*

See Map 9 on p. 80.

Quai Ouest (p. 76) SUBURBAN PARIS *FRENCH* This vast, airy warehouse-type space is industrial chic, with rough plank flooring, aluminum lights, and a fashionable clientele. The Sunday brunch is great for children, and dishes like scrambled eggs with smoked salmon are nicely done.... *Tel 01-46-02-35-54. 1200, Quai*

Marchel-Dassault, 92210 St-Cloud. Métro Boulogne Pont de St-Cloud. Reservations recommended. Daily noon–3pm and 8pm–midnight. AE, DC, MC, V. $$

Restaurant de l'Astor (p. 62) CHAMPS-ELYSEES *MODERN FRENCH* The brilliant Laurent Delarbre (voted Meilleur Ouvrier de France in 2005) concocts the sublime cuisine at this Art Deco restaurant where the menu changes with the season. French government ministers flock here from the Elysées Palace to sample the likes of tartare of pig's foot with slices of foie gras. Hotel Saint-Honoré.... *11, rue de l'Astorg, 8e. Tel. 01-53-05-05-05. Metro: Champs-Elysées Clemenceau. Open Mon-Fri noon-2pm and 7:30-10pm. AE, DC, MC, V. $$$*

See Map 9 on p. 80.

Restaurant du Palais-Royal (p. 72) LOUVRE/LES HALLES *TRADITIONAL FRENCH* This restaurant looks out upon the gardens of the Palais-Royal; some tables are actually in the peaceful gardens. A sampling from the menu: tuna carpaccio and cod with tomatoes and olive oil.... *Tel 01-40-20-00-27. 110, Galerie de Valois, Jardins du Palais Royal, 1er. Métro Palais-Royal. Reservations recommended. Mon–Sat 11:45am–2:15pm and 7:15–10:15pm. AE, DC, MC, V. $$*

See Map 8 on p. 78.

Restaurant Petrossian (p. 61) EIFFEL TOWER *CAVIAR/SEAFOOD* Occupying an elegant dove-gray dining room over the boutique of this famous supplier of caviar and smoked fish, this is the place for anyone looking to encounter some delicious and thrillingly out-there cooking. Chef Philippe Conticini won his first Michelin star for sublime dishes like smoked salmon with white-salmon sorbet and smoked swordfish with a compote of corn and a ragout of turnips. Desserts are amazing, too, including "Teaser, five explosions of taste," a colorful mixture of fruit coulis, jellies, and creams garnished with sugared pistachios.... *Tel 01-44-11-32-32. www.petrossian.fr. 18, bd. de La Tour Maubourg, 7e. Métro Invalides or La Tour Maubourg. Reservations required. Tues–Sat noon–2:30pm and 7:30–10:30pm. AE, DC, MC, V. $$$–$$$$*

See Map 11 on p. 84.

Restaurant Plaza Athénée (p. 69) CHAMPS-ELYSEES *TRADITIONAL FRENCH* The more casual restaurant in the Hôtel Plaza Athénée still has its original Art Deco decor. The menu features everything from salads, omelettes, and pasta to grilled meats and seafood.... *Tel 01-53-67-65-00. Hôtel Plaza Athénée, 25, av. Montaigne, 8e. Métro Franklin D Roosevelt. Reservations required. Daily 12:45–2pm and 7:45–10pm; closed in Aug. AE, MC, V. $$$*

See Map 9 on p. 80.

Rue Balzac (p. 63) CHAMPS-ELYSEES *MODERN FRENCH* Chef Michel Rostang and fading rocker Johnny Hallyday (it's a French thing) have created this stylish bistro that serves modern French cuisine by chef Yann Roncier. The decor's a bit clownish, but the crowd's interesting.... *Tel 01-53-89-90-91. 3, rue Balzac, 8e. Métro George V. Reservations recommended. Mon–Fri 12:15–2:15pm, daily 9:30–11:15pm. AE, DC, MC, V. $$$*

See Map 9 on p. 80.

Spoon, Food and Wine (p. 64) CHAMPS-ELYSEES *INTERNATIONAL* This extremely popular bistro pulls a lot of models and media people along with a surprising following of middle-aged voyeurs who come for the thrill of eating such unknown delicacies as barbecued spare ribs and charred squid with a curry dipping sauce, washed down with—*mon Dieu*—a Californian wine. Reserve well in advance.... *Tel 01-40-76-34-44. www.spoon.tm.fr. 14, rue Marignan, 8e. Métro Franklin D Roosevelt. Reservations required. Daily noon–2pm and 7–10pm. AE, DC, MC, V. $$–$$$*

See Map 9 on p. 80.

Taillevent (p. 57) CHAMPS-ELYSEES *HAUTE CUISINE* At this three-star gem, the masterpieces of Provençale maestro Alain Solivérès compliment impeccable service and superb wine list.... *Tel 01-44-95-15-01. www.taillevent.com. 17, rue Lamennais, 8e. Métro Charles de Gaulle Etoile. Reservations recommended. Daily 12:30–3:30pm and 7:30–10pm. AE, DC, MC, V. $$$$$*

See Map 9 on p. 80.

Terminus Nord (p. 65) GARE DU NORD *FRENCH/ALSATIAN* If you are starving when you arrive at the Gare du Nord from London via the Chunnel, you can't go wrong with the Terminus Nord, a classic brasserie serving shellfish, *choucroute*, grilled meats, and fish in handsome decor dating from 1925.... *Tel 01-42-85-05-15. 23, rue de Dunkerque, 10e. Métro Gare du Nord. Reservations recommended. Daily 11am–1am. AE, DC, MC, V. $$*

See Map 8 on p. 78.

Willi's Wine Bar (p. 73) LOUVRE/LES HALLES *FRENCH* A British-owned wine bar and restaurant. Willi's has become a fashionable institution, with an excellent selection of wines and nouvelle-ish cuisine and good art on the walls.... *Tel 01-42-61-05-09. 13, rue des Petits-Champs, 1er. Métro Bourse. Reservations recommended for restaurant. Restaurant Mon–Sat noon–2:30pm and 7–10:30pm; bar Mon–Sat 11am–midnight; closed 2 weeks in Aug. MC, V. $$*

See Map 8 on p. 78.

DIVER

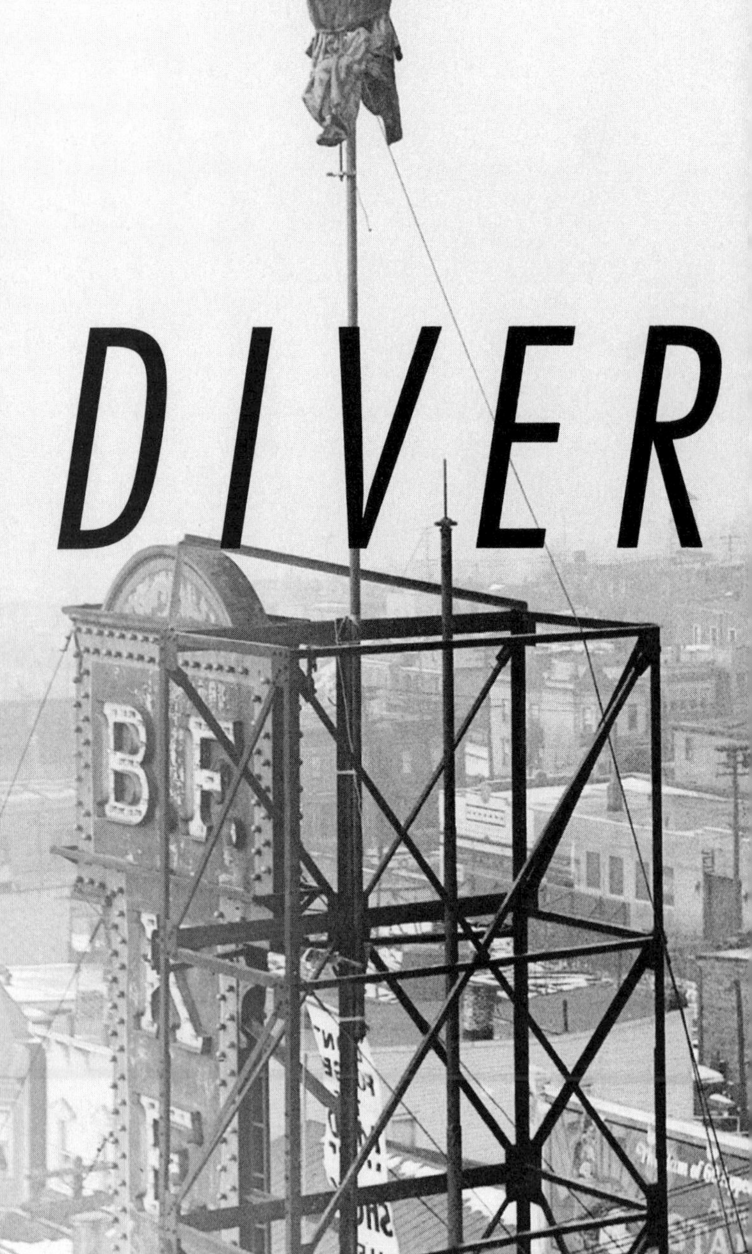

SIONS

3

Map 12: Paris Diversions—Orientation

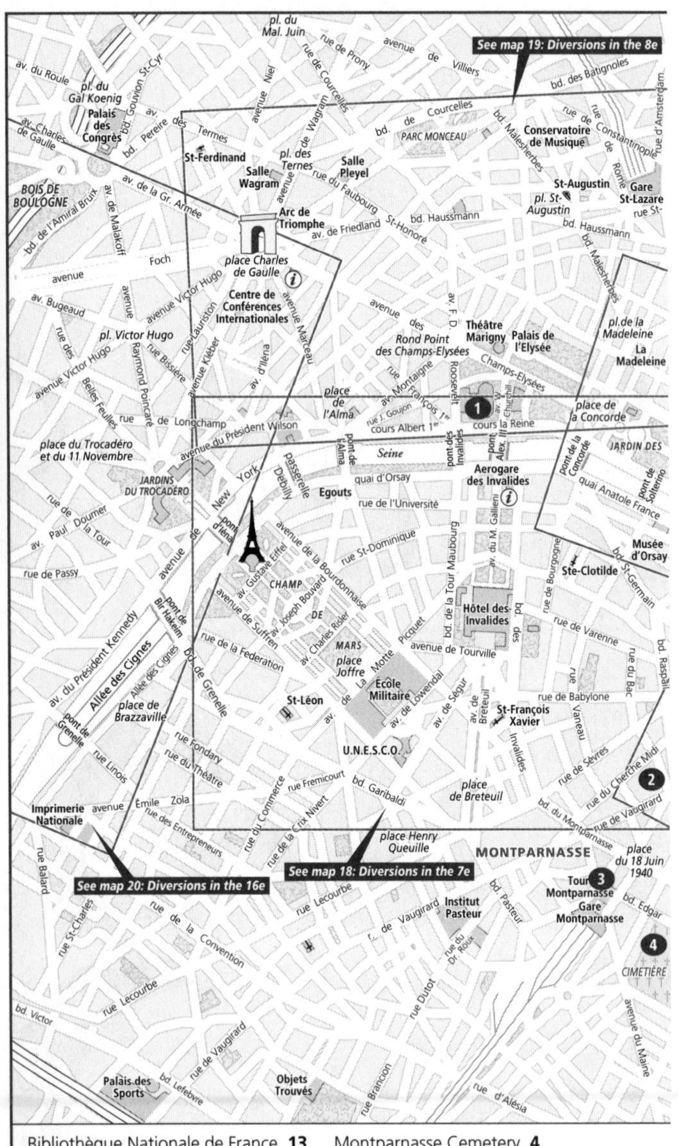

Bibliothèque Nationale de France **13**
Catacombs **5**
Fondation Cartier pour l'Art Contemporain **2**
Grand Palais **1**
Montparnasse Cemetery **4**
Musée de la Vie Romantique **8**
Musée de l'Erotisme **7**
Musée des Arts d'Afrique et d'Océanie **12**
Musée Edith Piaf **10**

DIVERSIONS

Parc de Belleville **9**
Père-Lachaise Cemetery **11**
Sainte-Chapelle **6**
Tour Montparmasse **3**

Information

Basic Stuff

Face it: The main reason you come to Paris is just to be in Paris. It's an incredibly seductive place—anyone who visits is likely to be spellbound by its beauty. The truth is, contrary to its popular image as a boisterous, giddy city, Paris can be a somber and lonesome place sometimes. Despite all the "Paris is for lovers" hype, more than half of the city's residents live alone. The good part about that is that Paris is a great place to visit if you are traveling by yourself—you'll fit right in. Parisians themselves are not even remotely self-conscious about being solitary. Anyone with the money for a cup of coffee can lay claim to a café table and watch the people pass by on the sidewalk for hours on end. Paris's glamour gets you going with all sorts of romantic expectations, but don't be offended if they are promptly cold-shouldered by the natives. Parisians tend to be nervous and reserved, unlikely to strike up a conversation with a stranger. In general, they'd rather be spectators than participate in what goes on around them. Part of this stems from the language itself, which distinguishes between the formal and familiar. The trick is to figure out how to move into the familiar without abandoning respect for the all-important formal.

Another thing that puts a damper on local spontaneity is that Paris is probably the most bourgeois city in the world; individuality is regarded with skepticism here. In Paris, there is a right way and a wrong way to do absolutely everything. Browse around any of the city's wonderful street markets, for example, and note how every batch of strawberries has been neatly piled into the requisite little pyramid and each pear has been wrapped in tissue paper. This tells you all you need to know about the degree to which Parisians are addicted to form. Here too, the key is to push the outer edges of form, but do not break the mold lest you be perceived as too weird. Sometimes you'll get away with your over-the-top energy simply because you're an American. That can be an excuse.

Fortunately, the Parisian obsession is not with form for its own sake, as is the German penchant for order. It is more precisely a preoccupation with *agréments (de la vie),* the adornments of life. This fixation with aesthetic minutiae may sometimes be irritating to foreigners who have made their home here, but at the same time it is exactly what makes Paris such a beautiful city to visit. Some of the most rewarding things to do here are the most ordinary. There's no better movie-going city in the world, for example, and there are few experiences better than strolling the banks of the Seine at night and admiring the city's artfully illuminated bridges.

Oddly, Paris is at its loveliest when it's most empty, so rise early and stay up late. Paris is more intimate, mysterious, and relaxed after dark than it is during the day. Wander around and you can catch the city unawares—say, a glimpse into the fluorescent-lit kitchen of a *boulangerie* (bakery) where a pastry chef is spooning preserves into the middle of neat triangles of dough. It may be just a moment, but it can be your window into the soul of Paris.

Getting Your Bearings

Paris has been cleverly divided by city officials into 20 arrondissements, with the 1st arrondissement situated at its heart. The other arrondissements snail around it clockwise, ending with the 20th arrondissement in the northeast. The Seine River arcs through the city, entering in the southeast and exiting in the southwest, and dividing it in two: the **Right Bank** (Rive Droite) in the north and the **Left Bank** (Rive Gauche) in the south. Métro lines are numbered, with line 1 running east-west across the city. They are also known by the end stations—line 1 is the La Défense–Château de Vincennes line, for example. The RER suburban train network is also handy for getting around more quickly in Paris. (See the Hotlines & Other Basics chapter for details on public transportation.)

The **1st arrondissement,** in the heart of the city, contains some of the city's biggest attractions: the Louvre, the Palais-Royal, the Jardin des Tuileries, and the très chic place Vendôme for shopping (not to mention the ugly underground Forum des Halles shopping mall and the sleazy rue St-Denis nearby). The 1st arrondissement's main artery is the traffic-choked rue de Rivoli. North of the 1st is the heavily commercial **2nd arrondissement,** home of the Paris Bourse and the old Bibliothèque Nationale. Moving east, you come to the **3rd arrondissement,** the northern part of the Marais, with its ancient buildings and narrow streets. To the south is the **4th arrondissement,** which takes in the rest of the Marais (including the place des Vosges and the Centre Pompidou), part of the Ile de la Cité (where Notre-Dame stands), and picturesque Ile Saint-Louis. The former Jewish quarter centers on the rue des Rosiers (the Marais still has the highest concentration of synagogues in the city), but nowadays the Marais is known as the gay ghetto. At night the area around the rue Vieille du Temple between the rue de Rivoli and the rue des Francs-Bourgeois bustles with restaurant- and bar-goers.

Across the river, you come to the **5th arrondissement,** the famous Latin Quarter, home of the Sorbonne, the Panthéon, the Jardin des Plantes, and many small, inexpensive restaurants. From place Saint-Michel, just south of the Seine, Boul' Mich (bd. St-Michel) rolls south, sluggish with traffic; the side streets east of the Boul' Mich are the true Latin Quarter. Go west for the **6th arrondissement,** home of cafés, restaurants, antiques shops, art galleries, and clothing boutiques of Saint-Germain-des-Prés. This neighborhood is what most visitors think of as the Left Bank, peopled by the *gauche caviar* (wealthy leftist intellectuals) as well as the simply rich and lots of artsy types. Its landmark is the graceful steeple of the Eglise Saint-Germain-des-Prés; the Jardin du Luxembourg is here, too. The **7th arrondissement** abuts Saint-Germain-des-Prés to the west and shares some of its characteristics—a wealthy, sedate residential area containing the Assemblée Nationale, the Musée d'Orsay, the Musée Rodin, the Hôtel des Invalides, and, most famously, the Eiffel Tower. The ritzy **8th arrondissement** faces the 7th from the Right Bank of the Seine. The avenue des Champs-Elysées bisects the area, littered with overpriced cafés, tourists, and pickpockets. Landmarks here include the Arc de Triomphe, the Grand Palais, and many of the palace hotels. Tree-lined avenue Montaigne is full of designer boutiques, and the rue du Faubourg-Saint-Honoré is fashion central for top designers. On the northern edge of the arrondissement is the lovely Parc Monceau, surrounded by the 19th-century homes of the discreet bourgeoisie. To the east, the **9th arrondissement** is primarily residential, with an emphasis on artsy types; along its grand boulevards you'll find the ornate Opéra Garnier and the big department stores, Printemps and Galeries Lafayette. A lively nightlife scene has developed along its northern edge, just below the strip joints of Pigalle.

East of the 9th is the **10th arrondissement,** a lower-middle-class residential area that visitors hardly ever see unless they're coming and going from its train stations, the Gare de l'Est and the Gare du Nord. The **11th arrondissement,** to the southeast, has a similar profile until it reaches the hip rue Oberkampf and the Bastille, the area around the modern opera house, where hectic nightlife around the rue de Lappe and rue de la Roquette draws rowdy suburbanites into town on weekend nights. Further south, sprawling as far east as the Bois de Vincennes is the **12th arrondissement,** the site of Paris's new development at Bercy, with the Palais d'Omnisports de Paris-Bercy, the new Ministry of Finance, and the newest nightlife area, Cour St. Emillion, which is filled with upmarket bars, restaurants, wine shops, and cinemas all inspired by Bercy's traditional activity as a wine-producing village.

The outer ring of arrondissements is primarily residential and commercial. Across the Seine is the **13th arrondissement**—a mix of traditional Paris (on its border with the 5th) and modern high-rises (of very uneven architectural value) at the place d'Italie and beyond. It is also home to Paris's largest Chinese community (and many good Asian restaurants), as well as the low-rise, almost bucolic area around the rue de la Butte aux Cailles. Along the Seine an impressive outcrop of glass and steel make up the Bibliothèque Nationale François Mitterrand and a host of restaurants and shops. West of the 13th lies the **14th arrondissement,** Montparnasse. Boulevard Montparnasse, with its legendary cafés, lies at its northern edge. The middle-class **15th arrondissement** continues on west to the Seine. Across the river is the aristocratic **16th arrondissement,** which fills in the area between the river and the Bois de Boulogne in the west. Originally the village of Passy, this is the bastion of the French "BCBG" (*bon chic, bon genre*): moneyed, traditional, culturally and politically conservative folk. North of it lies the **17th arrondissement,** a mixed bag housing the wealthy and the bourgeoisie in the area between the Arc de Triomphe and Villiers, and elsewhere the much less wealthy. To the east, the heterogeneous **18th arrondissement** spans Montmartre (home to the rich and famous), the trendy Abbesses area, the tourist mecca that is the Sacré-Coeur, sleazy-but-trendy Pigalle, large African communities around Barbès-Rochechouart, and the Goutte d'Or, a poor neighborhood notorious for its drug dealers. The working-class **19th and 20th arrondissements** lie to the east; tourists rarely come here except to visit Père-Lachaise Cemetery, but the area's low rents have attracted many young people and artists, which, of course, means that these neighborhoods are gradually becoming trendy and more expensive.

Discounts & Passes

Discounts for children, students, senior citizens, and teachers are offered at many attractions; be sure to ask before buying your ticket. A pass good for multiple visits to 70 museums and monuments over a given period of time (1, 3, or 5 consecutive days, at 18€/$23, 36€/$45, and 54€/$68, respectively), called the **Carte Musées et Monuments,** is available at major Métro stations, participating museums and monuments, tourism offices in the railway stations, and the Paris Tourism Office l 08-92-68-31-12 for recorded information in French and glish; www.paris-touristoffice.com; 127, av. des Champs-Elysées, 8e; open daily 9am–8pm). The beauty of the pass is that you don't have to wait in line at most attractions, a tremendous advantage at such favorite art shrines as the Louvre and the Musée d'Orsay.

The Lowdown

Must-sees for first-time visitors... Centre Pompidou, the popular museum of modern art in the heart of Paris, reopened in 1999 after a $90-million renovation. Inaugurated in 1977, the museum, which looks like a refinery turned inside out, was receiving 8 million visitors annually before it closed, and this huge crowd had worn out a structure designed to receive half that number. Aside from having its physical plant renewed, the museum was enlarged by 50,000 square feet, which allows it to put 1,400 works from its permanent collections on display, as opposed to just 800 when it closed. The museum is now home to a bookstore and boutique, both of which are run by the Printemps department store. Georges (p. 91), the critically acclaimed restaurant on the sixth floor, is run by local trendsetters the Costes Brothers. One much-loved attribute of the Centre was changed during the museum's makeover, though: The ride up the escalators used to be free—now you need your ticket to the museum.

The centuries-old **Louvre,** on the other hand, is still standing firm, and ongoing renovations have made it more beautiful than ever. The more modern addition is the Sackler Wing, housing 2,000 works of ancient Iranian and Arabian art. The Louvre can be dazzling, overwhelming, irritating, or exhausting, depending on your point of view. Many visitors to Paris just skip it or go only to the adjacent underground shopping mall.

What is there to say about the **Eiffel Tower,** known the world over as the symbol of Paris and the ultimate tourist attraction? That its lacy ironwork is lovely to look at; that riding the glass elevator slantwise upward is exciting and kind of scary; that the views are just a little disappointing because you're so high up and Paris is so flat. Unless you're going to eat at its first-rate restaurant Le Jules Verne (p. 98), you might want to skip the long lines for the elevator.

Some Louvre Tips

The long lines outside the Louvre's pyramid entrance are notorious, but there are some tricks for avoiding them:

- *Order tickets by phone at* **Tel 08-92-68-46-94,** *and pay with a credit card; then pick them up at any FNAC store. This gives you direct entry through the Passage Richelieu, 93, rue de Rivoli.*
- *Enter via the underground shopping mall, the Carrousel du Louvre, at 99, rue de Rivoli.*
- *Enter directly from the Palais Royal–Musée du Louvre Métro station.*
- *Buy Le Carte Musées et Monuments (Museums and Monuments Pass), which allows direct entry through the priority entrance at the Passage Richelieu, 93, rue de Rivoli.*

Tourists also flock to **Sacré-Coeur,** a Byzantine-style church on a Montmartre hilltop consecrated in 1919. The second symbol of Paris, it draws more visitors than the Cathedral of Notre-Dame, but many are disappointed by its tacky wedding-cake architecture and boring interior. Visitors to **Notre-Dame,** on its own little island in the Seine, admire the grandeur of the interior, the rose window, the magnificent flying buttresses, and the wonderfully grotesque gargoyles, which can be better appreciated from the cathedral towers, 387 steps up. The **Arc de Triomphe,** with its Empire architecture and colossal high-relief sculptures, is yet another symbol of Paris you won't want to miss.

Only in Paris... Across the Seine from the Tuileries is the **Musée d'Orsay,** a magnificent conversion of one of Paris's splendid train stations, with a grand collection of those Impressionist paintings most people associate with the city. Then there's the **Musée National Picasso,** which gives a comprehensive overview of the 20th-century master's work. Even if you aren't a great Picasso fan, come for the setting, a beautiful 17th-century *hôtel particulier* (mansion) in the Marais.

Paris's big cemeteries are nothing like those in the United States: Graves stand crowded together, and many of the older ones have tiny chapels—some fallen into eerie ruin, others well-kept and decorated with flowers, photos of the deceased, and/or sacred images. If you have time to see just one, go to **Père-Lachaise,** out on the city's eastern fringes. With its little stone chapels on most of the graves, it is truly a city of the dead (Jim Morrison,

Marcel Proust, Oscar Wilde, Colette, and Edith Piaf are among its residents); see "The big sleep," later in this chapter, for more details.

Just as you must have your photo taken feeding the pigeons in the Piazza San Marco in Venice, in Paris you must ride on one of the ***bateaux mouches*** (literally, "fly boats"), à la Audrey Hepburn and Cary Grant in the film *Charade*. It's a good way to get off your tired feet for an hour and take in an overall impression of the monumental buildings that line the Seine. It's most fun at night, when the boats' high-powered floodlights illuminate the banks of the river, blinding the residents (most of whom, strangely enough, don't seem to mind at all—they're generally fond of the *bateaux mouches*). The disadvantage is that you're accompanied by 300 other tourists and are forced to listen to a superficial multilingual commentary on a scratchy sound system. In the summertime, an alternative way to see Paris from the Seine is on the **Bat-O-Bus,** a hop-on-hop-off riverboat service run by the RATP.

Choice churches... **Notre-Dame,** built on the site of a Gallo-Roman temple, marked the beginnings of the classic Gothic style. Of course, it took nearly 2 centuries to erect this pile, which was finished around 1330, and over the subsequent centuries it suffered many alterations—particularly during the Revolution, when the public, mistaking the facade's statues of kings of Israel for French monarchs, decapitated them. (What's left of the originals—they've been replaced by replicas on the facade—can be seen in the Musée de Cluny.) Many kings of France were married or crowned in the cathedral, and Napoléon crowned himself Emperor here. These days, the most famous church in Paris is looking rather swell after a multimillion-dollar clean-up of its soot-blasted facades, and for the first time in many generations, you can see how astonishingly delicate much of its stonework actually is.

Sacré-Coeur came much later, finally consecrated in 1919. It was built at the instigation of two conservative Catholic businessmen to commemorate Paris's survival of the Franco-Prussian War of 1870 and the Paris Commune, a workers' uprising that took control of the city for a few weeks in 1871. For more than 100 years, relays of volunteers have continually prayed here to expiate the sins of humanity. But the reason most visitors come here is for the views of Paris from its dome and from the hilltop on which it resides and for walks around the winding streets and steep stairways of Montmartre.

The lovely 11th-century church of **Saint-Germain-des-Prés** is the oldest in Paris; its graceful Romanesque bell tower defines the skyline of its namesake neighborhood. Try to come here for one of its frequent, inexpensive chamber-music concerts. Universally referred to as a "jewel," the 13th-century Gothic **Sainte-Chapelle,** hidden inside the Palais de Justice on the Ile de la Cité, should be visited in the daytime to appreciate its incredible stained-glass windows, but evening concerts of classical music here are a treat, too.

Out-of-the-ordinary religious experiences... On the Left Bank's rue du Bac, there's a brisk business in "miraculous medals" at the **Chapelle Notre-Dame-de-la-Médaille-Miraculeuse.** Hordes of supplicants pray to the body of a young nun, Catherine Labouré, who is perfectly preserved under glass. In 1830 she had a vision of the Virgin Mary, for which she was later beatified by the Catholic Church. The chapel has a glowing statue of the Virgin.

For a truly eerie experience, go at midnight to the candlelit **Saint-Gervais-Saint-Protais** church in the Marais, sandwiched between the rue François-Miron and the rue des Barres behind the Hôtel de Ville. This 17th-century church, a flamboyant example of Gothic-style construction with a classical facade, is home base for a devout Catholic sect whose adherents keep up a round-the-clock vigil, kneeling silently in their robes on the cold, hard stones before the altar. At night, enter through the ordinary-looking door at the back of the church on the rue des Barres.

"Buddhamania" is sweeping France, and those with Buddhist leanings might want to visit the **Centre Bouddhique,** a Tibetan Buddhist temple in the Bois de Vincennes with a 9m- (30-ft.) high gilded statue of the Buddha. It's open to the public during Buddhist festivals. It's a bit of a hike, though, from the closest Métro stops, Château de Vincennes or Porte d'Orée.

Most hated architecture... Parisians are a funny bunch. When something new arrives in their city, they bitch and complain about it, claim to hate it, and then, within a very short period of time, learn to love it. Even the **Eiffel Tower,** now the universally beloved symbol of Paris, was considered a hideous eyesore when it was built more than 100 years ago. *Plus ça change....*

The late president François Mitterrand got endless flak for his *grands projets* program—people accused him of seeking kinglike immortality in a series of monumental structures that changed the face of Paris. At the height of the controversy over the **Opéra Bastille,** rumors circulated that an error had been made—that the building constructed after Carlos Ott's design was not the one that Mitterrand had selected from an architectural competition. People still complain halfheartedly about it, but they flock to performances (which are nearly always sold out). I.M. Pei's glass pyramid in the Cour Napoléon of the **Louvre** also raised an initial storm of protest, but the day that the pyramid was unveiled, curious Parisians came in droves to see it, and they had to admit that the airy structure actually added to the beauty of the refurbished palace surrounding it, offering a focal point in the courtyard and new perspectives through its glass. Likewise, the sharp-edged, open cube of the **Grande Arche de la Défense,** which on completion turned out to be a graceful addition to the city's western perspective, looking somehow delicate in spite of its massive size. (It is high enough to tower over Notre-Dame.) Architect Dominique Perrault's design for the **Bibliothèque Nationale de France,** the last of Mitterrand's projects, was harshly attacked because its four glass towers—meant to resemble open books—were devoted to storing fragile volumes, while visitors were relegated to the basement. The design had to be revised, at great cost, to add special wooden paneling that protects the books from light. The final result is impressive, thanks primarily to the natural woods and other materials, but still seems cold and impersonal.

Mitterrand can't be blamed for the **Forum des Halles,** the tacky, cheap-looking shopping center that replaced Victor Baltard's lovely 19th-century wrought-iron market building in the heart of Paris. No one dares to admit liking it, but at least the newest part of the development, on the western side, has been attractively landscaped and provided with imitation Baltard structures. The **Centre Pompidou** horrified many Parisians when it was completed in 1977. Designed by Renzo Piano and Richard Rogers, it's a textbook example of "high-tech" architecture that exposes a building's innards, a briefly popular style that was already out of vogue by the time the building opened. Now, however, the Centre Pompidou is a fixture in Paris, a lovable oddity that's already been through a major renovation. The architecture of the **Maison de la Culture du Japon,** on the quai Branly, is so discreet that it has raised few eyebrows. Architect Masayuki Yamanaka made a successful attempt to blend it into its surroundings with a curved facade of jade-colored glass. The interior, with its warm wood fittings, is spacious and airy. The American Center cost so much to build that the organization, strapped for funds, sold off the edifice and went out of business right after the building was finished, but fans of architect Frank Gehry might want to check out the building's wacky, sculptural exterior.

Museums to get lost in... It's almost shocking to see the excess of riches on display at the **Louvre**—shelves and shelves loaded with painted Greek vases, for example, or masterpiece paintings crowded together and hung one above the other. And as if the massive art collections weren't mind-boggling enough, there are also the added distractions of the book and gift shops and a modern adjacent underground shopping mall (complete with a horrible, very un-French cafeteria with an "international food court"). Plan your visit carefully: Use a museum map, available at the reception desk in the Hall Napoléon, under I.M. Pei's once-controversial but now well-loved glass pyramid, the museum's main entrance. There's rarely a line at the second entrance through the shopping gallery at 99, rue de Rivoli or via the stairway next to avenue du Carrousel. If you're going just to see the *Mona Lisa* (LA JOCONDE on museum signs) as many visitors do, you may be disappointed to find the enigmatic smile hidden behind bulletproof glass and your view obstructed by hordes of gawkers. The beautifully renovated Richelieu Wing is a bright, spacious section, where two courtyards under glass roofs have been turned into sculpture gardens complete with trees. If you don't want to tackle the museum on your own, ask about guided tours in English.

Most tourists visit the **Musée d'Orsay** to see the works of the Impressionists, and that's a good choice, except for the fact that Renoir and company are housed in anonymous rooms that don't take advantage of this magnificent turn-of-the-20th-century structure, with its vast spaces and lofty glass roof. Italian architect Gae Aulenti's conversion of the Left Bank train station into a museum is obtrusive but can't be termed a complete failure. Be sure to pick up a map of the museum—the signage here is very confusing.

Built for the Universal Exhibition of 1900, the **Grand Palais** (between the Champs-Elysées and the Seine) has a beautiful glass roof that's been repaired after several wobbly years. This is one of the most important venues in Paris for temporary art shows.

Museums to find yourself in... Lovers of medieval art and history will rejoice in the **Musée de Cluny,** full of tapestries (including *The Lady and the Unicorn* series), illuminated manuscripts, jewelry, paintings, and sculptures. Possibly the most serene museum in Paris, it's housed in a 15th-century Gothic mansion built in the Latin Quarter on the ruins of a 3rd-century Roman bathhouse, the remains of which are visible in the basement. Out in Passy, the **Musée Guimet** houses a major collection of art from Asia, including China, Japan, India, Vietnam, Cambodia, Tibet, Thailand, Laos, and Indonesia. There is also an annex, with a collection of Japanese Buddhas and a Japanese garden. The **Musée des Arts Décoratifs,** near the Jardin des Tuileries, traces the history of the decorative arts from the Middle Ages on; the Art Deco and Art Nouveau displays are the real winners. Favorite nooks here include the bedroom of Hector Guimard, the Art Nouveau designer who created the emblematic Métro entrances. (One of the best remaining examples can be seen at Métro Abbesses.) In the same wing of the Louvre is the **Musée de la Mode et du Textile,** with a permanent exhibition covering the history of fashion (which changes every 6 months) and occasional temporary exhibitions. The collection at the **Musée d'Art Moderne de la Ville de Paris** is housed along the Seine to the west, in a building constructed for the Universal Exhibition of 1937. Since the works of the Impressionists were moved across the river to the Musée d'Orsay, their former home, **Jeu de Paume** in the Jardin des Tuileries, has been revamped and turned into a gallery for exhibitions of contemporary art. But here's the good news: The huge windows have been uncovered, letting light into the once gloomy space.

Late arrivals on the museum scene... An important addition to Paris galleries is the **Maison Européenne de la Photographie,** in the Marais, which holds quality temporary photo exhibitions in a renovated mansion with a modern addition. The **Musée de la Musique,** in the La Villette complex, traces the history of music from the 17th century to the present with a collection of 900 instruments. The **Fondation Cartier pour l'Art Contemporain,** near Montparnasse, is notable for its appealing modern architecture by Jean Nouvel and its creative theme exhibitions.

Dina Vierny, who owns an important art gallery, met the sculptor Maillol when she was 15 and was his model for the next 10 years. In 1995, she opened the **Musée Maillol** in a beautifully restored 18th-century town house on the Left Bank. In addition to Maillols, there are also works by Picasso, Rodin, Gaugin, Bonnard, and Degas, as well as a variety of Russian artists.

One-man museums... Housed in a graceful 17th-century mansion in the Marais, the **Musée National Picasso** is high on the list of Paris attractions. In lieu of paying inheritance taxes after the artist's death, the family gave the French government first choice of his works. A later donation by his widow Jacqueline added to this exceptional collection, which spans the artist's entire career. The handsome light fixtures and bronze banquettes, chairs, and tables were designed by Diego Giacometti. An equally marvelous setting is the **Musée Rodin,** which shows off the sculptor's most famous works, including *The Kiss* and *The Thinker,* in the 18th-century mansion where he once lived and worked, near the place des Invalides. If you don't have the time to see the whole collection, or if you're not all that keen on statues, come here anyway to stroll around the lovely rose-filled English garden where some of the statues are; it can be visited for a token fee without entering the museum. If you happen to be in the 16th arrondissement, peek into the **Maison de Balzac,** which showcases the French Dickens' manuscripts, letters, and original editions of his novels.

Little-known museums... In the Latin Quarter, the handsome **Institut du Monde Arabe,** by French architect Jean Nouvel, includes an architectural novelty: One wall (on the courtyard side) has a set of apertures that react to light like a camera lens, opening and closing to let in just the right amount of natural light, creating a beautiful pattern reminiscent of Arab designs. If you happen to be out in the vast Bois de Vincennes park, you may want to drop by the **Musée des Arts d'Afrique et d'Océanie,** housed in a building in the Bois de Vincennes left over from the Colonial Exhibition of 1931, with a striking frieze depicting the history of colonialism on the facade. If you're with kids, skip the African and South Pacific art and head straight for the aquarium of gaudy tropical fish.

The **Musée Edith Piaf** houses a collection of memorabilia—letters, photos, clothing—from the life of France's beloved chanteuse, who was born in this same working-class Bastille neighborhood. Cinema critic Henri Langlois nurtured the careers of François Truffaut and Jean-Luc Godard and coined the term "New Wave," and the **Musée du Cinéma Henri Langlois,** out in Passy at the **Cinémathèque Française,** displays his exhaustive collection of some 5,000 objects illustrating the history of film around the world. You'll see Edison's kinescope, costumes, magic lanterns, posters, and a set from that enduring 1945 French classic, *Les Enfants du Paradis* (*Children of Paradise*).

Best museum cafés... The wealthy 19th-century art collector Edouard André married the artist who came to paint his portrait, Nellie Jacquemart. Together they indulged their passion for art, traveling throughout Europe and coming back with such treasures as the fabulous Tiepolo fresco that adorns the ceiling of the café in their mansion-turned-museum, the **Musée Jacquemart André** near the Champs-Elysées. Have lunch or afternoon tea after admiring works of the Italian Renaissance and 18th-century French school. On a warm day, get thee to another rich man's home: the **Musée Albert Kahn,** just outside Paris. Modest exhibitions of anthropological interest are held here, but the main draw is the variety of vegetation in the French, English, and Japanese gardens, the rose garden, the fruit orchard, the "blue" forest, the pine forest, and the swamp. The café is in the glass "palmarium," where you can take tea indoors under the palm trees or on the terrace with a view over the gardens.

Sexy stuff... Where else but in Pigalle would you find the **Musée de l'Erotisme?** This museum—just down the street from the Moulin Rouge—eschews the surrounding sleaze and goes for the arty approach to porn, with a fascinating collection of works from Africa, the Americas, Asia, Europe, and Oceania, many of which will raise a giggle.

Modish museums... It's only fitting that the fashion capital of the world would have two museums dedicated to the couturier's art. The renovated **Musée de la Mode et du Textile** has a huge collection of haute couture clothing, costumes, and accessories. The **Musée de la Mode et du Costume,** housed in the Palais Galliera, a 19th-century Italian Renaissance–style mansion near the Champs-Elysées, holds temporary exhibitions on the history of fashion, sometimes going back as far as the 18th century. (Yes, there was fashion before Coco Chanel.)

Where the Impressionists are... Everybody knows that the most extensive collection of the Impressionist masters is in the **Musée d'Orsay**—and that's the problem. If you can't bear to fight the crowds, try the **Orangerie** in the Jardin des Tuileries; it's a little treasure of a museum that's often overlooked by tourists. Here, in an intimate setting, you can peacefully view Claude Monet's renowned water lily series, as well as works by Cézanne, Renoir, Picasso, Rousseau, and Utrillo. Another often-neglected museum is the **Musée Marmottan,** set in a handsome 19th-century mansion, out by the Bois de Boulogne, that was the home of French art collector Paul Marmottan. Along with his Empire paintings, furniture, and objets d'art, there are plenty of Monet paintings, including some of his water lilies and the exceptional *Impression, Sunrise,* which gave the movement its name. Part of Monet's personal collection is exhibited here, including works by Renoir, Caillebotte, Pissarro, Morisot, and Boudin. The **Petit Palais**—a small-scale version of the Grand Palais, across the street—houses the art collection of the City of Paris, including works by Delacroix, Ingres, Courbet, Cézanne, and Impressionists Monet, Pissarro, Sisley, and Morisot.

Literary pilgrimages... The **Musée de la Vie Romantique** is dedicated to George Sand, the iconoclastic 19th-century writer. This Pigalle villa wasn't Sand's home, but artist Ary Scheffer lived here. Sand, who lived in the neighborhood, was a frequent visitor to Scheffer's salon, along with Chopin, Liszt, Ingres, and Delacroix. Decorated in the style of the period, the house is full of Sand memorabilia, including her jewels, furniture, and family portraits. The French Dickens, Honoré de Balzac, lived for 7 years in the house out in the Passy area, now called the **Maison de Balzac.** The museum's holdings include Balzac portraits, a collection of books, and the desk at which he wrote. The **Musée Carnavalet's** permanent collection, covering the history of Paris, is fairly inconsistent in quality, but the reason to visit here is the building itself. This handsome Marais *hôtel particulier,* reconstructed in the 17th century by Mansart (the man primarily responsible for the architectural style of Paris), was once the home of the witty Madame de Sévigné, whose prolific letters to her daughter give us a priceless insider's view of the court of Louis XIV. Don't get the idea that Marcel Proust wrote his epic novel here—his cork-lined bedroom was located on the other side of town.

Views for free... Paris is mostly flat, and most of its buildings are the same height, so you need to scout out a really tall building or one of the few hills to get a panorama of the city. The fun is in picking out landmarks such as the Eiffel Tower, the golden dome of **Invalides,** the Panthéon, the skyscraping **Tour Montparnasse,** and Notre-Dame Cathedral. You don't have to visit the boring interior of the **Sacré-Coeur** to enjoy the view of Paris from the Montmartre hill on which it sits. The **Samaritaine** department store is right in the heart of the city, and from the top floor of Magasin 2 you get a close-up view of the Seine and the Left Bank, with the Eiffel Tower in the background. The top floor of the **Institut du Monde Arabe** on the Left Bank offers great views of the Seine and the flying buttresses of Notre-Dame. The **Parc de Belleville,** a small neighborhood park in the out-of-the-way 20th arrondissement, offers views of Paris from an unusual angle, with the Eiffel Tower far in the distance.

Views for sale... The daytime view from the top of the **Eiffel Tower** can be a bit disappointing because you are so high up that the flat world far below becomes a boring blur. It's better to stop on the second floor for a closer view—or better yet, go at night when the ***bateaux mouches*** light up the buildings along the Seine with high-powered beams. Just as the top of the **Arc de Triomphe** offers a sweeping perspective on the city's architectural sightlines, straight down the place de la Concorde to the Tuileries and the Louvre, so too does the farther-out **Grande Arche de la Défense,** former president François Mitterrand's contribution to the French love of form and symmetry. From the Grande Arche, you will also have a good look at the modern architecture of the office complex La Défense—but the problem is you have to go all the way out west of the city to reach it. And then there's nothing else to do there—unless you want to shop in one of the largest malls in Europe. If your time's precious, stick to the Arc de Triomphe. The Ferris wheel at the carnival that springs up next to the **Jardin des Tuileries** twice a year offers a charming view of Paris, with the added thrill of swinging in the breeze when you're stopped at the top. It's especially fun at night.

Secret gardens... You go through a tunnel to reach the Jardin Alpin, a miniparadise hidden in a little valley in the **Jardin des Plantes,** along the Seine east of the Latin Quarter. In the alpine garden's moist microclimate, some 2,000 species of mountain plants and flowers from all over the world thrive, and a little stream runs through its artificial miniature mountains to form a pool in the center. Tucked away in a corner of the Jardin du Luxembourg is the rarely visited **Verger du Luxembourg,** or National Conservatory of Apples and Pears, founded by Napoléon in 1809, with its bewildering variety of apple and pear trees—come in spring for profusions of blossoms. Out west in the 15th arrondissement, the **Parc André Citroën** has a whole range of hidden miniature gardens, from rock gardens to fields of wildflowers. At the **Parc de Bagatelle,** a magical English garden within the Bois de Boulogne, peacocks strut across the wide lawns while summertime visitors inhale the perfume of the extravagant rose garden and enjoy gazing at the irises and water lilies. Many tourists "discover" the lovely English garden of the **Musée Rodin,** where his famous statue, *The Thinker,* sits surrounded by roses; if only they'd known ahead of time that they could visit the garden for a token fee and skip the rest of the museum completely.

The stars at your feet... Right behind the Sacré-Coeur there is a secret that most visitors never discover. The last block of the rue du Chevalier-de-la-Barre (Métro

Abbesses) turns into one of those Montmartre staircases that Utrillo liked to paint, with iron railings and a row of old-fashioned street lamps in the center. This one has an expanse of cobblestones on each side of the stairs, giving sculptor Patrick Rimoux and cinematographer Henri Alekan the wacky idea of implanting constellations in the cobblestones, reflecting the way the sky looks on July 1 and January 1. You have to see it from below at night: The twinkling lights in various shades of blue and white (made of fiber optics and glass) look truly magical, especially on a misty night with the towers of the Sacré-Coeur rising behind it.

Best hidden courtyard... If you lived in Paris, you would want to stay in the cour de Rohan, a series of three utterly calm, picturesque courtyards accessible from the rue du Jardinet or the medieval cour de Commerce Saint-André in the 6th arrondissement (Métro Odéon). Diane de Poitiers once lived here, and the archbishops of Rouen (whence "Rohan") were based here in the 15th century. Look around and you'll spot rare vestiges of old Paris, including a mule-mounting block and a well.

Mlle. Liberty in Paris... The small-scale replica of Auguste Bartholdi's Statue of Liberty that stands next to the pont de Grenelle (crossing the Seine between the 15th and 16th arrondissements) had its back turned to the United States until 1937, when she was spun around to face the mother country. Another miniature Liberty can be seen in a garden in the northwest corner of the **Jardin du Luxembourg.**

Where to meet your lover... The pont des Arts, a wooden pedestrian bridge that spans the Seine between the Louvre and the Institut de France, is a magical place in the heart of Paris. Linger as long as you like, soaking in the beauty of the buildings that line the banks and watching the Paris sky, a scene straight out of a 19th-century painting of the city. Bring a bottle of champagne and watch the sun set—if you're lucky, it'll light up the glass roof of the Grand Palais with a rosy glow. Some couples even bring a table, dishes, wine, and a real meal for a candlelit dinner on the bridge.

How to find the real Latin Quarter... For the *American in Paris* vision of the city, head straight for the Left Bank's Quartier Latin, which is still lively despite being touristy as all get-out. Around the fountain in place Saint-Michel, unsavory young *clochards* (street people) accompanied by their sleepy German shepherds mingle with folks from Vancouver, Melbourne, and Des Moines, listening to street musicians sing Beatles tunes. Along the tourist-clogged rue Saint-Séverin and rue de la Harpe nearby, mediocre Greek and French restaurants send multilingual touts out into the streets to lure gawking out-of-towners. Boulevard Saint-Michel (Boul' Mich, as it's affectionately known to students) is lined with cheap clothing boutiques, record shops, and bookstores. **Shakespeare & Company** (p. 199 in the Shopping chapter), a musty, English-language bookstore whose name was reverently borrowed from Sylvia Beach's renowned establishment and is now embarking on another renaissance with the arrival of owner George Whitman's daughter and co-manager Sylvia, is a big draw for visiting Americans who think they've found a bit of old Paris.

There's still real magic in the quarter, though, in the crooked little streets beyond this touristic triangle—jazz clubs, bookstores, cinemas showing classic films, little restaurants, and bars. After all, the Latin Quarter has been the student part of town from time immemorial; it's home to the Sorbonne and the elite Ecole Normale Supérieure, where legendary philosophers such as Jean-Paul Sartre and Simone de Beauvoir led the intellectual life. In the 12th century, the theologian and legendary lover Abélard (best known for his tragic affair with Héloïse) settled his students here after a scholarly spat with his colleagues on the Ile de la Cité; it's called the Latin Quarter because until the Revolution, students were required to speak Latin because their education was being provided by the church. (Of course, that never stopped students from being rowdy and decadent.) This was the battlefield of the student uprising of 1968, though you can no longer see the paving stones of the Boul' Mich, which were pried up and slung at the police in the great Parisian tradition—the authorities have prudently covered the street with a thick layer of tar, a wise precaution because student revolts still regularly occur in the neighborhood.

Among the Latin Quarter's sights, a top attraction is the **Musée de Cluny,** with its medieval treasures and remains of Roman baths. Also worth seeing are two churches: the Flamboyant Gothic Saint-Séverin (rue des Prêtres) and Saint-Julien-le-Pauvre (rue St-Julien-le-Pauvre), one of the oldest churches in Paris, now a Greek Orthodox chapel. (Both are near Métro St-Michel.) The landmark dome of the Panthéon (RER Luxembourg) rises in this neighborhood, but there's not much to see inside, even though Voltaire, Rousseau, Hugo, Zola, and other major figures are interred here.

Hanging out in Saint-Germain-des-Prés... It all began with a Benedictine abbey and a church built to house a fragment of the Cross, but the abbey was mostly destroyed by the Revolution and was finished off in the 19th century. Visitors now make pilgrimages to the boulevard Saint-Gemain's famous cafés, Deux-Magots (no. 170) and Café de Flore (no. 172), where Jean-Paul Sartre and Simone de Beauvoir used to hang out. (The waiters at the Flore would complain about how long de Beauvoir would sit writing over one cup of coffee.) Today, you're better off spending an hour or two on the terrace with a favorite person and ordering a chilled bottle of the house champagne. It'll be the best 50 bucks you ever spent. Brasserie Lipp (no. 151) was where François Mitterrand and other political honchos hung out. At 27, rue du Fleurus, Gertrude Stein and Alice B. Toklas entertained Picasso, Hemingway, and others.

Eugène Delacroix, Albert Camus, Antoine Artaud, and Jacques Prévert were other habitués of this Left Bank neighborhood, and in the 1950s, it was the hot spot for the jazz generation. Many of its tenants are now antiques dealers selling bits of the past, but there are also art galleries, publishing houses, cafés, restaurants, and boutiques of all sorts, from haute couture to mass-market rags. Just to soak up atmosphere, visit the lovely and peaceful square on the rue de Furstemberg; the Marché Saint-Germain, once a fairground, now a covered market with an international flavor; or the colorful little marketplace on the rue de Buci. Around the Odéon Métro station are several cinemas showing new releases in V.O. (*version originale,* or the language in which they were made).

The many faces of the Marais... During the last three decades, the Marais, once a poor quarter destined for urban renewal, has become totally chic—for better or for worse. Dozens of ancient buildings have been saved from destruction and beautifully renovated, but gentrification has sent property prices skyrocketing. Boutiques and art galleries open and close in the blink of an eye, pushing out the little bakeries and other food shops that make a neighborhood livable.

The Marais has many different identities. The area around the rue de Vieille du Temple has become the city's gay ghetto, but this culture coexists quite happily with straight nightlife and the ancient Jewish quarter around the rue des Rosiers, where you can still buy newspapers in Hebrew, not to mention fantastic rye bread, smoked salmon, and falafels. Check out the strange-looking synagogue on the rue Pavée, designed by Hector Guimard, who also created the famous Art Nouveau Métro entrances. Unfortunately, the trendy clothing boutiques have already invaded rue des Rosiers and its Jewish flavor may soon be lost forever. A mini-Chinatown has grown up around the rue au Maire and the rue de Gravilliers, where many of the wholesale shops are owned by Chinese immigrants. The rue Rambuteau and the rue de Bretagne are food-market streets where you can still find great little *boulangeries* (bakeries), cheese shops, wine shops, and restaurants among the incursions of boutiques.

Once a swamp (that's what the word *marais* means), the Marais has gone in and out of style many times over the centuries. In the 13th century, the Knights Templar and other religious communities built monasteries here; in the 14th century, Charles V set up housekeeping in the Hôtel Saint-Paul. Aristocratic families took over the area in the 17th century, after Henri IV had the lovely place des Vosges built; the graceful *hôtels particuliers* of that era give the Marais much of its charm. For a look inside one, stop in the **Musée Carnavalet,** where the famous letter-writer Madame de Sévigné once lived. By the time of Louis XVI, the nobles had moved on to the Ile Saint-Louis, the Faubourg Saint-Honoré, and the Faubourg Saint-Germain, and the Marais eventually became a slum—as recently as the early 1970s, a majority of the apartments here still didn't have private toilets or hot running water.

All that has changed now, of course, but the Marais is still rakish enough to thumb its nose at Sunday-closing laws, making it the best place in the city to stroll around on a Sunday afternoon.

Up and away in Montmartre... Parisians hear it so often that it's become a cliché: *"Montmartre, c'est un village."* But it is true that Montmartre has somehow remained a little world apart, up on its hill with its steep staircases lit by old-fashioned street lamps and its narrow, winding cobblestone streets. A creeping trendiness is invading the area around place des Abbesses (come here to check out one of the few remaining and intact Art Nouveau Métro entrances designed by Hector Guimard), but there is still a feeling of Old Paris here, accompanied by the strains of accordion music in the streets and restaurants.

Explore the wonderful market streets, the rue des Abbesses and the rue Lepic, with their dozens of bakeries, cheese shops, butchers, and fishmongers. Visit the **Montmartre Cemetery,** where François Truffaut and the French pop singer Dalida are buried, then follow the winding rue Lepic up the hill (Vincent van Gogh lived at number 54 with his brother Theo a century ago), past the Moulin de la Galette and the Moulin du Radet, the sole survivors of Montmartre's 30 windmills. On avenue Junot, where the wealthy Montmartois live, take a look at number 15, once the home of Dadaist writer Tristan Tzara. It was designed in 1926 by Austrian architect Adolf Loos. In keeping with his functionalist principles, it gives no ground to frivolous decoration: A white block sits, set back, on a beige stone block, looking like two different buildings, while recesses contain windows of varying sizes. If you continue upward and eastward, you will end up at the place du Tertre, overrun with caricature portrait artists and tourists (some 6 million per year visit this tiny square), and the **Sacré-Coeur.** You have now left the village and entered touristland.

Tourist-free neighborhoods... Few tourists venture into Butte aux Cailles, a bucolic area in the 13th arrondissement near the place d'Italie, with its trendy music bars and inexpensive restaurants. "Rue de Butte aux Cailles" translates as

Quail Hill Street, although the word *cailles* used to refer to the prostitutes who trolled the streets (the area was considered too dangerous for the police to enter). In 1783, when the world's first hot-air balloon flight set down here in what is now the place Paul-Verlaine, the hilltop was still countryside dotted with windmills. In 1871, however, it was a hotbed of insurrection, with the Communards fighting off government troops. Some restaurants and bars on the street still hark back to those times, with names borrowed from the Communards' anthem "Le Temps des Cerises" (the Merle Moqueur and La Folie en Tête, for example); the Marxist Library is located on the nearby rue Sigaud. For sheer local color, check out the rue des Cinq-Diamants, Passage Barrault, Passage Boiton, and rue Daviel, with their little houses and gardens.

Another hilltop village is in the Belleville area, in the 20th arrondissement, a working-class area where ugly high-rise apartment buildings set a general theme of god-awful modernization. But the **Parc de Belleville** gives a wonderful view of Paris from its summit, and a few pockets of the old neighborhood still survive. Right next to the hideous housing project on the place des Fêtes (Métro Place des Fêtes), a peaceful alleyway leading off 11, rue des Fêtes is occupied by adorable little houses, each with its own flower garden—if only city life were always like this. For more of the same, try the little passageways off the rue de Bellevue. This area is called L'Amérique, and no one really knows why, but legend has it that the products of the former quarry site were exported to the United States. Near Métro Porte de Bagnolet, between the boulevard Mortier and the place Octave-Chanute, is an area called La Campagne à Paris, which has more little houses and gardens—originally workers' cottages and now coveted real estate among Parisians who'd rather be living in the country. Belleville has only been "discovered" by the young and trendy.

The nearby suburb Montreuil-sous-Bois (Métro Mairie de Montreuil) has become highly sought after by artists, writers, theater and cinema people, and those after funky loft and industrial spaces to set up house and make art. Come here now before the boutiques invade and take over.

Where to read a book... Bring a novel by Colette to the gardens of the **Palais-Royal,** where she lived until her death. Though in the heart of the city (the Palais-Royal lies across the rue de Rivoli from the Louvre), the gardens are sheltered from the noise of traffic—all you'll hear is the soothing sound of water rushing from the fountain. The Medicis Fountain in the **Jardin du Luxembourg** is a peaceful and romantic place to sit and read or just watch the goldfish swimming languidly in the pool. From the hillside **Parc de Belleville,** you will have a panoramic view before you when you lift your eyes from your book. There is also a charming and discreet gazebo to discover on the Jussieu side of the **Jardin des Plantes.**

For indoor reading, the **Bibliothèque Mazarine** in the Institut de France will transport you to another time. After mounting a gem of a 19th-century marble staircase, you enter the calm precincts of the library, with its wood paneling and Corinthian columns, green-shaded reading lamps, and busts of famous men. Bring a passport-size photo and ID, and you can get a *carte de lecteur* (reader's card).

X-rated street scenes... It's not on most tourist itineraries, but many visitors stumble on it by accident. The rue Saint-Denis, in the center-city district of Les Halles, is one of the prime marketplaces for prostitution, which is tolerated—but not legal—in France. Almost all the doorways are draped with women (of all ages) dressed in costumes ranging from schoolgirl to dominatrix, designed to appeal to the varying tastes of their clients. In Montmartre, on the rue des Martyrs, rue André-Antoine, and rue Germain-Pilon, some very aggressive transvestite prostitutes openly ply their trade. The specialty of the Bois de Boulogne is Brazilian transvestites, known for their beauty and style. For something even more lurid and bizarre, take a taxi down the little street right behind the Russian Embassy (40, bd. Lannes, 16e), known to the French as the rue des Branleurs ("Jerk-off Street"), where exhibitionists live up to the nickname. While puritanical Americans may cluck and stare, Parisians just chuckle. On the whole, the French do not moralize or judge when it comes to issues of the heart or pelvis; they either partake or just keep walking.

The big sleep... **Père-Lachaise Cemetery** is the premier resting place for the illustrious dead—the roster includes Colette, Honoré de Balzac, Frédéric Chopin, Guillaume Apollinaire, Abélard and Héloïse, Molière, and La Fontaine, along with many other long-gone celebrities. Some of them, however, are not necessarily resting in peace. Jim Morrison's grave is always surrounded by pilgrims (not always of the most savory kind); the bust that used to adorn his grave has long since been stolen, and surrounding gravestones are covered with handwritten messages of love to him. There are even rumors of Satanic rituals taking place around his grave at night. Marcel Proust's grave is touchingly simple and elegant; Edith Piaf's is always heaped with flowers. Sexual scandal surrounds Oscar Wilde even in death: The handsome sculpture of a sphinx on his grave had its testicles chopped off by two scandalized visitors. (The offending parts were thereafter used for years by the cemetery's director as a paperweight.) The statue on the grave of Victor Noir has kept its genitalia, which are so awesome that visitors have rubbed them shiny, in hopes of increasing their own sexual powers. The atmosphere around mystic Allan Kardec's grave is truly spooky, with his followers (his philosophy of spiritism is wildly popular in Brazil) silently waiting their turn to touch his gravestone and commune with his spirit, departed from this world more than 100 years ago. Apart from the departed, the other permanent inhabitants of the cemetery are wild cats, who are regularly fed by kindly old ladies. Since Père-Lachaise is a city unto itself, be sure to purchase a map from one of the street vendors stationed outside of the cemetery to help find your way around and, more importantly, your way out before the 5:15pm closing time.

Parklike **Montmartre Cemetery** has its share of celebs too, including Hector Berlioz, Heinrich Heine, Stendhal, Vaslav Nijinsky, Edgar Dégas, Jacques Offenbach, Sacha Guitry, Aldolphe Sax (inventor of the saxophone), and Alphonsine Plessis (the model for the heroine of *La Dame aux Camélias*). François Truffaut, who once sneaked into the cemetery to shoot a scene for a film after the authorities refused him permission, specified that he wanted to be buried here. Left Bank intellectuals who wound up in the **Montparnasse Cemetery** include Jean-Paul Sartre and Simone de Beauvoir, along with Samuel Beckett, Charles Baudelaire, Tristan Tzara, Brancusi, Alfred Dreyfus,

Marshall Pétain, Guy de Maupassant, and Americans Man Ray and Jean Seberg (the incandescent Iowa beauty who tramped up and down the Champs-Elysées in Godard's *Breathless,* hawking the *Herald Tribune*).

Go backstage... A tour behind the scenes of the **Opéra Bastille** is a fascinating experience: The spaces are unbelievably immense, the huge sets make you feel like a Lilliputian, and the stage machinery is the most sophisticated of any opera house in the world. This "opera of the people" (with sky-high ticket prices) has been plagued with controversy since its inception in 1989. Just about no one admits to liking its exterior; two beloved international musical stars, Daniel Barenboim and Myung Whun-Chung, were fired from their posts with great public uproar; and its super-high-tech stage machinery has been beset with technical problems. If you want "the Phantom's" opera, however, you've got to go to its predecessor, the opulent **Opéra Garnier.** It's your classic, late 19th-century opera house, with a lavish interior rife with gilt, marble, crystal, and sculpting. The auditorium ceiling, painted by Marc Chagall in 1963, is beautiful in itself but clashes with the rest of the look. Mostly dance performances are held here now, and in the daytime you can go inside on your own to peek at the grand staircase, the public rooms, the auditorium, and the exhibition space (guided tours are also available). There's also an opera history museum, located in what was once the emperor's private entrance. Listen closely for the strains of the Phantom's organ drifting up from the underground lake beneath the opera house.

For a behind-the-scenes look at how a radio station operates, take a guided tour of the **Maison de Radio France**'s futuristic aluminum-faced circular building—actually three concentric circles, with the middle housing 70 recording studios (the round shape solved the acoustical problem of how to avoid parallel walls in the studios). An on-site museum covers the history of recording, with re-creations of early radio and television stations.

For *cinéphiles* and *cinéastes*... The favorite topic of conversation at any French dinner party is movies, and not just the latest ones—the French are fans of everything from Ernst Lubitsch films to *Rambo* or the latest Godard. The number of films made in Paris is mind-boggling, and they can all be seen in Les Halles at the **Vidéothèque de Paris,** an archive of videos and films related to Paris. For a small fee, you can stay all day, plunked in an armchair beside your own individual video screen, watching anything from *The 400 Blows* to silent footage of street life in Paris at the turn of the 20th century. Out west near Trocadéro, the **Cinémathèque Française,** another archive, has an enormous collection of classic and rare films and holds festivals on themes like Charlie Chaplin or film noir. It is also the home of the Musée du Cinéma Henri Langlois, with its amazing collection of film memorabilia. The **Cinémathèque de la Danse** has a collection of 400 films and 2,000 videos related to dance, with everything from Nureyev to Fred Astaire (private viewings are possible by appointment). Eccentric **Studio 28** in Montmartre is the most wonderful movie theater in Paris, with camp chandeliers in the auditorium that were supposedly designed by Jean Cocteau.

Kid-pleasers... The best overall place to go is the **Jardin d'Acclimatation** on the northern side of the Bois de Boulogne—it's a combination park, carnival, zoo, and playground. With its bears and bumper cars, donkey rides and boat rides, hall of mirrors and shooting galleries, it has something that every kid and adult can enjoy. Then there's Parc de la Villette's **Cité des Sciences et de l'Industrie,** a museum in a former slaughterhouse, which is full of things that kids love: a full-size model of a supersonic bomber, rocket and space station exhibits, a planetarium, and educational computer games. The science-oriented kids' section, Cité des Enfants, is so popular that it's sometimes hard to get in; thank goodness there are plenty of other attractions in the park, including a real submarine and eight fascinating theme gardens, including one with a monster slide. And the **Foire du Trône** carnival (in the Bois de Vincennes from March to the end of May) is like a wholesome version of an American midway, with Ferris wheels and other rides and shooting galleries. The Bois de Vincennes also has the largest zoo in Paris, the **Parc Zoologique de Paris,** where the wild beasts live in nearly natural habitats. The Chinese government donated a panda that has had a hard time staying cool in the summers.

If you'd rather stick to the center of town, there are the tried-and-true favorites: sailing rented wooden boats in the pools of the **Jardin des Tuileries** and **Jardin du Luxembourg.** The Luxembourg also has a marionette theater and a large, well-equipped playground, and twice a year the Tuileries hosts a carnival with a super Ferris wheel. It's all so Parisian, you almost expect to see Madeleine and her convent school chums filing past. Little monsters (and their parents) adore the colorful monsters in the Stravinsky Fountain next to the **Centre Pompidou.** The wacky sculptures by Jean Tinguely and Niki de Saint-Phalle—each named after one of the great composer's works—spin and spout water in all directions (when it's working). Nearby, the **Musée de la Poupée,** a private doll museum, has a collection of some 200 dolls dating from between 1860 and 1960 (yes, Barbie is included). Down on the Left Bank, the Ménagerie in the **Jardin des Plantes** is a fascinating little zoo with everything from panthers, monkeys, and bears to wild goats and insects. Want to drop your kids off? Try the **Jardin des Enfants aux Halles,** a high-tech, kid-pleasing playground for ages 7 to 11 in the newer part of the Forum des Halles, with labyrinths, tunnels, climbing walls, toboggans, and a "mysterious island." Kids can stay for 1 hour at a time, and no adults are allowed (there is adult supervision within). Younger children can visit with adults on Saturdays. Show up early (beginning at 10am) if you don't want a disappointed child on your hands because limited numbers of kids are admitted each hour. In summer, the **Louvre** runs some English-language classes about art history in its Atelier des Enfants (call 01-40-20-52-63 at 9am that morning to reserve).

If they insist, take your kids to **Disneyland Paris,** reachable by suburban train (RER A4). You know what to expect: Mickey, Goofy, Main Street U.S.A., Frontierland, Discoveryland, and so on. The Disney Studio is devoted to cinemagraphic extravaganzas. On a nice day, expect to wait in long lines for most attractions.

Keeping surly teenagers happy... Nothing will amuse them if they have to do it with adults. For those with macabre tastes, whip up to Denfert-Rochereau near Montparnasse for the **Catacombs,** old quarries where the city dumped leftover skeletons from Paris's overcrowded cemeteries (at one point, bones were actually jostling up out of the soil). Various skeletal parts have been decoratively arranged into walls and other frightening formations—awesome, if not disturbing. If their minds are in the gutter, haul them over to the Quai d'Orsay to explore the famous **Sewers of Paris** (*égouts*), although they won't dig the musty smell. Not so long ago, having fancy-dress parties in the sewers was the chic thing to do for young upper-class Parisians—talk about slumming.

Traces of Rome... The name Paris comes from the Parisii, a Celtic people who were holed up on the Ile de la Cité in 52 B.C., when the Romans hit town. The Romans conquered the Parisii's settlement, Lutetia (Lutèce), and stuck around for more than 5 centuries, when invaders from the north finally made the Romans clear out. The Roman influence still lurks in some parts of Paris, especially at the well-preserved **Arènes de Lutèce,** the ruins of an amphitheater that could hold up to 10,000 people to watch gladiators fight off wild beasts or be eaten by them. (There was also a stage to regale the populace with less-bloody theatrical performances.) Uncovered in 1869, the ruins today host modern-day gladiators: old men playing *boules.* Under the **Musée de Cluny** have been unearthed the remains of Roman baths, including the frigidarium and bits of the mosaics and frescoes that once decorated it. You don't have to pay the price of a museum ticket to see them, however—just peer through the iron fence from the boulevard Saint-Michel. Further archaeological excavations are now underway here. At the **Crypte Archéologique de Notre-Dame de Paris,** parts of the wall built to defend the Parisians from barbarian invaders in the 4th century can still be seen, along with other Gallo-Roman remains, including two rooms heated by the Romans' early version of a central-heating system. You can see the basements of medieval houses here too, but that's another era.

Map 13: Diversions in the 1er

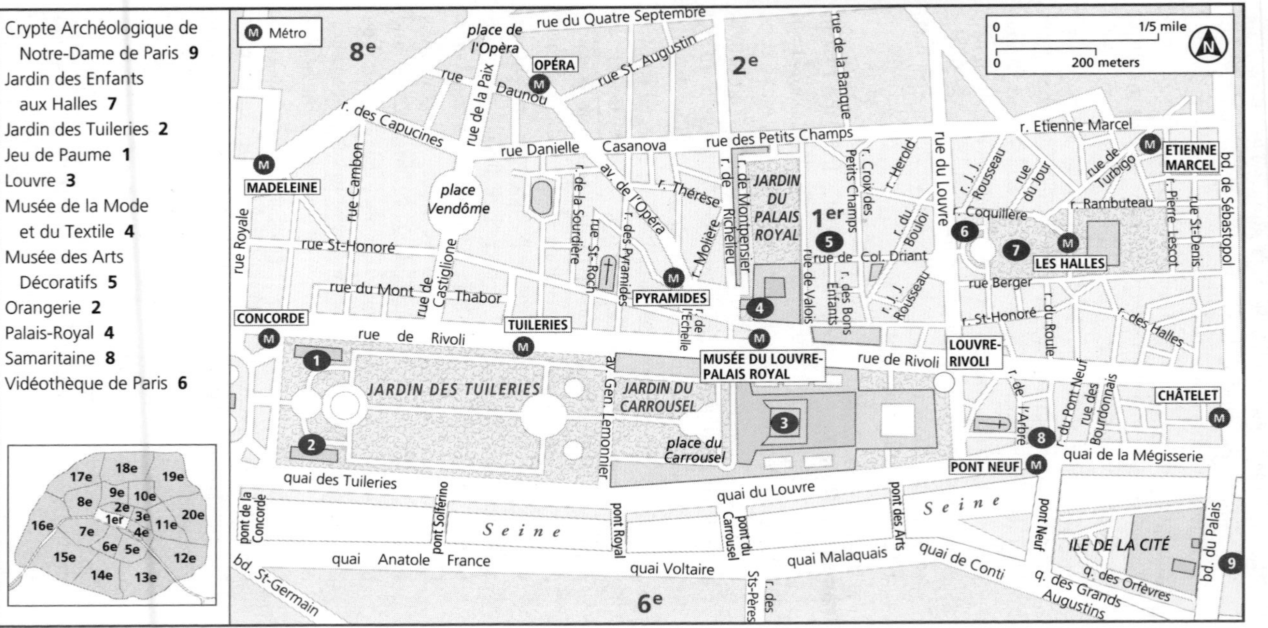

Map 14: The Louvre

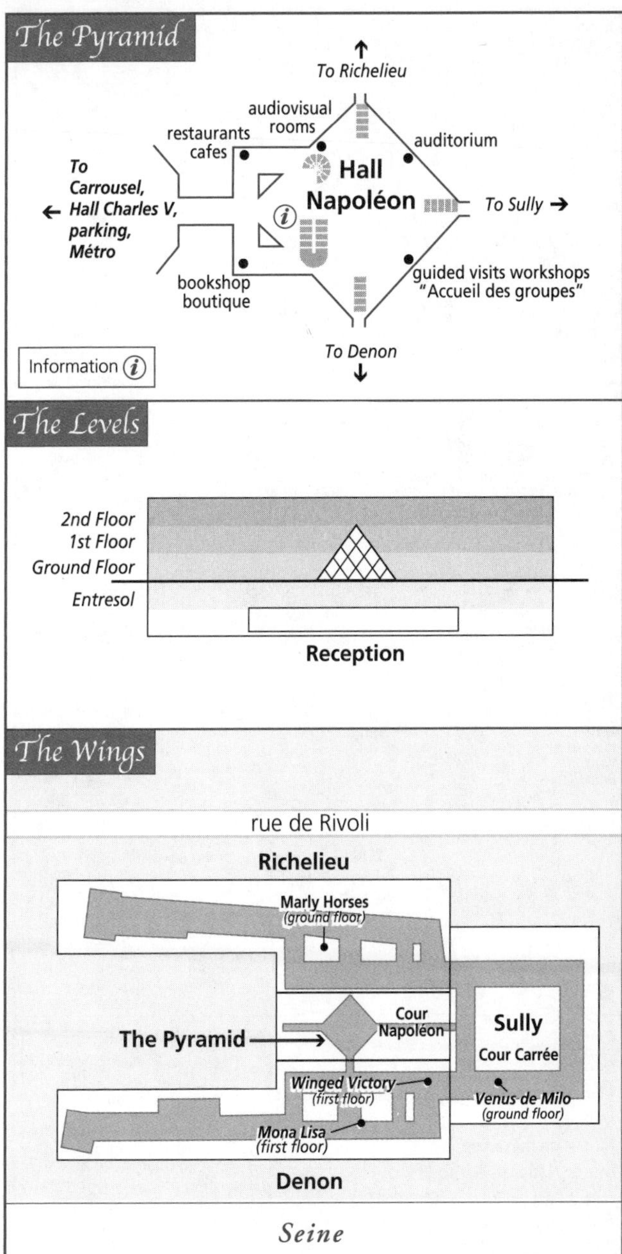

Map 15: Diversions in the 3–4e

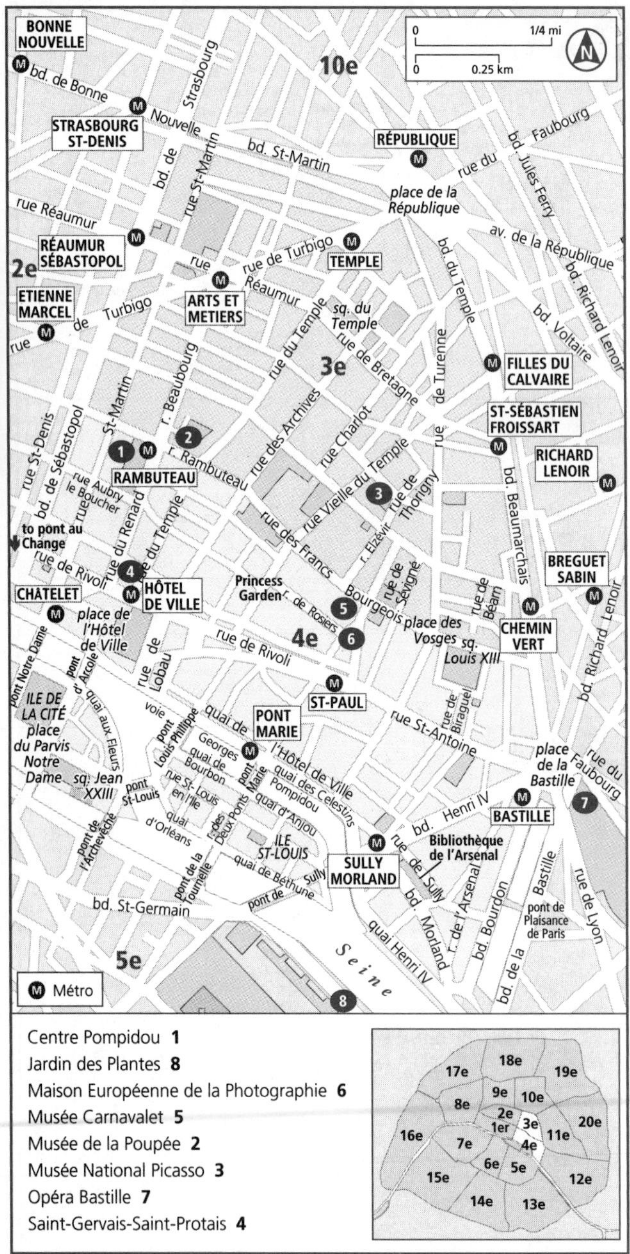

Map 16: Notre-Dame

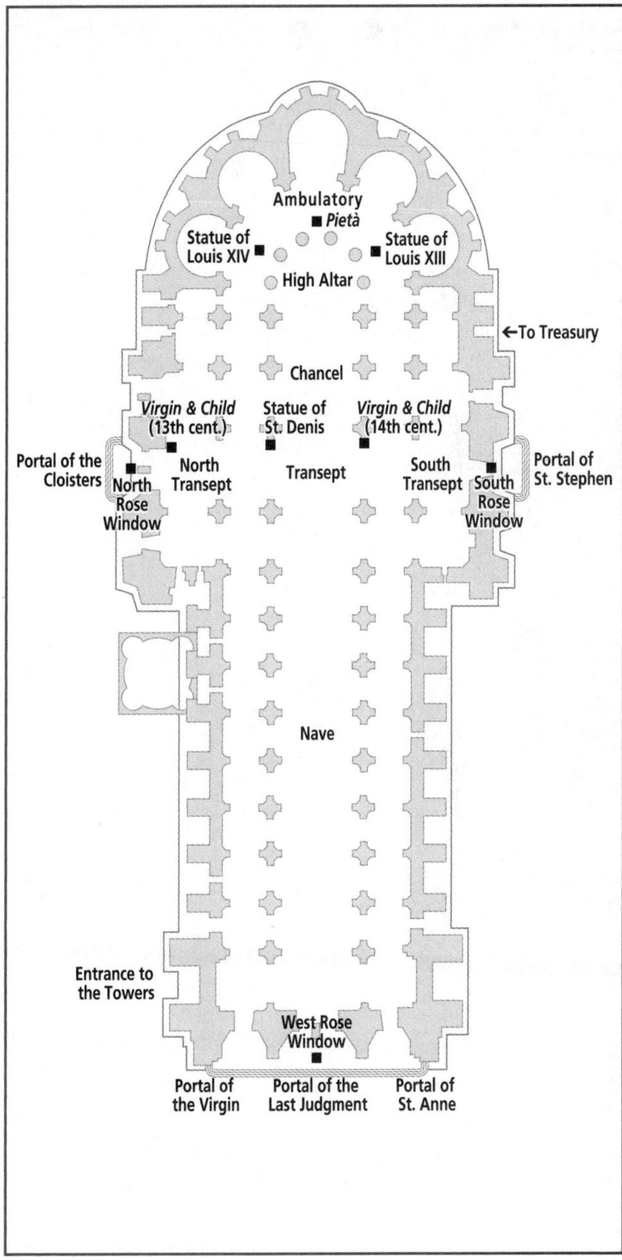

Map 17: Diversions in the 5–6e

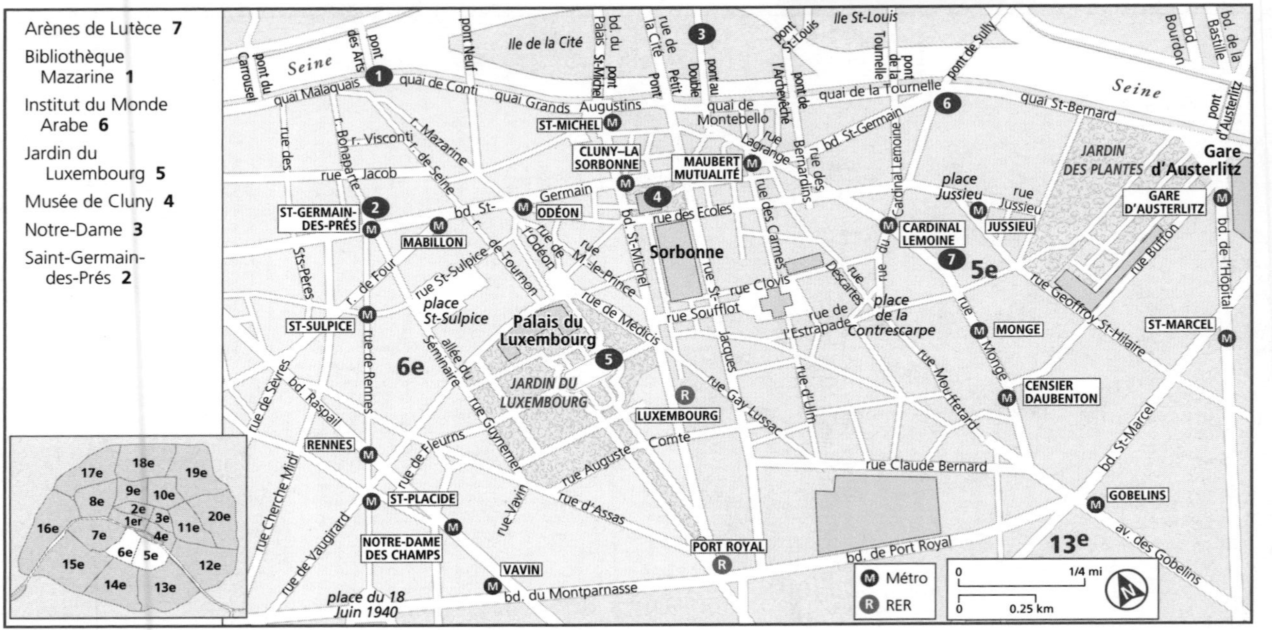

Map 18: Diversions in the 7e

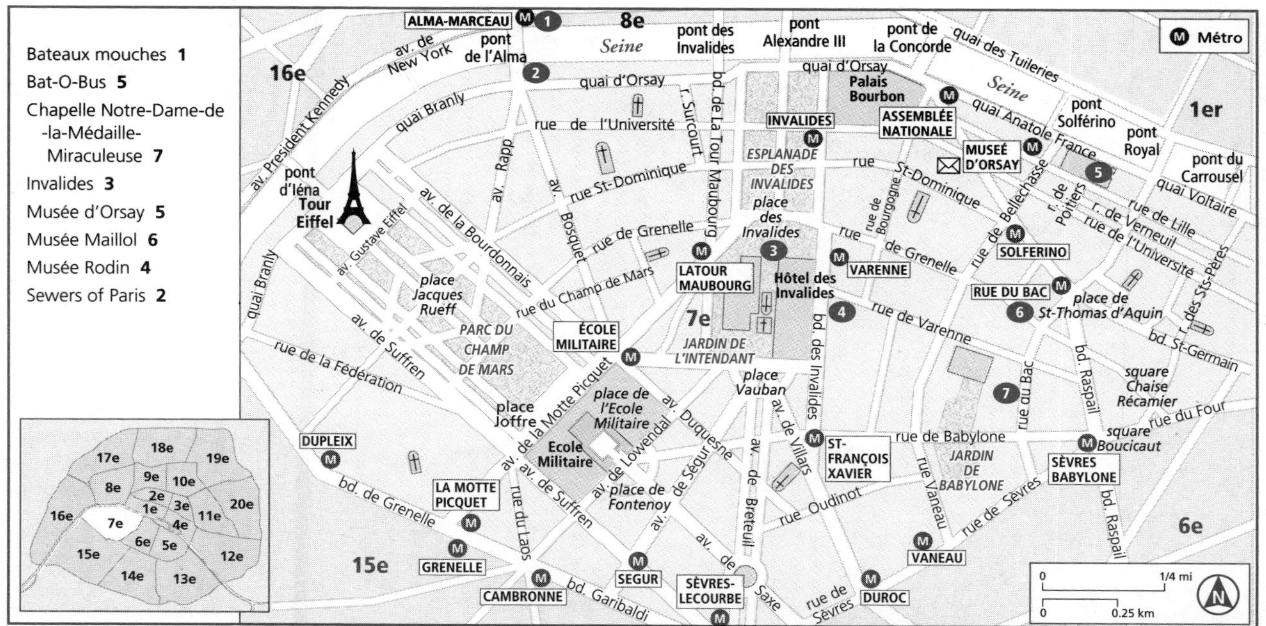

Map 19: Diversions in the 8e

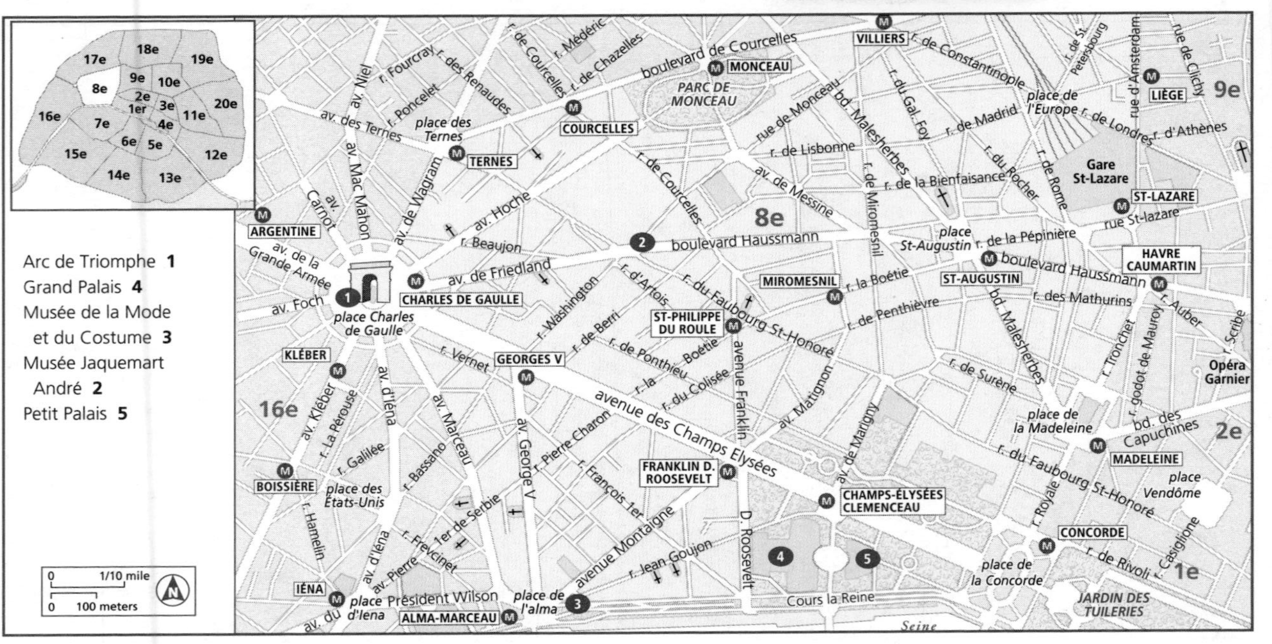

Map 20: Diversions in the 16e

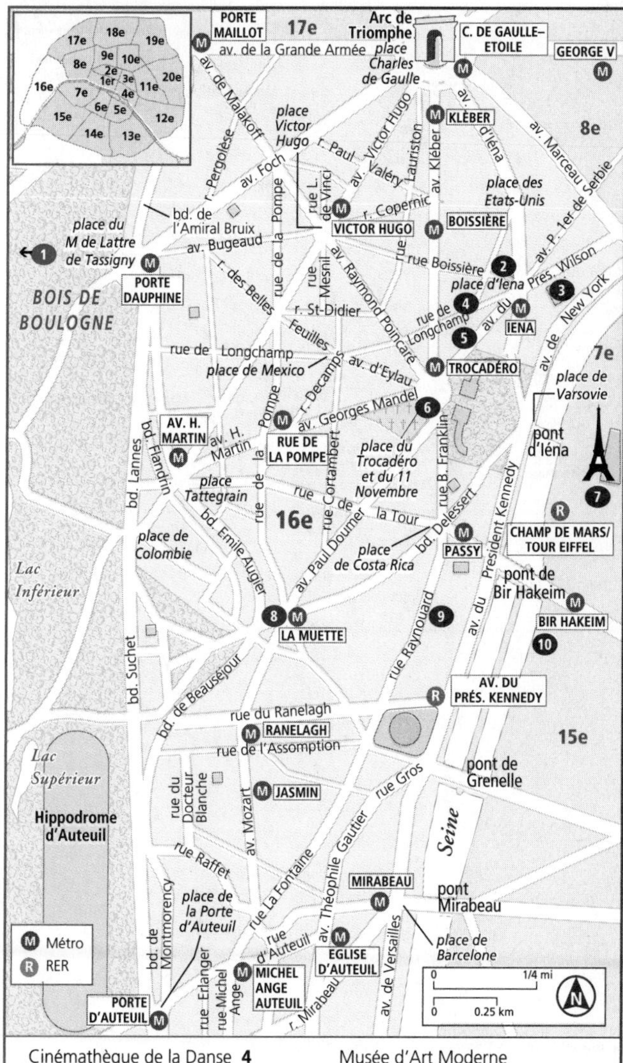

Cinémathèque de la Danse **4**
Cinémathèque Française **4**
Eiffel Tower **7**
Jardin d'Acclimatation **1**
Maison de Balzac **9**
Maison de la Culture du Japon **10**
Maison de Radio France **3**
Musée d'Art Moderne de la Ville de Paris **5**
Musée du Cinéma Henri Langlois **6**
Musée Guimet **2**
Musée Marmottan **8**

Map 21: Bois du Boulogne

Map 22: Diversions in the 18e

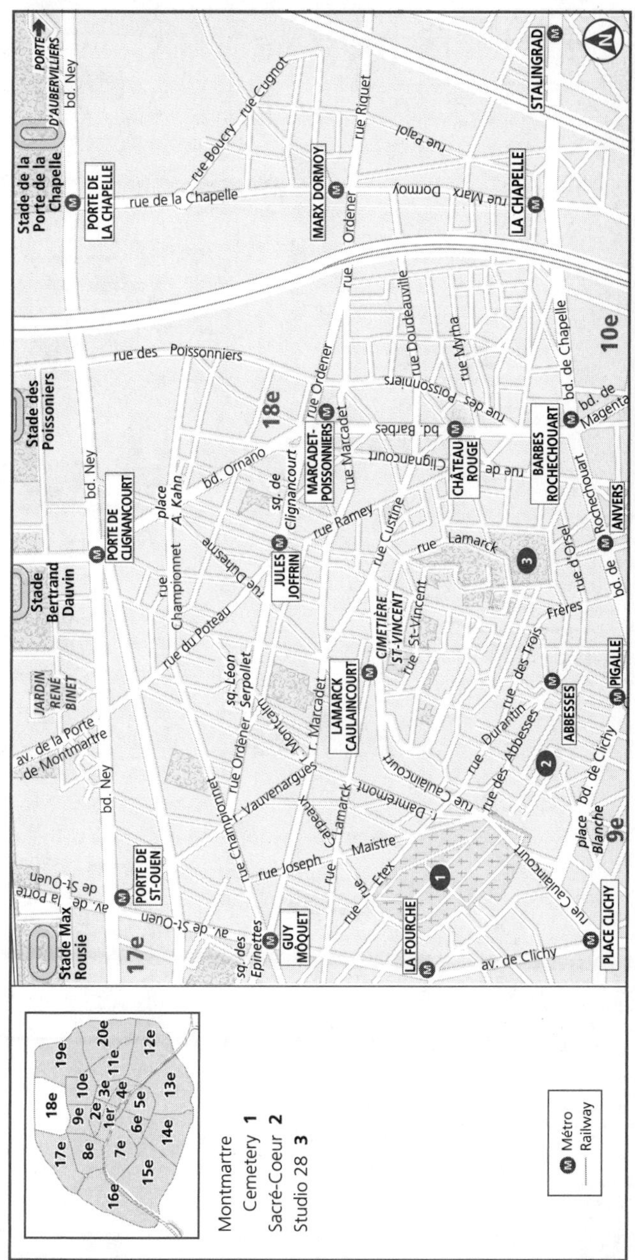

DIVERSIONS

Map 23: Père-Lachaise Cemetery

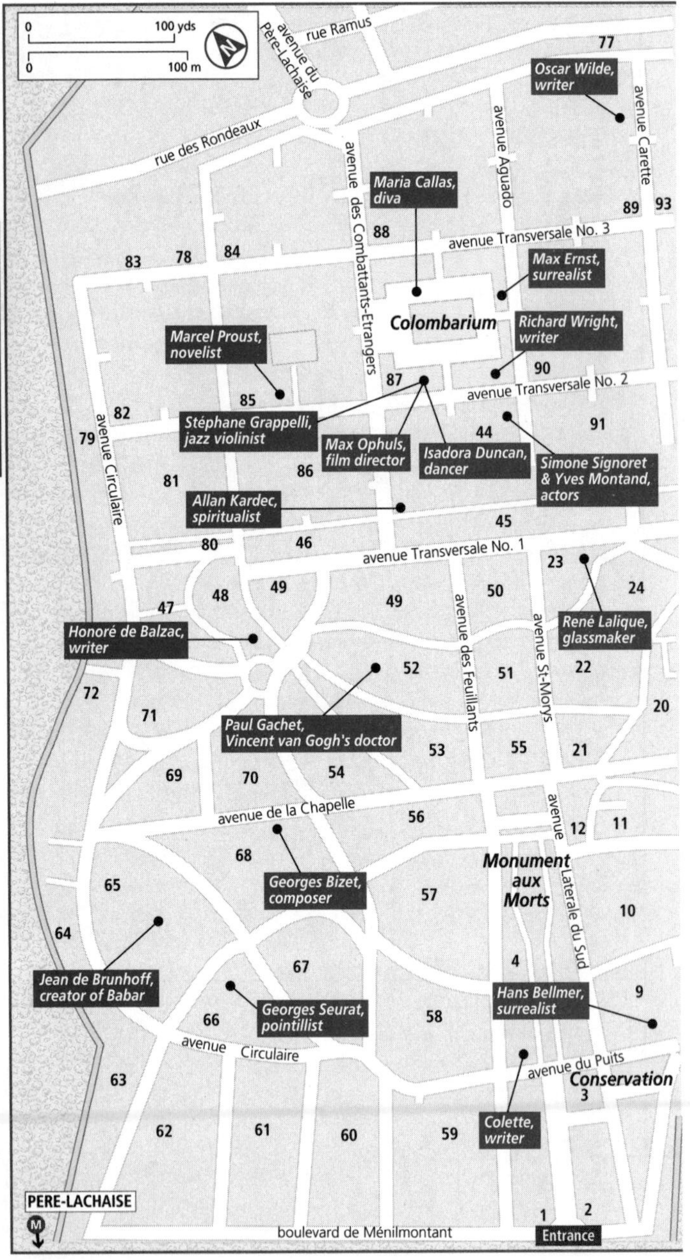

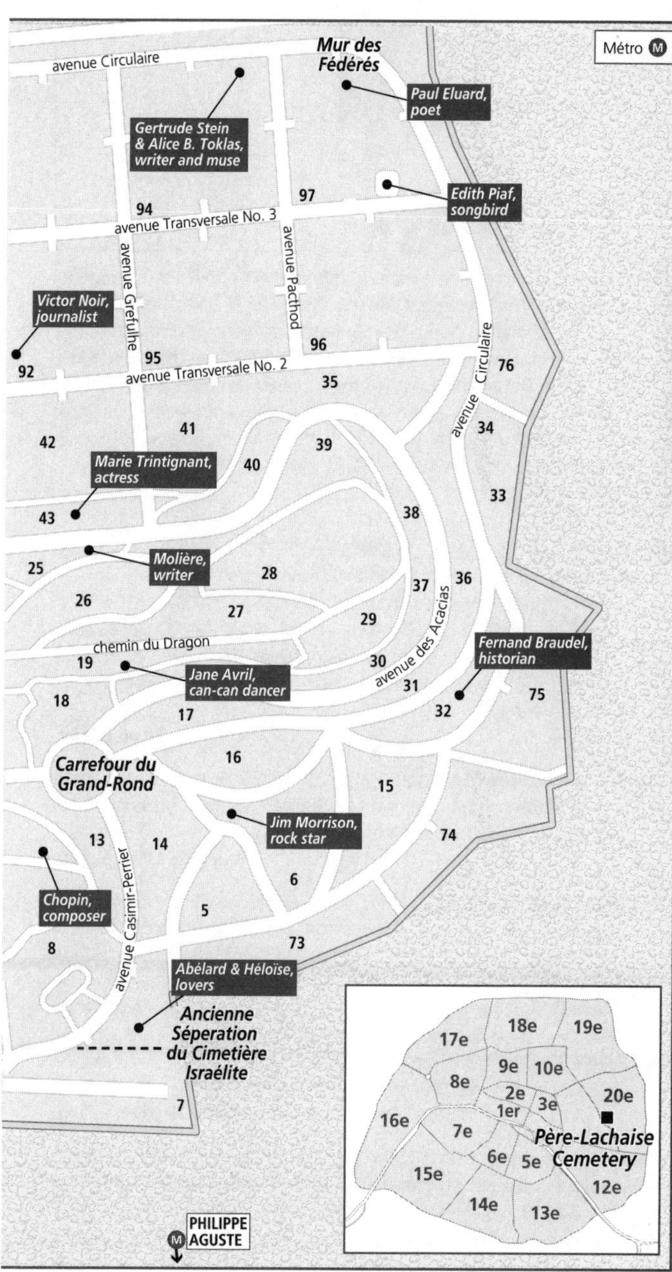

Métro
Mur des Fédérés
avenue Circulaire
Paul Eluard, poet
Gertrude Stein & Alice B. Toklas, writer and muse
Edith Piaf, songbird
avenue Transversale No. 3
avenue Grefulhe
avenue Pacthod
Victor Noir, journalist
avenue Transversale No. 2
avenue Circulaire
Marie Trintignant, actress
Molière, writer
chemin du Dragon
avenue des Acacias
Fernand Braudel, historian
Jane Avril, can-can dancer
Carrefour du Grand-Rond
Jim Morrison, rock star
avenue Casimir-Perrier
Chopin, composer
Abélard & Héloïse, lovers
Ancienne Séperation du Cimetière Israélite
PHILIPPE AGUSTE
17e
18e
19e
9e
10e
8e
2e
3e
20e
1er
16e
7e
Père-Lachaise Cemetery
6e
5e
15e
12e
14e
13e

The Index

There is no shortage of online information about Paris's sights. Often the best websites are *not* the official ones belonging to the tourist sights; do an online search for your favorite sight and see what fellow Paris-lovers have posted for you (the private visits to the Catacombs, for example, might enchant you). For the more beaten track, check www.parisinfo.com; the French Ministry of Culture also has excellent sites in English at www.monum.fr and www.culture.fr. All national monuments, museums, and sights are included.

Arc de Triomphe (p. 115) CHAMPS-ELYSEES The famous triumphal arch originally ordered by Napoléon provides visitors with a view of the Champs-Elysées from its rooftop.... *Tel 01-44-09-89-94. Place Général-de-Gaulle, 8e. Métro Etoile. April–Sept daily 9:30am–11pm; Oct–March daily 10am–10:30pm. Admission charged. Use underground passage from Champs-Elysées sidewalks to enter.*

See Map 19 on p. 144.

Arènes de Lutèce (p. 137) LATIN QUARTER Ruins of a Roman amphitheater.... *Entrances at 49, rue Monge and on rue Navarre, 5e. Métro Jussieu. Admission free.*

See Map 17 on p. 142.

Bateaux mouches (p. 116) CITYWIDE Several different companies provide this tour-boat service on the Seine. Boats can be boarded at the pont de l'Alma (Métro Alma Marceau), Port de la Bourdonnais (Métro Trocadéro), Quai de Montobello (Métro St-Michel), Port de Suffren (Métro Bir-Hakeim), and the square du Vert-Galant on the Ile de la Cité (Métro Pont Neuf).... *Boats run every 30 min, 10am–10:30pm; some close at lunchtime. Fare 7€ ($8.75) adults, 4€ ($5) children 5–15.*

See Map 18 on p. 143.

Bat-O-Bus (p. 116) CITYWIDE A bus-boat that plies the Seine in the summer. Board at the Eiffel Tower (Métro Bir-Hakeim), the Musée d'Orsay (Métro Solferino), Saint-Germain-des-Prés (Métro St-Germain-des-Prés), Notre-Dame (Métro St-Michel or Maubert Mutualité), Jardin des Plantes (Métro Jussieu or Cardinal Lemoine), Hôtel de Ville (Métro Hôtel de Ville), the Louvre (Métro Louvre Rivoli), or Champs-Elysées (Métro Champs-Elysées or

Clémenceau).... *Boats run every 30 min, 10am–7pm, May–Sept. All-day flat fare 11€ ($14) adults, 5€ ($6.25) children 3–11.*

See Map 18 on p. 143.

Bibliothèque Mazarine (p. 132) ST-GERMAIN-DES-PRES A lovely 17th-century library in the eastern wing of Institut de France.... *Tel 01-44-41-44-06. 23, quai de Conti, 6e. Métro Pont Neuf. Mon–Fri 10am–6pm. Admission free.*

See Map 17 on p. 142.

Bibliothèque Nationale de France (p. 118) GARE D'AUSTERLITZ The super-high-tech national library.... *Tel 01-53-79-59-59. www.bnf.fr. 11, quai François-Mauriac, 13e. Métro Quai de la Gare. Tues–Sat 10am–7pm, Sun noon–6pm. Admission free.*

See Map 12 on p. 108.

Catacombs (p. 137) MONTPARNASSE The spooky repository of thousands of skeletons moved from Paris's overcrowded cemeteries to old underground quarries.... *Tel 01-43-22-47-63. 1, place Denfert-Rochereau, 14e. Métro Denfert Rochereau. Tues–Fri 2–4pm, Sat–Sun 9–11am and 2–4pm. Admission charged.*

See Map 12 on p. 108.

Centre Bouddhique (p. 117) BOIS DE VINCENNES A Tibetan Buddhist temple, open to the public for meditation sessions. Call first.... *Tel 01-40-04-98-06. Bois de Vincennes, 12e. Métro Porte Dorée.*

See Map 12 on p. 108.

Centre Pompidou (p. 114) MARAIS A renovated cultural center with a modern-art collection, open-access library, cinema, bookstore, and children's center.... *Tel 01-44-78-12-33. www.centrepompidou.fr. Rue Rambuteau and rue St-Merri, 4e. Métro Rambuteau or Hôtel de Ville. Mon, Wed–Fri noon–10pm, Sat–Sun 10am–10pm. Closed Tues. Admission charged for permanent collection and some temporary exhibitions.*

See Map 15 on p. 140.

Chapelle Notre-Dame-de-la-Médaille-Miraculeuse (p. 117) EIFFEL TOWER Pilgrims come to this chapel to pray to a saint whose body is preserved under glass and to buy "miraculous medals"..... *Tel 01-49-54-78-88. 140, rue du Bac, 7e. Métro Sèvres Babylone. Wed–Mon 7:45am–1pm and 2:30–7pm, Tues 7:45am–7pm. Admission free.*

See Map 18 on p. 143.

Cinémathèque de la Danse (p. 135) BOIS DE BOULOGNE A collection of 400 films and 2,000 videos related to dance. Call to schedule a private viewing on a Friday.... *Tel 01-53-65-74-70. www.cinemathequefrancaise.com. 4, rue de Longchamp, 16e. Métro Iéna. By appointment only.*

See Map 20 on p. 145.

Cinémathèque Française (p. 122) BOIS DE BOULOGNE The French film archive shows retrospectives of often rare films.... *Tel 01-55-65-74-74. www.cinemathequefrancaise.com. 4, rue de Longchamp, 16e. Métro Iéna. Admission charged.*

See Map 20 on p. 145.

Cité des Sciences et de l'Industrie (p. 135) LA VILLETTE A kid-pleasing science museum with rocket and space station exhibits, a planetarium, and educational computer games. The Cité des Enfants has organized educational activities for children.... *Tel 01-40-05-72-23. www.cite-sciences.fr. 30, av. Corentin-Cariou, 19e. Métro Porte de la Villette. Tues–Sat 10am–6pm, Sun 10am–7pm. Admission charged.*

See Map 12 on p. 108.

Crypte Archéologique de Notre-Dame de Paris (p. 137) LATIN QUARTER 4th-century defensive walls, Gallo-Roman artifacts, and the basements of medieval houses in the crypt of Notre-Dame.... *Tel 01-55-42-50-10. Place du Parvis-Notre-Dame, 5e. Métro Cité. Daily 10am–4:30pm; closed public holidays. Admission charged.*

See Map 13 on p. 138.

Disneyland Paris (p. 136) SUBURBAN PARIS A morsel of Americana in the French countryside.... *Tel 01-60-30-60-30. www.disneylandparis.com. Marne-la-Vallée, RER line A to Marne-la-Vallée. Mon–Fri 10am–6pm, Sat–Sun 9am–8pm. Admission charged.*

See Map 12 on p. 108.

Eiffel Tower (p. 114) EIFFEL TOWER The symbol of Paris.... *Tel 01-44-11-23-45. www.tour-eiffel.fr. Champs de Mars, 7e. Métro Bir-Hakeim, RER Champs-de-Mars. Daily 9:30am–11pm. Admission charged.*

See Map 20 on p. 145.

Foire du Trône (p. 135) BOIS DE VINCENNES A carnival held in the Bois de Vincennes from March to June. You pay 1.50€ or 3€ ($1.85 or $3.75) for each ride.... *Tel 01-46-27-52-29. www.foiredutrone.com. Bois de Vincennes, 12e. Métro Château de Vincennes. Daily noon–midnight (Sat till 1am).*

See Map 12 on p. 108.

Fondation Cartier pour l'Art Contemporain (p. 121) MONTPARNASSE Modern art museum in a handsome modern building by Jean Nouvel.... *Tel 01-42-18-56-50. 261, bd. Raspail, 14e. Métro Raspail. Tues–Sun noon–8pm. Admission charged.*

See Map 12 on p. 108.

Forum des Halles See "Target Zones" in the Shopping chapter.

See Map 25 on p. 178.

Grande Arche de la Défense (p. 118) MONTPARNASSE A monumental arch providing views of Paris and La Défense from its rooftop.... *Tel 01-49-07-27-57. Place du Parvis-de-la Défense, 15e. Métro/RER La Défense. Daily 10am–7pm. Admission charged.*

See Map 20 on p. 145.

Grand Palais (p. 120) CHAMPS-ELYSEES A glass-roofed structure built for the Universal Exhibition of 1900 hosts traveling exhibitions and occasional blockbuster shows.... *Tel 01-44-13-17-17. 3, av. du Général-Eisenhower, 8e. Métro Champs Elysées Clemenceau. Wed–Mon 10am–8pm, until 10pm Wed. Admission charged.*

See Map 19 on p. 144.

Institut du Monde Arabe (p. 121) LATIN QUARTER Architect Jean Nouvel's handsome building houses a museum showcasing the arts of the Arab world and a Lebanese restaurant.... *Tel 01-40-51-38-38. 1, rue des Fossés-St-Bernard, 5e. Métro Jussieu. Tues–Sun 10am–6pm. Admission charged.*

See Map 17 on p. 142.

Invalides (p. 124) A 17th-century architectural masterpiece that occupies a quadrilateral, housing the Musée de l'Armée, the Musée d'Histoire Contempraine, the Musée de l'Ordre de la Libération, and the Musée des Plans et Reliefs.... *Tel 01-44-42-37-72. www.invalides.org. Esplanade des Invalides, 7e. Métro Varenne. Oct–March daily 10am–5pm; April–May and Sept daily 11am–6pm; June–Aug daily 10am–7pm. Admission charged.*

See Map 18 on p. 143.

Jardin d'Acclimatation (p. 135) BOIS DE BOULOGNE A park, carnival, zoo, and playground.... *Tel 01-40-67-90-82. In the Bois de Boulogne, 16e. Métro Sablon. The Petit Train also leaves from behind the Orée de Bois restaurant at Porte Maillot after 1:30pm every 10 min on Wed, Sat, Sun (every day during French school holidays). Daily 10am–6pm, 10am–7pm in summer. Admission charged. Extra charge for some attractions.*

See Map 20 on p. 145.

Jardin des Enfants aux Halles (p. 136) LOUVRE/LES HALLES A state-of-the-art playground in the western side of Les Halles, for children ages 7 to 11. Supervised 1-hour visits; no adults allowed, except on Saturday from 10am–2pm, when younger children are also admitted.... *Tel 01-45-08-07-18. 105, rue Rambuteau, 1er. Métro Les Halles. Call for opening times; closed Sun and when it rains. Admission charged.*

See Map 13 on p. 138.

Jardin des Plantes (p. 125) LATIN QUARTER Botanical garden, home of the newly refurbished National Museum of Natural History; the Jardin d'Hiver, a tropical garden in a greenhouse; the Jardin Alpin; a reptile house; a small zoo; and galleries of mineralogy, paleontology, entomology, and paleobotany....

Tel 01-40-79-30-00. 57, rue Cuvier, 5e. Métro Gare d'Austerlitz. Galleries 10am–5pm. Closed Tues. Garden daily 7:30am–8pm, 7:30am–5:30pm in winter; hrs vary for other attractions. Admission charged for some attractions.

See Map 15 on p. 140.

Jardin des Tuileries (p. 125) LOUVRE/LES HALLES 63 acres of the city's most formal gardens, designed by Le Nôtre.... *1er. Métro Tuileries or Concorde. Daily 7:30am to dusk. Admission free.*

See Map 13 on p. 138.

Jardin du Luxembourg (p. 126) ST-GERMAIN-DES-PRES Classic French formal gardens on the Left Bank.... *6e. Métro Odéon/RER Luxembourg. Admission free.*

See Map 17 on p. 142.

Jeu de Paume (p. 120) LOUVRE/LES HALLES A gallery of contemporary art in Napoléon III's former tennis court.... *Tel 01-47-03-12-50. Place de la Concorde, 1er. Métro Concorde. Tues noon–9:30pm, Wed–Fri noon–7pm, Sat–Sun 10am–7pm. Admission charged.*

See Map 13 on p. 138.

Louvre (p. 114) LOUVRE/LES HALLES The fabled museum in a palace. Home of the *Mona Lisa*.... *Tel 01-40-20-51-51 for general information. www.louvre.fr. Rue de Rivoli, 1er. Métro Palais Royal. Wed–Mon 9am–6pm, until 9:45pm Wed (Richelieu Wing open Mon until 9:45pm); closed some public holidays. Admission charged.*

See Map 13 on p. 138.
See Map 14 on p. 139.

Maison de Balzac (p. 121) BOIS DE BOULOGNE Balzac's former home is a museum containing many of his belongings.... *Tel 01-42-24-56-38. www.paris.fr/musees/balzac. 47, rue Raynouard, 16e. Métro Passy. Tues–Sun 10am–5:45pm. Admission charged.*

See Map 20 on p. 145.

Maison de la Culture du Japon (p. 119) EIFFEL TOWER Japanese cultural center, with art exhibitions, performances, and a library.... *Tel 01-44-37-95-00. 101 bis, quai Branly, 7e. Métro Bir-Hakeim. Tues–Sat noon–7pm. Admission charged.*

See Map 20 on p. 145.

Maison de Radio France (p. 134) BOIS DE BOULOGNE The headquarters of the French national radio stations.... *Tel 08-20-82-08-20. 116, av. du Président-Kennedy, 16e. Métro Iéna. Guided tours Mon–Sat at 10:30am, 11:30am, 2:30pm, 3:30pm, and 4:30pm. Admission charged.*

See Map 20 on p. 145.

Maison Européenne de la Photographie (p. 121) MARAIS This photo museum shows works by everyone from Pierre et Gilles to Helmut Newton.... *Tel 01-44-78-75-00. 5–7, rue de Fourcy, 4e.*

Métro St-Paul. Wed–Sun 11am–8pm; closed public holidays. Admission charged.

See Map 15 on p. 140.

Montmartre Cemetery (p. 130) MONTMARTRE A parklike cemetery where François Truffaut and Dalida, among others, have found their final resting place.... *Tel 01-43-87-64-24. Entrance on av. Rachel, 18e. Métro Place de Clichy or Abbesses. Mon–Fri 8am–5:30pm, Sat 8:30am–5:30pm, Sun 9am–5:30pm. Admission free.*

See Map 22 on p. 147.

Montparnasse Cemetery (p. 133) MONTPARNASSE An impressive roster of Left Bank notables, including Jean-Paul Sartre, Simone de Beauvoir, and Samuel Beckett are buried here.... *Tel 01-44-10-86-50. 3, bd. Edgar-Quinet, 14e. Métro Edgar Quinet. Mon–Fri 8am–5:30pm, Sat 8:30am–5:30pm, Sun 9am–5:30pm. Admission free.*

See Map 12 on p. 108.

Musée Albert Kahn (p. 122) SUBURBAN PARIS Anthropological exhibitions and fantastic gardens, with a tearoom in the palmarium.... *Tel 01-46-04-52-80. 14, rue du Port, 92100 Boulogne-Billancourt. Métro Boulogne Pont du St-Cloud. Tues–Sun 11am–6pm. Admission charged.*

See Map 20 on p. 145.

Musée Carnavalet (p. 124) MARAIS The museum of the history of Paris is located in the mansion where Madame de Sévigné once lived. Good temporary photography exhibitions, a nice gift shop.... *Tel 01-44-59-58-58. 23, rue de Sévigné, 3e. Métro St-Paul. Tues–Sun 10am–5:40pm; closed public holidays. Admission charged.*

See Map 15 on p. 140.

Musée d'Art Moderne de la Ville de Paris (p. 120) BOIS DE BOULOGNE The city of Paris's modern-art museum often holds good temporary exhibitions.... *Tel 01-53-67-40-00. 11, av. du Président-Wilson, 16e. Métro Iéna. Tues–Fri 10am–5:30pm, Sat–Sun 10am–6:45pm. Admission charged.*

See Map 20 on p. 145.

Musée de Cluny (p. 120) LATIN QUARTER A museum of medieval art, with a collection of tapestries, paintings, and sculptures. Housed in a 15th-century Gothic mansion built on the ruins of a 3rd-century Roman bathhouse.... *Tel 01-53-73-78-00. 6, place Paul-Painlevé, 5e. Métro Cluny La Sorbonne or RER St-Michel–Notre Dame. Wed–Mon 9:15am–5:45pm. Admission charged.*

See Map 17 on p. 142.

Musée de la Mode et du Costume (p. 123) CHAMPS-ELYSEES Temporary exhibitions about the history of fashion.... *Tel 01-56-52-86-00. 10, av. Pierre-1er-de-Serbie, 8e. Métro Alma Marceau. Tues–Sun (during exhibitions) 10am–5:40pm. Admission charged.*

See Map 19 on p. 144.

Musée de la Mode et du Textile (p. 120) LOUVRE/LES HALLES An extensive collection of haute couture, costumes, and accessories.... *Tel 01-44-55-57-50. 107, rue de Rivoli, 1er. Métro Palais Royal. Tues, Thurs, Fri 11am–6pm, Wed until 10pm, Sat–Sun 10am-6pm. Admission charged.*

See Map 13 on p. 138.

Musée de la Musique (p. 121) LA VILLETTE Collection of 900 musical instruments from the 17th century to the present. Research library.... *Tel 01-44-84-44-84. www.cite-musique.fr. 221, av. Jean-Jaurès, 19e. Métro Porte de Pantin. Tues–Thurs noon–6pm, Fri–Sat noon–7:30pm, Sun 10am–6pm. Admission charged.*

See Map 12 on p. 108.

Musée de la Poupée (p. 136) MARAIS A private collection of some 200 dolls dating from 1860 to 1960.... *Tel 01-42-72-73-11. Impasse Berthaud (entrance at 22, rue Beaubourg), 3e. Métro Rambuteau. Tues–Sun 10am–6pm. Admission charged.*

See Map 15 on p. 140.

Musée de la Vie Romantique (p. 123) PIGALLE George Sand memorabilia in a period setting.... *Tel 01-55-31-95-67. 16, rue Chaptal, 9e. Métro Pigalle. Tues–Sun 10am–5:40pm; closed public holidays. Admission charged.*

See Map 12 on p. 108.

Musée de l'Erotisme (p. 122) PIGALLE Erotic art collection from around the world in the heart of sleazy Pigalle.... *Tel 01-42-58-28-73. 72, bd. de Clichy, 18e. Métro Pigalle. Daily 10am–2am.*

See Map 12 on p. 108.

Musée des Arts d'Afrique et d'Océanie (p. 122) BOIS DE VINCENNES Art from Africa and Oceania and an aquarium with some 300 species of tropical fish.... *Tel 01-43-46-51-61. 293, av. Dausmesnil, 12e. Métro Porte Dorée. Mon–Fri 10–11:45am and 1:30–5:20pm, Sat–Sun 10am–5:45pm. Admission charged.*

See Map 12 on p. 108.

Musée des Arts Décoratifs (p. 120) LOUVRE/LES HALLES A museum tracing the history of the decorative arts from the Middle Ages to the recent past. Also has large collections of dolls and posters.... *Tel 01-44-55-57-50. 107, rue de Rivoli, 1er. Métro Palais Royal. Wed–Mon 12:30–6pm; closed major holidays. Admission charged.*

See Map 13 on p. 138.

Musée d'Orsay (p. 115) EIFFEL TOWER A magnificent collection of art from the second half of the 19th century, housed in a beautiful turn-of-the-20th-century converted train station.... *Tel 01-40-49-48-14. 1, rue de Bellechasse, 7e. Métro Solférino, RER Musée d'Orsay. Open Tues–Sun 10am–6pm, until 9:30pm Thurs. Admission charged.*

See Map 18 on p. 143.

Musée du Cinéma Henri Langlois (p. 122) PALAIS DE CHAILLOT The history of moving pictures from their beginnings to today.... *Tel 01-47-04-79-34. 1, place du Trocadéro, 16e. Métro Trocadéro. Guided tours offered Wed–Sun 10am, 11am, 2pm, 3pm, 4pm, and 5pm. Admission charged.*

See Map 20 on p. 145.

Musée Edith Piaf (p. 122) BASTILLE Letters, photographs, and clothing belonging to France's beloved chanteuse.... *Tel 01-43-55-52-72. 5, rue de Crespin-du-Gast, 11e. Métro Menilmontant. By appointment Mon–Thurs 1–6pm. Admission charged.*

See Map 12 on p. 108.

Musée Guimet (p. 120) BOIS DE BOULOGNE A major Asian art museum with an especially fine Khmer art collection and a bamboo garden in the annex.... *Tel 01-56-52-53-00. 6, place d'léna, 16e. Métro léna. Mon and Wed–Sat 10am–5:45pm.*

See Map 20 on p. 145.

Musée Jacquemart André (p. 122) CHAMPS-ELYSEES A private art collection displayed in the restored 19th-century mansion of its owners, who raided Europe for Italian Renaissance art and more.... *Tel 01-45-62-11-59. 158, bd. Haussmann, 8e. Métro St-Philippe-du-Roule. Daily 10am-6pm.*

See Map 19 on p. 144.

Musée Maillol (p. 121) LATIN QUARTER Interesting and atmospheric museum in a beautifully restored 18th-century town house mainly devoted to the works of the sculptor Maillol but also exhibiting works by Degas, Picasso, and others.... *Tel 01-42-22-59-58. 59–61, rue de Grenelle, 5e. Métro Rue du Bac. Mon, Wed–Sun 11am–6pm. Admission charged.*

See Map 18 on p. 143.

Musée Marmottan (p. 123) BOIS DE BOULOGNE A 19th-century mansion, with a large collection of Impressionist paintings and a fine assemblage of illuminated medieval manuscripts.... *Tel 01-42-24-07-02. 2, rue Louis-Boilly, 16e. Métro Muette. Tues–Sun 10am–5:30pm. Admission charged.*

See Map 20 on p. 145.

Musée National Picasso (p. 115) MARAIS Works spanning the artist's entire career on display in a 17th-century mansion.... *Tel 01-42-71-25-21. Hôtel Salé, 5, rue de Thorigny, 3e. Métro St-Sébastien-Froissart or St-Paul. Wed–Mon 9:30am–5:50pm. Admission charged.*

See Map 15 on p. 140.

Musée Rodin (p. 121) EIFFEL TOWER The sculptor's most famous works, including *The Kiss* and *The Thinker,* in an 18th-century mansion.... *Tel 01-44-18-61-10. 77, rue Varenne, 7e. Métro Varenne. Tues–Sun 9:30am–5:15pm. Admission charged.*

See Map 18 on p. 143.

Notre-Dame (p. 115) MARAIS The 14th-century Gothic cathedral has suffered many indignities over the centuries but still stands in all its glory and has been cleaned up for the new millennium.... *Tel 01-42-34-56-10. Place du Parvis-Notre-Dame, 4e. Métro Cité. Cathedral 8am–6:45pm, closed Sat 12:30–2pm; towers 10am–6pm in summer, hrs vary slightly throughout the year. Admission charged for tower visits.*

See Map 16 on p. 141.
See Map 17 on p. 142.

Opéra Bastille (p. 118) BASTILLE The controversial and technologically sophisticated new opera house. For details about performances, see the Entertainment chapter.... *Tel 01-40-01-19-70. 120, rue de Lyon, 11e. Métro Bastille. Guided 75-min tours begin at 1pm; call for dates. Closed 2 weeks in July and all of Aug. Admission charged.*

See Map 15 on p. 140.

Opéra Garnier (p. 134) OPERA GARNIER This ornate theater is the venue for dance performances and some opera.... *Tel 01-40-01-17-89. 8, rue Scribe, 9e. Métro Opéra. Daily 10am–5:30pm, guided tours at 1pm (except during matinees); closed Jan 1 and May 1. Admission charged.*

See Map 27 on p. 226.

Orangerie (p. 123) LOUVRE/LES HALLES A small museum that houses a fine collection of Impressionist works.... *Tel 01-42-97-48-16. Jardin des Tuileries (on the Seine side near the place de la Concorde), 1er. Métro Concorde. Wed–Mon 9:45am–5:15pm. Admission charged.*

See Map 13 on p. 138.

Palais-Royal (p. 132) LOUVRE/LES HALLES Originally the residence of Cardinal Richelieu, Louis XIII's prime minister, the Palais-Royal today houses government offices. The draw here is the garden, which is bordered by arcades. Check out the controversial 1986 Buren sculpture in the main courtyard.... *Rue St-Honoré, 1er. Métro Palais Royal–Musée du Louvre. Daily 8am–7pm. Admission free.*

See Map 13 on p. 138.

Parc André Citroën See "Taking the air, part three: city parks," in the Getting Outside chapter.

See Map 24 on p. 164.

Parc de Bagatelle (p. 125) BOIS DE BOULOGNE An English garden within the Bois de Boulogne.... *Tel 01-40-67-97-00. 16e. Route de Sèvres-à-Neuilly and route de la Reine-Marguerite. Métro Pont de Neuilly, then take no. 43 bus, or Métro Porte Maillot, then take no. 244 bus. Daily 8:30am–8pm in summer; hrs vary in other seasons. Admission charged.*

See Map 21 on p. 146.

Parc de Belleville (p. 124) MENILMONTANT An off-the-beaten-track hillside park with views over the city.... *Rue Piat, 20e. Métro Pyrénées. 8:30am–5pm. Admission free.*

See Map 12 on p. 108.

Parc Zoologique de Paris (p. 135) BOIS DE VINCENNES A zoo in the Bois de Vincennes where the animals live in natural habitats.... *Tel 01-44-75-20-10. 53, av. de St-Maurice, 12e. Métro Porte Dorée. Daily 9am–6pm, until 5pm in winter. Admission charged.*

See Map 12 on p. 108.

Père-Lachaise Cemetery (p. 115) PERE-LACHAISE The permanent resting place of everyone from Abélard and Héloïse to Jim Morrison.... *Tel 01-43-79-02-69. Entrance at corner of rue de la Roquette and bd. Ménilmontant, 20e. Métro Père Lachaise. Daily 8am–5:15pm. Admission free.*

See Map 12 on p. 108.
See Map 23 on p. 148.

Petit Palais (p. 123) CHAMPS-ELYSEES Home of the City of Paris's art collection. Often holds good temporary exhibitions.... *Tel 01-42-65-12-73. av. Winston Churchill, 8e. Métro Champs Elysées Clemenceau. Tues–Sun 10am–5:40pm. Admission charged.*

See Map 19 on p. 144.

Sacré-Coeur (p. 115) MONTMARTRE The famous hilltop church looks like a white wedding cake and has great views of Paris.... *Tel 01-53-41-89-00. 35, rue Chevalier-de-la-Barre, 18e. Métro Anvers. Church daily 6–11am; dome and crypt open 9am–7pm, until 6pm in winter. Admission charged for dome and crypt.*

See Map 22 on p. 147.

Sainte-Chapelle (p. 117) LOUVRE/LES HALLES A gorgeous 13th-century Gothic church hidden inside the Palais de Justice, with incredible stained-glass windows.... *Tel 01-53-73-78-51. 4, bd. du Palais, 1er. Métro Cité. Daily 10am–4:30pm Oct–April, 9:30am–6:30pm May–Sept. Admission charged.*

See Map 12 on p. 108.

Saint-Germain-des-Prés (p. 117) ST-GERMAIN-DES-PRES The oldest church in Paris dates to the 11th century.... *Tel 01-55-42-81-33. 3, place St-Germain-des-Prés, 6e. Métro St-Germain-des-Prés. Daily 7am–7:30pm. Admission free.*

See Map 17 on p. 142.

Saint-Gervais-Saint-Protais **(p. 117)** MARAIS A 17th-century Flamboyant Gothic church that is open 'round the clock.... *Place St-Gervais, 4e. Métro Hôtel de Ville. Admission free.*

See Map 15 on p. 140.

Samaritaine **(p. 124)** LOUVRE/LES HALLES Free views of Paris from the top floor of Magasin 2 of this venerable department store.... *Tel 01-40-41-20-20. La Samaritaine, Magasin 2, 2, quai du Louvre, 1er. Métro Louvre Rivoli. Mon–Sat 9:30am–7pm, until 10pm Thurs. Admission free.*

See Map 13 on p. 138.

Sewers of Paris **(p. 137)** EIFFEL TOWER Sophisticated yet stinky sewage system originally constructed under Napoléon III. Don't wear your Sunday best.... *Tel 01-47-05-10-29. Entrance at 93, quai d'Orsay, 7e. Métro Alma Marceau. Sat–Wed 11am–5pm, until 4pm in winter. Admission charged.*

See Map 18 on p. 143.

Shakespeare & Company See the Shopping chapter for a complete description.

See Map 25 on p. 178.

Studio 28 **(p. 135)** MONTMARTRE A charming and eccentric movie theater with a bar and garden.... *Tel 01-46-06-36-07. 10, rue Tholozé, 18e. Métro Blanche or Abbesses. Most days, screenings begin at 3, 5, 7, and 9pm. Closed last 2 weeks of July and all Aug. Admission charged.*

See Map 22 on p. 147.

Tour Montparnasse **(p. 124)** MONTPARNASSE Great view of Paris from 209m (686 ft.) high on the 56th and 57th floors.... *Tel 01-45-38-69-96. Rue de l'Arrivée, 15e. Métro Montparnasse or Montparnasse Bienvenüe. Winter 9:30am-10:30pm; summer 9:30am-11:30pm. Admission charged.*

See Map 12 on p. 108.

Verger du Luxembourg See "Taking the air, part two: city gardens" in the Getting Outside chapter.

See Map 24 on p. 164.

Vidéothèque de Paris **(p. 135)** LOUVRE/LES HALLES A video archive with a huge selection of films concerning Paris.... *Tel 01-44-76-62-00. 2, Grande Galerie du Forum des Halles, Porte St-Eustache, 1er. Métro Les Halles. Tues–Sun 1–9pm, until 10pm Thurs. Admission charged.*

See Map 13 on p. 138.

GETTING

OUTSIDE

Map 24: Getting Outside

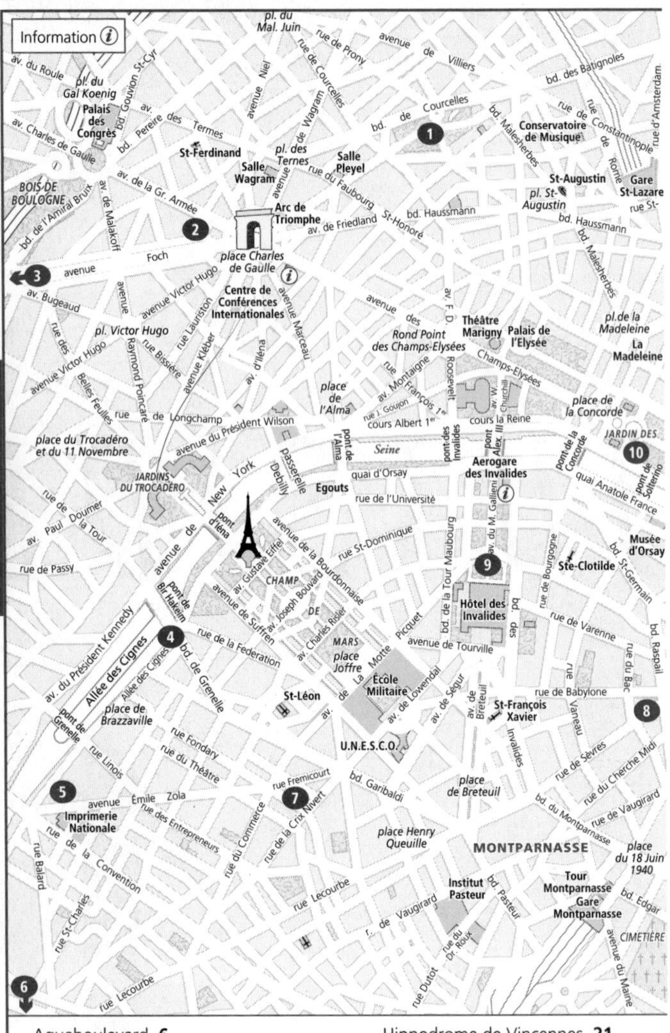

Aquaboulevard **6**
Bike 'n Roller **9**
Bois de Boulogne **3**
Canal Saint-Martin **16**
Club Med Gym **7, 14**
Club Quartier Latin **19**
Esplanade des Invalides **9**
Golf Club d'Etoile **2**
Hippodrome de Vincennes **21**
Jardin des Tuileries **10**
Jardin du Carousel **12**
Parc André Citroën **5**
Parc de Bercy **21**
Parc des Buttes-Chaumont **15**
Parc Monceau **1**
Paris à Vélo, C'est Sympa! **17**

Paris Plages **18**
Piscine d'Auteuil **3**
Piscine de Pontoise **19**
Piscine Nouveau Forum des Halles **13**
Réserve Ornithologique **3**
Ritz Club **11**
Société d'Equitation de Paris **3**
Société Equestre de l'Etrier **3**
Squash Front de Seine **4**
Squash Rennes-Raspail **8**
Tennis Luxembourg **20**
Verger du Luxembourg **20**

The French idea of a garden dictates that nature be tortured and tamed into symmetrical shapes and designs. Instead of green expanses of lawn, you get dirt. If there is grass, you're usually not allowed to sit on it—it's only to be looked at. This produces beautiful gardens, not places where you go to have fun. Paris does have a few wide-open green spaces, but they're so civilized—and in good weather so crowded with people—that you hardly feel you're outdoors.

And then there's the traffic. There are often pollution alerts in the summer, but the city government seems unwilling to take action to cut down on the number of cars. (The strongest measure so far has been to restrict traffic to odd or even license-plate numbers on the day after a pollution alert.) There are some improvements, however. A prime example is Paris Plage, whereby the city converts 3km (1.86 miles) of the Right Bank of the Seine into a waterfront playground for 2 months in the summer.

If you know where to go, it's possible to find a bit of tranquillity and greenery in Paris and its environs. Just don't expect to "get in touch" with nature.

The Lowdown

Taking the air, part one: city forests... Wandering aimlessly through the vast forest of the **Bois de Boulogne** (main entrance near Métro Porte Dauphine) is not very interesting unless, of course, you are intrigued by public sexual activities, often practiced in broad daylight. Whole books and dissertations have been written on the subject of prostitution in the park, with special interest paid to all the Brazilian transvestites who ply their trade in the Bois. If this sort of stuff isn't your priority, head for less sordid areas of the forest, such as the **Pré Catelan,** a pristine little park within the Bois de Boulogne, where a 200-year-old beech tree provides a huge sprawl of shade, and nannies watch their little charges cavorting over great expanses of green. The gourmet restaurant Le Pré Catelan (p. 98) is located here, as is the **Jardin Shakespeare,** which has an outdoor theater surrounded by all sorts of trees and plants mentioned by the Bard. Even lovelier is the **Bagatelle,** an English-style garden with peacocks, a spectacular rose garden, and art exhibitions held in a tiny château. The child-oriented **Jardin d'Acclimatation,** a park in the Bois with zoo animals and carnival rides, is fun for adults as well. Boats can be rented for paddling around on **Lac Supérieur.**

Unlike the wooded Bois de Boulogne, the large **Bois de Vincennes** (Métro Château de Vincennes), at the eastern edge of Paris, sometimes seems too civilized and overbuilt. Take a walk in its **Parc Floral** (small admission charged), which has a little train running around its perimeter. Rent a rowboat and go out on one of the two lakes, **Lac des Minimes** (Métro Porte Dorée) or **Lac Daumesnil** (RER Nogent-sur-Marne). Stroll through the **Parc Zoologique** or visit the Foire du Trône (an annual carnival); the **Centre Bouddhique,** a Tibetan Buddhist temple; the **Château de Vincennes** and its dungeon that inspired Alexandre Dumas; or the **Musée des Arts d'Afrique et d'Océanie.**

Taking the air, part two: city gardens... The **Jardin du Luxembourg** (Métro Odéon or RER Luxembourg), a residential area in Roman times and later a private royal property, was liberated during the Revolution and is now open to everyone. Visitors no longer have to pay to rent one of the pretty green metal chairs that are traditional in French parks—they're free to all. You'll have to pay for a wooden toy boat if your child wants to sail one in the pool in the center of the park, but it's worth it, both to appease the kid and to see the brightly colored sails zipping around in the water. This park is so kid-friendly, it has chess tables, a large playground, a marionette theater—even a *pelouse* (lawn) on which children are allowed to play. (In some Paris parks a law allows you to sit on some lawns, but not in the Luxembourg, which is owned by the Senate rather than by the city.) In addition to the lawns and café under the chestnut trees near the place du Luxembourg, there are various gardens graced with statues. (Look for George Sand to the left of the Saint-Michel entrance and the queens of France surrounding the large, open space in the center.) The most scenic part of the park is the **Medicis Fountain,** built by Marie de Medicis to improve the view from her bedroom window in the Luxembourg Palace, built in 1612; goldfish swim in the long, rectangular pool flanked by Italian-style vines, as a statue of an amorous couple looks on. Tucked away in the southwest corner of the garden is the rarely visited **Verger du Luxembourg,** or the National Conservatory of Apples and Pears, founded by Napoléon in 1809. Here, 360 species of apple trees and 270 types of pear trees are tortured into those unnatural shapes so beloved by French gardeners. And who gets to eat the fruit? Members of the Senate, of course, who meet in the palace on the other side of the park. (Leftovers are given to a soup kitchen.) Nearby is an apiary, which sells its honey at the end of September in the garden near the intersection of rue de Vaugirard and rue Guynemer.

Once a place for "elegant rendezvous," **Jardin des Tuileries** (Métro Tuileries), stretching along the right bank of the Seine between the place de la Concorde and the Louvre, is now a gay cruising ground at night. In the daytime, however, this statue-studded formal garden—created by Catherine de Medicis in the 16th century and revamped by Louis XIV's architect, Le Nôtre, in the 17th—is a reasonable spot for a stroll. Some of the statues here date back to the 17th century, and four of them were sculpted by Auguste Rodin. Children love the round pool toward the western end of the garden, where they can sail wooden boats rented from a nearby stand. Twice a year, for a few weeks in summertime and at Christmas, a carnival is set up between the garden and the rue de Rivoli; its main attraction is an immense Ferris wheel with stellar views of Paris from the top (well worth risking an attack of vertigo). Two major museums, the Orangerie (p. 158) and Jeu de Paume (p. 154), are in the Tuileries, and a renovated garden, the **Jardin du Carrousel** (which contains no carousel at all), has opened here next to the Louvre, with lawns adorned with statues by Aristide Maillol. Its flower beds are a treat for the eye, and its comfortable lawn chairs are a welcome place to take a load off.

Taking the air, part three: city parks... Climb to the top of the **Parc de Belleville** (Métro Pyrénées), a hillside park, and you have Paris at your feet. A monumental stairway leads down the hill, passing terraced lawns with fountains, waterfalls, and pools.

Parc de Bercy (Métro Bercy) is a good reason to visit this area on the eastern side of Paris, which the city has been unsuccessfully trying to redevelop for years. Located among abandoned wine warehouses along the Seine, the park has inherited hundreds of old trees and has a "jardin romantique," an aromatic garden, a rose garden, a "philosopher's" garden, a vegetable garden, fruit orchards, a small lake, a labyrinth, and the ruins of a small château.

Parc André Citroën (Métro Balard) in the southwest corner of the city is an urban park par excellence. It doesn't try to pretend it's not part of a city; instead, architectural elements are used to create hidden corners with varying miniature landscapes, ranging from rock gardens to mini-fields of wildflowers. Fountains and waterways, mazelike walkways, and several beautiful, modern greenhouses (one of which holds changing exhibitions) add more variety to this unusual park. In the center is a large stretch of lawn surrounded by a mock moat. In summer, children have a great time playing in the jets of a fountain between the two large greenhouses.

The ubiquitous Baron Haussmann, who in the late 19th century created the grand boulevards that give Paris its present form, also designed the **Parc des Buttes-Chaumont** (Métro Buttes Chaumont or Botzaris), set on a former hilltop quarry in the northeastern part of the city. All the "natural" features you see here—the "mountains" and the lake—are man-made. The temple situated on an outcropping in the lake offers good views of the city, topping off this romantic tableau. The whole scene is straight out of Wordsworth or Keats.

On the run... Don't be surprised if people stare at you when you lace up your Nikes and hit the pavement—jogging is still considered pretty odd here along city streets, although it is gradually becoming more popular among the stubbornly sedentary French. And while running along the **Seine** is a romantic idea, the health benefits are debatable; with three or four lanes of heavy traffic running alongside you, you'll be breathing lungfuls of exhaust fumes. The same goes for the Right Bank's **Canal Saint-Martin.** Happily, the city now closes the quays of the Seine and the streets along the canal to automobile traffic for a good part of the day on Sundays, leaving a clear, pollution-free path for joggers and bikers. The quays are traffic-free from around the Jardin des Tuileries to the Pont Charles de Gaulle in the 12th on the Right Bank, and from the quai Anatole France to quai Branly on the Left Bank.

Much more pleasant for running are the large parks: the **Jardin du Luxembourg,** the **Tuileries,** the **Parc des**

Buttes-Chaumont, the **Parc de Montsouris** (RER Cité-Universitaire), the **Bois de Vincennes,** or the **Bois de Boulogne** (see "Taking the air, part one: city forests" above). It's also possible to run in the pretty **Parc Monceau** (Métro Monceau), in the 8th arrondissement, but you'll have to circle the park many times to work up a good sweat. Jogging is not allowed in the city's other large green spaces, the cemeteries: You might rouse the dead.

Two-wheeling in Paris... Paris is not a city where you long for a bicycle (*vélo*), although it is how many city dwellers choose to get around. It is mostly flat, but there is just too much (terrifying) traffic and pollution to make cycling seem like a good idea. With proper guidance, though, it can be a wonderful experience. Luckily, Michele Nöe, a clever Belgian and owner of a company called **Paris à Vélo, C'est Sympa!** at 20, rue Alphonse Baudin, 11e (Tel 01-48-87-60-01; www.parisvelosympa.com; Métro Richard Lenoir), had the good idea of not only renting bicycles but also conducting 3-hour guided tours of Paris neighborhoods that take riders into little-known corners of the city, showing them delightful places that few residents, let alone visitors, know about. Noë knows the traffic-free streets, the tiny passageways, and the few bicycle paths in the city. He and his assistant provide ongoing commentary (in English, even) on the sights and architecture. He runs night tours of the city, too.

Bicycles can also be rented at stands in the **Bois de Boulogne,** near the Relais du Rois on the route de Suresnes (Métro Pont de Neuilly, bus 144), and in the **Bois de Vincennes,** either at the Lac des Minimes (Métro Porte Dorée) or at the entrance to the Parc Floral (Métro Château de Vincennes). Both parks have bicycle paths (*pistes cyclable*). If you'd rather not tire out your calf muscles, **Scooters** (Tel 01-48-70-13-40) rents motor scooters through some Paris hotels. Call for information, but be warned, no English is spoken. No driver's license is required, and insurance, two anti-theft devices, and the obligatory helmet are provided.

If you'd like to get out of town, **La Bicyclette Verte** (Tel 05-49-69-14-68; www.bicyclette-verte.com) organizes bicycle trips that last from 1 to 10 days and cover various parts of France outside Paris. One such trip goes to Ile de Ré, an island off La Rochelle where you can find white flower-covered houses, salt flats, and great Atlantic beaches. The company arranges for hotels and meals and meets you with ready-to-roll bicycles at the train station of your choice.

Back in the saddle... For a brisk gallop through the woods of the Bois de Boulogne, on the western edge of Paris, try the **Société d'Equitation de Paris,** route de Neuilly à la Muette (Tel 01-45-01-20-06; Métro Pont de Neuilly) or the **Société Equestre de l'Etrier,** route des Lacs à Madrid (Tel 01-45-01-20-02; Métro Porte Maillot, bus 244). The sprawling Bois de Vincennes, just to the east of Paris, also has the **Cercle Hippique du Bois de Vincennes,** 8, rue de Fontenay (Tel 01-48-73-01-28) and the **Centre Equestre de la Cartoucherie** (Tel 01-43-74-61-25; Métro Château de Vincennes).

Get all wet... The **Piscine d'Auteuil,** route des Lacs et Passy, 16e (Tel 01-42-24-07-59; http://piscine.auteuil.free.fr; Métro Ranelagh), an outdoor pool in the Bois de Boulogne, is open Monday from 1 to 4:15pm; Tuesday through Saturday from 7am to 4:15pm; and Sunday from 8am to 5:15pm. It costs 2.60€ ($3.25) per visit, 22€ ($28) for 10 visits. **Aquaboulevard,** 4, rue Louis-Armand, 15e (Tel 01-40-60-10-00; Métro Balard), is a leisure complex on the southwestern edge of the city that has a huge swimming pool (a small part of which extends outdoors) equipped with toboggans, waves, and rapids. There is also an outdoor "beach," a well-equipped gymnasium, a climbing wall, tennis and squash courts, table tennis, billiards, restaurants, snack bars, and shops. It's open daily from 9am to 11pm, and it costs about 18€ ($23) to use the pool.

If you don't feel like trekking all the way out to the 'burbs for your swim, there are some indoor options in town. **Club Med Gym,** the largest chain of gyms in Paris, has pools at three branches: 14, rue Vandrezanne, 13e (Tel 01-45-80-34-16; www.clubmedgym.fr; Métro Place de l'Italie); 10, place de la République, 11e (Tel 01-47-00-69-98; Métro Place de la République); and 8, rue Frémicourt, 15e (Tel 01-45-75-34-00; Métro Émile Zola). All are open daily well into the evenings, though they close at 5pm on Sundays. All charge about 32€ ($40) per day for use of all their facilities.

The Olympic-size **Piscine Roger-le-Gall,** 34, bd. Carnot, 12e (Tel 01-44-73-81-12; Métro Porte de Vincennes), also open daily, has a sliding roof that opens to let in the rays when the weather's good. It goes nudist twice a week, thanks to some dogged demonstrating on the part of a group of naturists (mostly men strip down at these 2-hour swim sessions, though all are welcome; call Tel 01-47-78-18-78 for more info). Another Olympic-size pool is the **Piscine Nouveau Forum des Halles,** 10, place de la Rotonde, 1er (Tel 01-42-36-98-44; Métro Les Halles), in the new part of the underground Forum des Halles shopping mall, right in the heart of the city. The indoor **Piscine de Pontoise,** at 19, rue de Pontoise, 5e (Tel 01-55-42-77-88; www.clubquartierlatin.com; Métro Maubert Mutualité or Jussieu), is the trendy place to take a dip before dancing all night at your favorite disco. It's open daily, and stays open until midnight 4 nights a week. Public pools usually charge 3.70€ ($4.65) for a dip. Swim on weekdays if possible—these pools are extremely crowded on weekends, especially in summer, and French people seem to have a hard time staying in their lanes when they swim (the same problem they have when they drive).

The **Ritz Club,** place Vendôme, 1er (Tel 01-43-16-30-30; www.ritz.com; Métro Concorde) is the Ritz's luxurious spa with a pool and gym. It is sometimes available for day use if the hotel isn't full. Call the day before you want to visit and be prepared to cough up as much as 100€ ($125).

The tennis racket... If you must swing a racket while you're in Paris, the municipal courts at **Tennis Luxembourg** in the Jardin du Luxembourg, boulevard Saint-Michel, 6e (Tel 01-43-25-79-18; RER Luxembourg) are available on a first-come, first-served basis. Go in the morning for the best chance of getting a court. The vast **Aquaboulevard,** 4, rue Louis-Armand, 15e (Tel 01-40-60-10-00; Métro Balard) has courts for both tennis and squash (pronounced "skwatch" by the French). Squash can also be played at the **Club Quartier Latin,** 19, rue de Pontoise, 5e (Tel 01-55-42-77-88; Métro Maubert Mutualité); **Squash Rennes-Raspail,** rue des Rennes, 6e (Tel 01-49-64-70-70; Métro St-Placide or Montparnasse); and **Squash Front de Seine,** 21, rue Gaston-de-Caillavet, 15e (Tel 01-45-75-35-37; Métro Bir-Hakeim). Reserve a court in advance if you can. Most facilities cost between 9€ and 12€ ($11 and $15) per person for a half-hour; prices are somewhat lower on weekday afternoons.

Birds of a feather... Did you bring your binoculars? Got that field notebook handy? Then visit the bird preserve in the Bois de Boulogne, the **Réserve Ornithologique,** Allée de Longchamp (Métro Porte Maillot, bus 244). Guided bird walks take place regularly in the **Bois de Vincennes;** call Christian Galinet (Tel 01-47-70-29-83) for details. The **Ligue pour la Protections des Oiseaux** (Tel 05-46-82-12-34) provides information on birds in the Paris regions and organizes bird-watching walks and trips. Otherwise, a Sunday morning stroll through the bird market at **Métro Cité** is always a good idea.

Best places for pickup... On weekend afternoons, there are usually pickup Frisbee and soccer games at the **Esplanade des Invalides** (Métro Invalides), soccer on the lawns of **Parc de la Villette** (Métro Porte de Pantin or Porte-de-la-Villette), baseball on the **Plaine de Pershing** (RER Joinville-le-Pont), and soccer and Frisbee on the fields near the **Château de Vincennes** (Métro Château de Vincennes) in the Bois de Vincennes. Don't bother going in the morning—the players don't show up until their hangovers have worn off.

Stretching your legs... Get out your backpack, fill it with pâté, cheese, fruit, a baguette, a bottle of water, and a bottle of wine, and hop on a train for a day's hike. The **Forêt de Fontainebleau,** the largest forest near Paris, is a favorite spot for rock climbers because of its marvelous rock formations, some of them 20m (more than 60 ft.) high. Even if you're not interested in hanging like a bat from a rock, you'll appreciate these as scenery—they come in fantastic shapes and all sizes, and some look like enormous Swiss cheese riddled with holes. You'll occasionally come across fountains inscribed with poetry as well. Take a suburban (*banlieue*) train from the Gare de Lyon to Fontainebleau-Avon (the trains leave every hour and a half during the day, and the ride takes 50 min). When you leave the station, turn right, go past the café, and take the stairs up to a busy road. You'll see the forest on the other side, behind the outdoor swimming pool (bring your bathing suit in summer and take a dip after your hike). Paths are clearly marked with colored paint on trees and rocks: A double line along the path means there's a change of direction, a curved line should be followed in the direction to which it points, and an "X" means you've headed in the wrong direction.

Good skates... Indoor ice rinks, open year-round, are the **Patinoire d'Asniéres-sur-Seine,** boulevard Pierre-de-Coubertin, 16e (Tel 01-47-99-96-06; Métro Gabriel Péri), or the **Patinoire de Saint-Ouen,** 4, rue du Docteur-Bauer, 93400 St-Ouen (Tel 01-40-11-43-38; Métro Mairie de Saint-Ouen), just outside Paris. Skate rental is included in the overall fee (8€/$10) at rinks, where packs of speeding kids and teenagers churn up the ice, accompanied in the indoor rinks by the incessant racket of disco music. From mid-December through early March there is a small, free **open-air ice rink** in the square in front of the Hôtel de Ville, Paris's city hall, in the 4th arrondissement (Métro Hôtel de Ville); they rent skates, too, for about 5€ ($6.25) a pair.

Rollerblading has taken Paris by storm, and every Friday night there's a city-run event called Paris Roller, which leaves the place d'Italie at 10pm and covers 30km (19 miles) of city streets with a police escort. This popular event attracts an average of 800 bladers a week, and since most of them are experienced, this is not an occasion to try a new sport. You can rent rollerblades at **Bike 'n Roller,** 38, rue Fabert, 7e (Tel 01-45-50-38-27; http://bikenroller.fr; Métro Invalides) for about 10€ ($13) a half day.

A day at the races... In the Bois de Vincennes, the **Hippodrome de Vincennes,** 2, route de la Ferme (Tel 01-49-77-17-17; RER Joinville-le-Pont), is a trotters' course; it attracts a working-class crowd. For information on horse racing in France, go to www.cheval-francais.com.

A day at the beach... Sponsored by the Mairie de Paris, **Paris Plages** creates a quasi-beach atmosphere on the banks of the Seine from the end of July to mid-August. For 3km (1.86 miles) on the Right Bank—from the Hôtel de Ville to the Pont Marie—there are sand volleyball courts, hammocks, reclining chairs, and umbrellas. Plenty of inexpensive refreshment stands as well, with draft beer that primarily fuels the bocce players.

Par for the course... While the kids are shaking hands with Mickey and Goofy, and spending your life's savings on Disney memorabilia, you can try to relax on the 27-hole course at **Golf Disneyland Paris** (Tel 01-60-45-68-90; RER Métro Marne-la-Vallée-Chessy). Greens fees are 25€ ($31) for nine holes (40€/$50) on weekends). Most other golf courses near Paris are for members only; for information on courses that accept nonmembers, contact the **Fédération Française du Golf,** 69, av. Victor Hugo, 16e (Tel 01-45-02-13-55). The **Golf Club d'Etoile,** 10, av. de la Grande-Armée, 17e (Tel 08-92-70-02-10; Métro Etoile) is a driving range.

Working up a sweat... If you didn't bring your personal trainer with you, **Home Gym** (Tel 01-45-77-60-62) will send one to your hotel (except in Aug) for 60€ ($75) an hour, or 52€ ($65) per hour for a two-session plan. Other services include massages and hair styling and cutting. For a touch of luxury (at a price), the elegant gymnasium at the Ritz, the **Ritz Club,** place Vendôme, 1er (Tel 01-43-16-30-30; Métro Concorde) sometimes accepts visitors who pay by the day (95€/$119 per day). For a single visit, the best bet in town is **Club Quartier Latin,** 19, rue de Pontoise, 5e (Tel 01-55-42-77-88; Métro Maubert Mutualité), where a day pass runs 15€ ($19) and includes access to the Piscine de Pontoise. They offer a complete range of well-maintained machines, plus a full schedule of aerobic, cardio, stretch, and other classes, and this place is frequented by a friendly young crowd. The leisure complex **Aquaboulevard,** 4, rue Louis-Armand, 15e (Tel 01-40-60-10-00; Métro Balard; 25€ ($31) per day for all facilities), has an enormous, well-equipped gym complete with a climbing wall.

SHOP

PING

5

Map 25: Paris Shopping

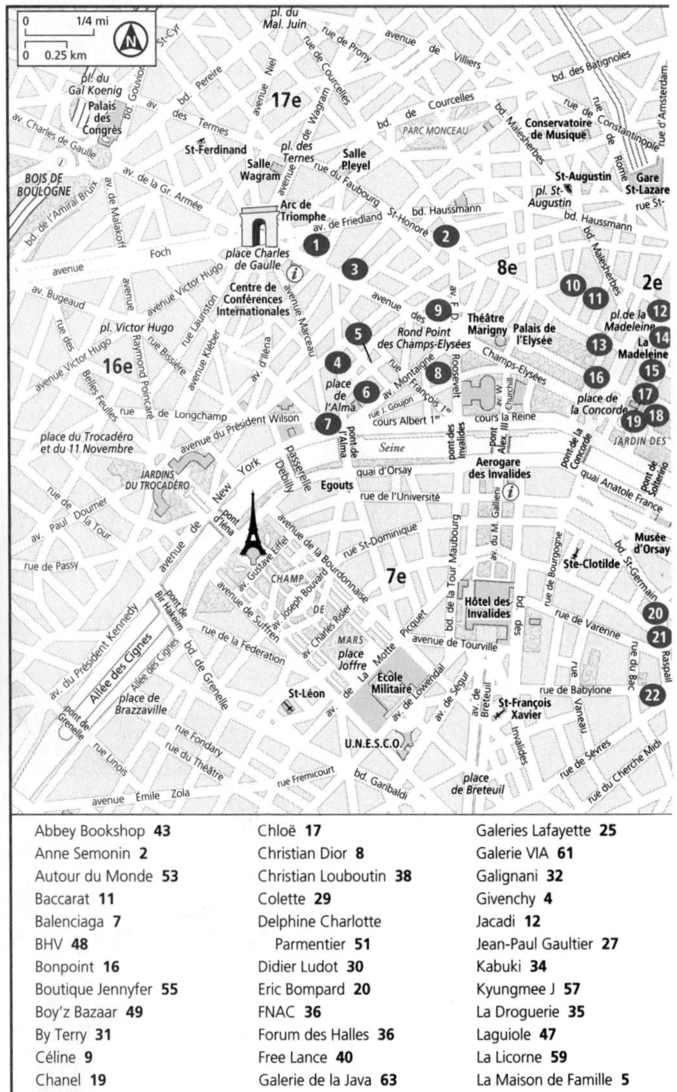

Abbey Bookshop **43**
Anne Semonin **2**
Autour du Monde **53**
Baccarat **11**
Balenciaga **7**
BHV **48**
Bonpoint **16**
Boutique Jennyfer **55**
Boy'z Bazaar **49**
By Terry **31**
Céline **9**
Chanel **19**
Charles Jourdan **3**
Chloë **17**
Christian Dior **8**
Christian Louboutin **38**
Colette **29**
Delphine Charlotte Parmentier **51**
Didier Ludot **30**
Eric Bompard **20**
FNAC **36**
Forum des Halles **36**
Free Lance **40**
Galerie de la Java **63**
Galerie Gaultier **60**
Galeries Lafayette **25**
Galerie VIA **61**
Galignani **32**
Givenchy **4**
Jacadi **12**
Jean-Paul Gaultier **27**
Kabuki **34**
Kyungmee J **57**
La Droguerie **35**
Laguiole **47**
La Licorne **59**
La Maison de Famille **5**

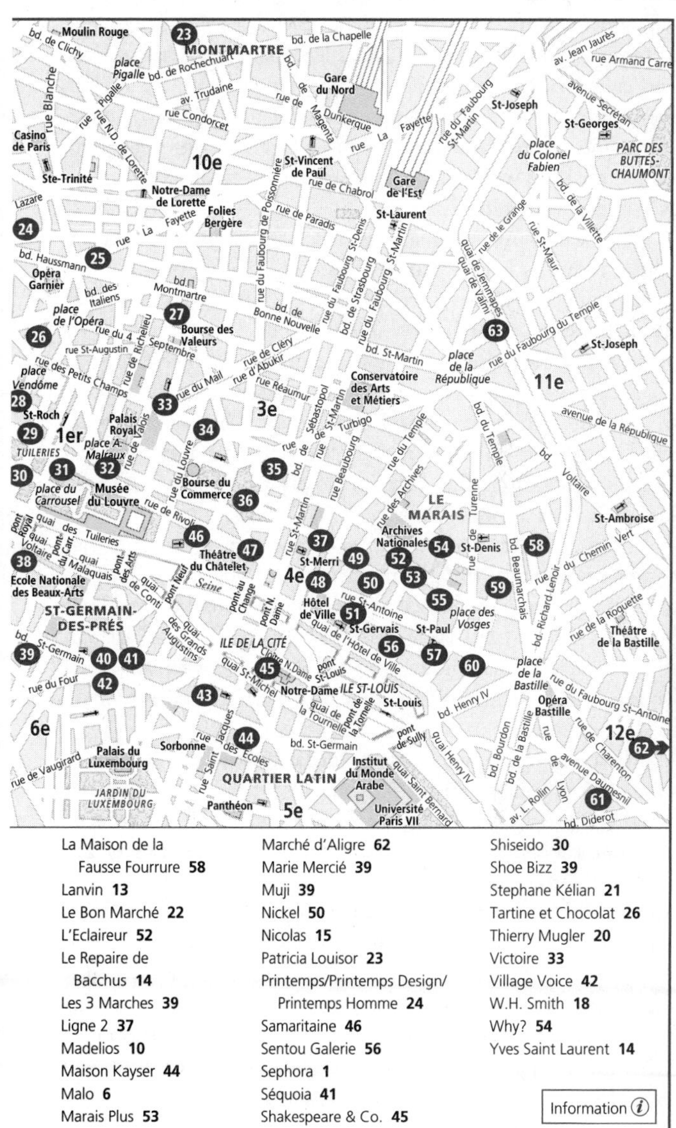

La Maison de la Fausse Fourrure **58**
Lanvin **13**
Le Bon Marché **22**
L'Eclaireur **52**
Le Repaire de Bacchus **14**
Les 3 Marches **39**
Ligne 2 **37**
Madelios **10**
Maison Kayser **44**
Malo **6**
Marais Plus **53**
Marché d'Aligre **62**
Marie Mercié **39**
Muji **39**
Nickel **50**
Nicolas **15**
Patricia Louisor **23**
Printemps/Printemps Design/ Printemps Homme **24**
Samaritaine **46**
Sentou Galerie **56**
Sephora **1**
Séquoia **41**
Shakespeare & Co. **45**
Shiseido **30**
Shoe Bizz **39**
Stephane Kélian **21**
Tartine et Chocolat **26**
Thierry Mugler **20**
Victoire **33**
Village Voice **42**
W.H. Smith **18**
Why? **54**
Yves Saint Laurent **14**

Information (i)

Basic Stuff

"Window-licking" is an *affaire d'intérêt* with Parisians, a matter of money, if not survival. It takes a bulging wallet (and at least one credit card or checkbook—the French write checks for everything) to actually make purchases at the chic department stores and trendy boutiques, so most locals satisfy their consumer fetishism with what Americans more prosaically describe as "window-shopping."

You can, however, get your hands on a designer original that already has been worn in a fashion show, or pick up reasonably priced designer "seconds" and used designer clothing at specialty stores around town (see "Bargain Hunting," below). Hip, young Parisians, like their American counterparts, put together their ultra-stylish anti-fashion statements with items from used-clothing stores and thrift shops. The bonus here is, even if you can do without the retro polyester jogging suits, recent castoffs from chic Parisian closets are often just coming into style back at home.

And of course you want to get some sort of souvenir that comes with a story you can repeat to all of your friends, especially if you found the little treasure after an hour-long trek to a local flea market (see "Watch out for fleas and fleecers," later in this chapter). Who knows, you may end up with an Eiffel Tower enshrined in a plastic altar and decorated with Christmas-tree lights.

If splurging on high-fashion (or tacky souvenirs) isn't your *raison d'être,* you can easily rid yourself of spare cash on other delights for which the French are famous: wine and champagne, gourmet kitchenware, sensuous perfumes, and fine sheets and pillowcases that make you understand a bit more clearly why Marcel Proust spent so much of his life in bed. Not to mention fine pens and desk supplies, terrific underwear, chocolate, and the hippest cheap gift on the globe: mustard. In general, French spending is down, and has been down for some time, so retailers are desperate to get some of your cash. That means clearance racks and flat-out bargaining are common, no matter where you shop. Twice a year look for Paris's famous *soldes,* the markdowns that are regulated by French law.

One final word of warning—watch out for the *vendeuses,* or female shop assistants, who usually come in one of three varieties: frosty, smarmy, or pushy! Many work on commission and will do Oscar-quality performances when it comes to convincing customers they can't live without the latest ludicrously expensive Starck-designed kitchen gadget. They can also be compliment sluts, so if anyone purrs "Madame! That non-dry-cleanable rubberized dress shows off your figure perfectly" leave the store immediately with a curt *"Et ta mère, cherie!"* ("And your mother, too, sweetheart!").

Le Pharmacie

The French are famous hypochondriacs—they just don't feel well if they're not dosing themselves with medications. At school-exam times, pharmacy windows are crammed with mysterious remedies for fatigue intellectuelle. Pharmacies also do a booming business in crèmes d'amincissements, products supposed to slim down thunder thighs and get rid of cellulite. French pharmacies can be pretty damn intimidating, though. All medicinal products are kept behind the counter, where you have to ask a clerk for them—and you may have to describe your symptoms in front of other customers. You could lurk outside until the pharmacy's empty, but someone's sure to walk in just as you reach the most intimate part. Many pharmacists speak at least some English, and they often serve as substitute doctors here, so if you have a minor problem, don't hesitate to ask the pharmacist for a cure. In fact, the French pharmacist plays an active role in the health-care process and is highly trained to provide solutions to many ailments, and can even sort the mushrooms you picked in the woods. Don't be surprised, however, if the druggist tries to sell you seven different creams, soaps, and pills for your acne. Homeopathy is widely accepted here, so don't think the guy's a quack if the ingredients read like a grocery list. The "parapharmacies" have somewhat lower prices.

Target Zones

The buzzword on the Paris shopping scene continues to be diversity, and the city truly does offer something for everyone. Fashion junkies on unlimited budgets should head straight for the **Triangle d'Or.** This classy quartier around rue du Faubourg Saint-Honoré and avenue Montaigne is the Parisian equivalent of Madison Avenue and boasts couture houses and luxury boutiques galore. Diamonds and watches are rich girls' best friends on the **place Vendôme** while **rue Royale** and **Place de la Madeleine** are target zones for crystal, chic tableware, and the ultimate in gourmet food.

Parisian department stores, known locally as *les grands magasins* (the Big Stores), are basically just that: multistory emporiums that are fun but confusing to shop in owing to the ongoing French obsession with procedures (which often has distraught shoppers dashing frantically from cash register to cash register waving multiple slips of paper!). If you prefer more personal, why, God forbid, even *friendly* service, try the new breed of ateliers-boutiques that are springing up all over the city. Shopping in these intimate studio/shops is low-key and relaxing, and you often have the added bonus of meeting the designer behind the clothes. Check out the **Marais,** a lively area crammed full of ateliers-boutiques, Jewish delis, and kitsch design shops. If, on the other hand, clubwear and funky bohemian styles are your thing, spend an afternoon combing the area around trendy **place des Abbesses.**

Once the favored hangout of Parisian intellectuals and black-clad existentialists, **Saint-Germain** is now famous for fashion boutiques. Bypass the ultra-touristy Deux Magots and join the crowd of modern-day de Beauvoirs sipping lattes in Emporio Armani. (Or become truly avant-garde again and return to Deux Magots and snub the Armani gig, which you can find in most high-end districts of major cities.) Comme des Garçons, Yohji Yamamoto, British knitwear master and minimalist Joseph, and cult second-hand store Kiliwatch can all be found on **rue Etienne-Marcel,** the street that leads to mini fashion mecca **Place des Victoires. Rue du Jour** is another fab fashion destination, but underground shopping mall **Forum des Halles** (just down the road) is best avoided, apart from a quick trip to mega-music-book-computer store FNAC. Home to tramps, pickpockets, and drug addicts, the Forum smells of cheap aftershave and urine on a good day (and, no, don't even ask about the bad!). The Nouveau Forum des Halles on the western side of the mall is far more savory and attractive, and, besides offering a wide range of shops, it also houses the huge UGC cinema complex and a very cool Olympic-size pool and a sprawling terrarium of wild vegetation.

For a classier version of the shopping mall, wander through the arcades of **Palais-Royal,** whose gorgeous covered galleries were built by the debt-ridden Duke d'Orléans in the 18th century. Nearby **Galerie Vivienne,** built in 1823, has also been lovingly restored and is now home to such fashion musts as the Gaultier boutique. Alternatively, enjoy the hustle and bustle of the city's vibrant market streets—**rue Montorgeuil** (Métro Sentier or Etienne Marcel) and **rue Mouffetard** (Métro Monge) are two of the most colorful—or pay a visit to the boisterous flea markets (*marchés aux puces*) on the city outskirts.

Bargain Hunting

The best fashion deals in town are found in *dégriffé* or *dépôt-vente* boutiques, which carry designer seconds and other covetable items with the label ripped out. Among those with the best selections are **Alternatives** in the Marais, which carries many outfits made for the fashion shows and never worn again;

Le Mouton à Cinq Pattes stores, where you can paw through a vast selection of men's and women's designer seconds; **Passé Devant** (women's only; new and used) in Montmartre; and **L'Habilleur,** also in the Marais (men's and women's; new only). **La Marelle** in the Galerie Vivienne has used clothing in fine condition, with top-designer labels. End-of-season sales are held in most boutiques and department stores in January and July.

Chain stores such as **Kookaï, Morgan,** and **H&M** (Hennes & Mauritz) are worth checking out for year-round bargains. These shops "translate"—that's fashion speak for *copy*—the latest runway trends and get them out on the rails for about a tenth of designer prices. Okay, so the clothes are often manufactured in crappy fabrics—but who cares when you can pick up a dress for around 35€ ($44) and toss it Kleenex style at the end of the season? The Spanish chain **Zara** and the sale-price annex shop of cult French label **APC** are also firm favorites with the fashion pack.

If you don't mind searching through racks of junky used clothes for that one fabulous find, and you're not allergic to musty polyester jogging suits, head for a **Guerrisold** outlet. Once frequented only by the down-and-out, this chain of used-clothing stores is now a regular haunt of stylish young hipsters and trendy designers looking for inspiration. Already-worn clothes and other secondhand treasures can also be found at Paris's many flea markets on the outskirts of town (see "Watch out for fleas and fleecers," later in this chapter). The **rue de Paradis** (Métro Poissonnière) in the 10th arrondissement is paradise for bargain hunters who want big-name tableware at discount prices. Try **Maison de la Porcelain** for Limoges porcelain or **Lumicristal** for crystal by Baccarat, Daum, and Limoges. **Baccarat** has a shop and museum on the street, but does not offer discounted prices.

Trading with the Natives

Bargaining is common for used goods and antiques, but not for new merchandise. If you're buying a high-priced item, however, don't hesitate to ask for *une petite réduction,* especially in small shops where you may be dealing directly with the owner or manager. You've got nothing to lose. Again, your success rate may have to do with your ability to charm.

Most stores are willing to mail purchases and will hold goods for a limited period of time (usually 24 hrs). Gift-wrapping services are provided almost everywhere; ask for *un paquet cadeau.* ***Remember:*** It's considered rude not to say *"bonjour"* when you enter a shop (*"bonsoir"* if after 6pm) and *"au revoir"* when you leave. Form counts for everything.

Business Hours

Most boutiques open at around 10am and close at 7pm. Smaller shops typically close at lunchtime, usually between 1 and 2:30pm. Major department stores are open from about 9:30am to 7pm, and most stay open until 10pm one night of the week. By law, retail stores, except those that sell food, must close on Sunday; Virgin Megastore on the Champs-Elysées challenged the law a few years back, but hardly started a consumer revolt. However, many boutiques, particularly in the Marais, flout the law and open on Sunday (usually starting at 2pm). Markets are also often open on Sundays. Some boutiques close on Monday mornings. Many shops close during August, some during July.

Sales Tax

France's TVA (*taxe sur le valeur ajouté* or value-added tax) is 19.6%. This astounding rate is actually an improvement; it was 20.6% but President Chirac lowered it to gain public favor. This tax has been factored into posted prices; in other words, sales tax is not added at the point of purchase. If you are visiting for less than 6 months, you can avoid paying this hefty tax on purchases that you take out of the country with you, but the catch is that you have to spend more than 182€ ($228) in one store on the same day to benefit from this law. Remember to have a form filled out at the *détaxe* office in the store of purchase, and present it (with your receipt) to the customs *détaxe* window at the airport when you leave the European Union. (Which means that you can't get a tax refund on your purchases in Paris if you are going to Amsterdam or Madrid before flying back to the U.S. or Canada.) Don't check your bags with your purchases before going to the *détaxe* window—the customs agents usually will want to eyeball whatever you're claiming. The form will be stamped, and then one copy is slid into an addressed envelope, which you need to post from the airport. Cash refunds are sometimes possible, but the easiest way to be refunded is to have the sum credited to your credit card account. There's no refund available for food products, services (such as your hotel stay), tobacco, medicines, firearms, and uncut gems—and you must be at least 15 years old to qualify for the cost break.

The Lowdown

Les grands magasins... Long renowned as a world center for retail therapy, Paris invented the department store in the 19th century. And the good news is that five of the city's original *grands magasins* still exist today. The oldest is **Le Bon Marché,** a temple of Left Bank chic and luxury goods, whose iron structure was designed by Gustave Eiffel. Le Bon Marché boasts a state-of-the-art beauty department offering everything from make-up lessons to aromatherapy. **Printemps** and the **Galeries Lafayette,** meccas of the Right Bank, just around the corner from the Opéra Garnier, have also undergone major facelifts to launch them into the 21st century. Printemps has an excellent men's department (complete with in-house bar designed by Paul Smith) and a divine Young Designer space, while Galeries Lafayette offers an unbeatable selection of perfume, jewelry, and lingerie. Both offer inexpensive and impressive dining rooms for lunching in shopping style.

The **BHV** next to Paris's city hall has traditionally had a dowdier image than its bigger, flashier brothers, but do-it-yourself freaks flock here in droves at the weekend, working themselves into near-religious ecstasy over the nuts and bolts in the hardware basement, by far France's most extensive hardware store. Check out the hidden and super-mignon smoke-free café in the basement called Café Bricolo. **Samaritaine** is worth a visit for its rooftop café and look-out terrace as well as its stylish and romantic 5th-floor restaurant Le Toupary and its gorgeous Art Deco staircase (Shop 2), but the staff are mind-bogglingly rude and overall the place just don't have no class—which may be one reason for checking it out.

Feet first... Paris is absolute heaven for foot fetishists—slip into strappy slingbacks and gravity-defying heels *chez* **Christian Louboutin,** France's answer to Manolo Blahnik, or pay a visit to French shoe guru **Stephane Kélian.** Kélian's famous for doing classics as well as trends, so you'll find everything from hand-woven pumps to kinky over-the-knee boots in his elegant boutiques. **Kabuki**'s a great address for one-stop trend shopping—you'll find the latest shoes from Prada, Miu Miu, and Sergio Rossi downstairs, and cutting-edge men's and women's fashion upstairs. **Charles Jourdan** designs seriously high fashion footwear for men and women while **Free Lance** styles are for wilder party girls who like lots of psychedelic colors and ponyskin. Meanwhile, shoppers with cash-flow problems can find this season's hottest looks with purse-friendly price tags at **Shoe Bizz.** If you're looking for the latest in trendy Pumas or Nikes, stroll down rue Saint Denis in the Les Halles district for discount athletic and shoe stores.

Designer dressing... You have to have serious Attitude to shop on Avenue Montaigne, the land of frosty blonde *vendeuses* who'd sooner impale themselves on a stiletto heel than wish you a nice day. If you're really not up to their withering looks, you can always dawdle outside the boutiques and be a window-licker. Begin with a visit to **Christian Dior**'s sumptuous flagship store, filled with the wildly flamboyant (and wildly expensive) collections dreamt up by in-house eccentric John Galliano. Up the road at **Givenchy,** designer Alexander McQueen—aka the inventor of "butt-crack" trousers—tones his style down for ladies-and-celebrities-who-lunch, while another British fashion talent, Phoebe Philo, tempts modern vamps at **Chloë. Céline**'s windows used to be full of prim little suits for prissy French madames, but New Yorker Michael Kors put the Céline logo back in style with a vengeance. Style slaves should also visit the beautifully revamped **Balenciaga** boutique, where Nicolas Ghesquière pulls the crowds with sexy little black dresses and collections inspired by heroines from *Alien* and *Star Wars.*

Chanel (as in Kaiser Karl reworking the Coco classics), **Jean-Paul Gaultier,** and **Thierry Mugler** (the high priest of hips and bosoms) are still firm French favorites. **Lanvin** is also worth a visit—if only to eat supermodel salads washed down with ludicrously expensive mineral water at Café Bleu—but the one to watch is **Yves Saint Laurent.** Now that Fashion god Tom Ford is no longer in control of the creative reins, it remains to be seen if the YSL logo will continue to be a smokin' property. **Victoire** and **L'Eclaireur** are good multi-label shops. Cashmere fans will think they've died and gone to heaven in **Malo**—that is, until they've seen the price tags. **Eric Bompard** is (slightly) cheaper and stocks an extensive selection for men and women. Don't be put off by the frumpy-looking vitrines! Fashion junkies who really want to splurge should pay a visit to vintage couture king **Didier Ludot.** Secondhand

SHOPPING

Dior and Chanel don't come cheap, but five-figure price tags are only to be expected now that Miuccia Prada's become one of Ludot's best clients. To find the perfect vintage Hermès bag to go with your new (old) Chanel suit, head to **Les 3 Marches.**

Jeunes créateurs... If you're looking for originality, it's better to avoid the Avenue Montaigne sector. Escape logo-land and check out the new wave of ateliers-boutiques, where if you're lucky you'll find the designer beavering away on a sewing machine at the back of the store. In the Marais, **Kyungmee J** puts on an impressive one-woman show in her cute little boutique, acting as designer, saleswoman, model, and cleaning lady. Around the corner, Franco-Japanese duo **Ligne 2** turn out impeccable minimalist fashion with a twist. Montmartre is another hotbed of young design talent. Worth checking out are **Patricia Louisor**—boho chic in a party atmosphere—and Fanche et Flo—a charming duo who go in for colorful, graphic prints on cashmere and blanket fabric.

Mix, match, 'n' accessorize... Oh do get real, Chanel bags and Hermès scarves are not the be-all and end-all when it comes to Paris accessories anymore. Why not be more adventurous and visit **La Licorne,** a quirky old-fashioned boutique full of fabulous costume jewelry from the 1920s to the '60s? **Marie Mercié** makes flamboyant hats for all occasions. Hot young French jewelry designer **Delphine Charlotte Parmentier,** whose elegant creations have sparkled on the couture catwalk for Chanel, Lacroix, and Ungaro, is also a must. Creative types will prefer to mix and match their own beads and baubles at **La Droguerie,** and handbag junkies will get their fill at **Séquoia,** a fabulous minimalist boutique that stocks great-looking but reasonably priced bags in all shapes and sizes. Stop off at **La Maison de la Fausse Fourrure** for fun fake fur bags, hats, and leopard-skin lampshades.

Marvelous markets... The outdoor food markets of Paris are full of wonders for visitors, especially those who like to cook. The **Marché d'Aligre,** an indoor/outdoor food and clothing market near Bastille, is reputed to have the lowest prices in town. On Sunday mornings, it's more like an Arab souk than a French marketplace, with vendors calling out their prices and offering samples of their wares to the crowds, and huge piles of fresh mint and coriander scenting the air. In the covered part of the market, one stand sells Portuguese and Spanish products, including Serrano ham, *vinho verde* (a delicious, light white wine), and excellent Portuguese bread made with cornmeal—great picnic ingredients.

Every morning except Monday, the lower part of rue Mouffetard (Métro Censier Daubenton or Monge), a Latin Quarter street dating to Roman times, becomes a food market. On Sunday mornings, the entire neighborhood turns out to do shopping and have coffee or a glass of wine at one of the little cafés; an accordion player even passes out song sheets so the crowd can join in.

The wine list... The wine-shop chain **Nicolas** has a wonderfully helpful, friendly staff; at the flagship store on the place de la Madeleine, you can buy such rarities as an 1869 Château d'Yquem—that is, if you're willing to pay a literal fortune. The charm of this French institution is that you can also find a great drinkable bordeaux for everyday use. Snobs are unwelcome. **Le Repaire de Bacchus** is another wine chain with excellent selections; the flagship store, in a fancy shopping alley off the rue Royale, has a friendly English manager and a super tasting-room upstairs.

Kid stuff... The French tend to go in for dressing their kids up like Little Lord Fauntleroy, bourgeois tots strutting the streets in togs from **Bonpoint** (luxury kids' clothes at luxury prices), **Jacadi** (cute classics at slightly more affordable prices), and **Tartine et Chocolat** (a fairly chi-chi brand that also does its own line of rather nauseating baby perfume). **Marais Plus** is a great address for wacky knick-knacks and unusual toys and also has a tearoom with fabulous chocolate cake for harassed mothers in need of a quick calorie fix.

Boys to men... Fashionable boys can shop the day away at **Madelios,** Paris's first mega-store for men where they'll find everything from Dior, YSL, and Givenchy to Helmut Lang jeans, not to mention a sleek in-store bar and massage studio (not for that muscle, darling). Needless to say, all the major department stores have followed Madelios's example, completely revamping their men's sections, and **Printemps Homme** is well worth a visit these days.

Wine Tip

If you're tempted to ship wine home, think again. The shipping costs can elevate the overall price above what you'd spend back home. However, when you love a wine that you can't get back home, the temptation is valid. Some travelers pack up to 20 bottles of their favorite burgundy in one of those hard-cased suitcases with strong wheels. The wine travels well, and the customs duty on excess bottles is surprisingly cheap—less than half a dollar per bottle.

Nothing beats **Boy'z Bazaar,** a gay institution in the Marais, for skimpy T-shirts and cute clubby looks.

Preening and pampering... The city's best one-stop shop for perfume has to be **Sephora,** a space-age beauty emporium that boasts wall-to-wall lipsticks, cosmetics, and fragrances arranged in neat alphabetical order. For head-to-toe hedonism you can't beat a trip to **Anne Semonin.** Famous for her revolutionary jetlag cure, France's new beauty guru customizes plant-based products, essential oils, and lashings of seaweed to suit all skin types. If you really want to splash out, pay a visit to **By Terry,** a chic little boutique where Yves Saint Laurent's former make-up artist Terry de Gunzberg will mix up your own unique shade of lipstick. Alternatively, drop in to **Shiseido**'s divine mirrored and mosaic-ed HQ and treat yourself to a bottle of personalized perfume. Well-groomed boys will love **Nickel,** a hip male beauty salon in the Marais offering everything from Shiatsu massage to body waxing.

For serious foodies... At **Maison Kayser,** Chocolatier Jean-Paul Hévin has mastered the fusion of *chocolat* with *fromage.* Sweet luscious chocolates are infused with tart cheese like Camembert and Roquefort to satisfy the chocolate lover's sweet tooth. Savory chocolates are also served without cheese, and the aroma leaves you captivated. Hordes of foodies also line up daily outside Maison Kayser for the best croissants in Paris. And their up-to-date stainless steel ovens produce mouth-watering baguettes and loaves of bread.

Lifestyle, gifts, and design... **Colette,** a hip multi-story boutique showcasing the latest trends in fashion, art, and design, sparked a citywide craze for lifestyle boutiques. Japanese label **Muji** is currently taking Paris by storm: Young hipsters on a budget flock there in droves to snap up ultra-functional kitchenware, furniture, and home accessories plus trendy stationery and clothing. **La Maison de Famille** and **Autour du Monde** are good one-stop shopping stores that carry everything from tasteful tableware to casual men's and women's clothing. **Galerie Gaultier** sells Jean-Paul's quirky furniture line, as well as his younger labels, JPG and Gaultier Maille. Fans of contemporary design can check out the latest in cutting-edge furniture at the **Galerie VIA** or browse through shelves of covetable lamps, vases, and design collectibles at **Sentou Galerie.** If you're more in the market for kitsch, try **Why?,** where you'll find the inflatable furniture and flower-shaped lamps you've been dreaming of. The branches of **Boutique Jennyfer** are fabulous for gift-shopping, offering everything from arty jewelry to reproductions of museum pieces, but the hottest address in Paris for groovy furniture and home furnishings has to be the **Printemps Design** boutique in the Centre Pompidou. If you're looking for classic French design gifts, take home a horn-handled knife from **Laguiole** or a crystal vase from **Baccarat.**

A good book (in English)... Paris has no shortage of English-language bookstores, and most news kiosks sell at least a few papers in English. Near the place de la Concorde, **Galignani** has a peaceful old-world look and a good choice of art and travel books; it holds the distinction of being the first English-language bookshop in Europe. Nearby is the British chain **W.H. Smith** with a large selection of literature and best sellers. But those with serious literary inclinations should head over to Saint-Germain-des-Prés and the **Village Voice,** whose well-read owner Odile Hellier is always happy to steer her customers to a good read. The reading series here is world class. Many visitors head to **Shakespeare & Company,** assuming that it's Sylvia Beach's famous shop of the same name that nurtured the Lost Generation back in the 1920s. Well, that's not exactly the story, although the taste of old-time bohemia is still present; for the real scoop ask young Sylvia Beach Whitman, the

TIP

Look for posters in the street advertising brocantes*—traveling flea markets (selling mostly antiques)—that set up in the streets for a few days at a time.*

owner's daughter and now co-manager. Around the corner you'll find Paris's only Canadian bookshop, the **Abbey,** with tempered bookman Brian Spence at the helm. For massive selections of books—although not all that much in English—head to any branch of the **FNAC** chain.

Watch out for fleas and fleecers... Since the Middle Ages, people in need of quick cash have sold used goods outside the city walls to avoid paying taxes; the three major *marchés aux puces* (flea markets) are still located on the edge of the city. Supposedly the largest flea market in the world, the Puces de Saint-Ouen (Métro Porte de Clignancourt, just follow the crowds), in northern Paris, officially opens at 7:30am, though some fanatics show up at 5am. You'll find old magazines, jewelry, antique furniture, and whatever else sellers have emptied from their closets. Along the avenue Porte de Clignancourt, between the Métro and the market proper, street vendors sell scads of tacky gewgaws, from leather jackets to used telephone cards. The market itself has been organized into sections according to the goods sold: Marché Vernais, period furniture and curios; Marché Biron, antiques; Marché Cambo, furniture and paintings; Marché Serpette, antique and rustic furniture, curios; Marché Paul Bert, secondhand goods and bronze objects; Marché Jules-Vallès, rustic furniture; Marché Malik, secondhand clothes, eyeglasses, records. Marked prices for antiques are generally not any cheaper than in the stores, but you can sometimes bargain for a great deal.

In eastern Paris, serious shoppers arrive at the smaller Puces de Montreuil (Métro Porte de Montreuil) at 6:30am sharp. You can pick up anything from a used car to an accordion as barbers shave customers in the street. It's open Saturday through Monday from 6:30am to 1pm; Monday is the day to go for used clothing. On the southwest edge of the city, the Puces de Vanves (avenues George Lafenstre and Marc-Sangnier, Métro Porte de Vanves) has 140 legitimate vendors selling antiques and secondhand stuff, but some of the best deals are from unlicensed merchants, who have to keep on the move to avoid the frequent police patrols. It's open Saturday and Sunday from dawn to 7pm. A small, manageable, and fun weekend flea market is held once a month in the **Galerie de la Java,** a classified historical monument dating from 1924, up in the 10th arrondissement. There's a café on the top floor where live jazz bands play between 5 and 9pm.

The Index

Paris shops and boutiques usually open at 10 or 10:30am and close at 7 or 7:30pm. Hours that veer from the norm as explained in "Business Hours," earlier in this chapter, are noted below.

For shops with multiple locations, only the first listed branch is mapped.

Abbey Bookshop (p. 191) LATIN QUARTER An English-language bookstore (used and new) with a good literature section and Canadian publications.... *Tel 01-46-33-16-24. 29, rue de la Parcheminerie, 5e. Métro St-Michel.*

See Map 25 on p. 178.

Anne Semonin (p. 189) CHAMPS-ELYSEES Luxury plant-based beauty treatments including the revolutionary "anti-jetlag special".... *Tel 01-42-66-24-22. 108, rue du Faubourg-St-Honoré, 8e. Métro St Philippe-du-Roule.*

See Map 25 on p. 178.

Autour du Monde (p. 190) MARAIS Get a designer lifestyle in this chic French boutique, which stocks everything from candles, clothes, and ceramics to tasteful soft furnishings.... *Tel 01-42-77-06-08. 8, rue des Francs-Bourgeois, 3e. Métro St-Paul.*

See Map 25 on p. 178.

Baccarat (p. 183) CHAMPS-ELYSEES The famous house of crystal.... *Tel 01-42-65-36-26. www.baccarat.fr. 11, place de la Madeleine, 8e. Métro Madeleine.*

See Map 25 on p. 178.

Balenciaga (p. 186) CHAMPS-ELYSEES Cutting-edge style from French wunderkind Nicolas Ghesquière.... *Tel 01-47-20-21-11. 10, av. Georges V, 8e. Métro Alma Marceau.*

See Map 25 on p. 178.

BHV (p. 185) MARAIS Modestly priced department store where you can find anything you could ever need—except shoes. Its famous basement is a paradise for *bricoleurs* (do-it-yourselfers).... *Tel 01-42-74-90-00. www.bhv.com. 52, rue de Rivoli, 4e. Métro Hôtel de Ville. Until 10pm Wed.*

See Map 25 on p. 178.

Bonpoint (p. 188) CHAMPS-ELYSEES Bourgeois kids—from tiny tots to young teens—dress in these well-cut clothes made from luxury fabrics. Luxury prices to match.... *Tel 01-47-42-52-63. www.bonpoint.com. 15, rue Royale, 8e. Métro Concorde.*

See Map 25 on p. 178.

Boutique Jennyfer (p. 190) MARAIS Postcards, books, and reproductions of art objects.... *Rue de Sévigné: Tel 01-42-74-08-00; Musée Carnavalet, 23, rue de Sévigné, 3e; Métro St-Paul; closed Mon. Rue des Francs-Bourgeois: Tel 01-42-71-67-00; 29 bis, rue des Francs-Bourgeois, 4e; Métro St-Paul; closed Mon morning. rue Pierre-Lescot: Tel 01-40-26-01-23; Forum des Halles, 1, rue Pierre-Lescot, 1er; Métro Les Halles; closed Mon morning.*

See Map 25 on p. 178.

Boy'z Bazaar (p. 189) MARAIS A full range of men's clothing for the gay market.... *Rue Sainte-Croix-de-la-Bretonnerie: Tel 01-42-71-67-00; 5, rue Sainte-Croix-de-la-Bretonnerie, 4e; Métro Hôtel de Ville. Tel 01-42-71-80-34; 38, rue Sainte-Croix-de-la-Bretonnerie, 4e; Métro Hôtel de Ville; Mon–Sat noon–midnight, Sun 2–9pm.*

See Map 25 on p. 178.

By Terry (p. 189) LOUVRE/LES HALLES YSL make-up artist Terry de Gunzberg mixes up custom-made cosmetics at her exclusive new boutique.... *Tel 01-44-76-00-76. 36, gal Véro Dodat, 1er. Métro Palais Royal.*

See Map 25 on p. 178.

Céline (p. 186) CHAMPS-ELYSEES So hip it hurts—collections based around masses of cashmere, fur, and minimalist chic.... *Tel 01-49-52-12-01. www.celine.com. 36, av. Montaigne, 8e. Métro Franklin D Roosevelt.*

See Map 25 on p. 178.

Chanel (p. 186) LOUVRE/LES HALLES Boutique where the famous interlocked C's reign.... *Tel 01-42-86-28-00. www.chanel.com. 31, rue Cambon, 1er. Métro Concorde.*

See Map 25 on p. 178.

Charles Jourdan (p. 185) CHAMPS-ELYSEES Sleekly fashionable shoes and capsule collection of ready-to-wear for men and women.... *Tel 01-47-20-81-28. www.charles-jourdan.com. 23, rue Francois, 8e. Métro Georges V.*

See Map 25 on p. 178.

Chloë (p. 186) CHAMPS-ELYSEES Phoebe Philo revived this boring old French fashion house with tarty frocks for modern-day vamps.... *Tel 01-44-94-33-00. www.chloe.com. 54, rue du Faubourg-St-Honore, 8e. Métro Concorde.*

See Map 25 on p. 178.

Christian Dior (p. 186) CHAMPS-ELYSEES The refurbished Dior empire.... *Tel 01-40-73-73-73. www.dior.com. 30, av. Montaigne, 8e. Métro Franklin D Roosevelt.*

See Map 25 on p. 178.

Christian Louboutin (p. 185) EIFFEL TOWER France's answer to Manolo Blahnik, which means super-chic mules and party shoes for clients like Princess Caroline of Monaco and Anna Wintour, editor of *Vogue*.... *Tel 01-42-22-33-07. 38, rue Grenelle, 7e. Métro Palais Royal or Louvre.*

See Map 25 on p. 178.

Colette (p. 189) LOUVRE/LES HALLES Minimalist temple to art, fashion, and design.... *Tel 01-55-35-33-90. 213, rue St-Honoré, 1er. Métro Tuileries.*

See Map 25 on p. 178.

Delphine Charlotte Parmentier (p. 187) MARAIS Arty little boutique where sought-after designer Delphine Charlotte showcases jewelry and accessories alongside handmade ceramics and pretty beaded sandals.... *Tel 01-44-54-51-72. 35, rue du Bourg-Tibourg, 4e. Métro Hôtel de Ville.*

See Map 25 on p. 178.

Didier Ludot (p. 186) LOUVRE/LES HALLES The French king of vintage couture sells everything from secondhand Dior and Balenciaga to snazzy Chanel suits made by Coco herself. There's a new space devoted to the Little Black Dress at 125, Galerie de Valois, 1er (Tel 01-40-15-01-04; Métro Palais-Royal).... *Tel 01-42-96-06-56. www.didierludot.com. 20/24, Galerie Montpensier, 1er. Métro Palais Royal.*

See Map 25 on p. 178.

Eric Bompard (p. 186) EIFFEL TOWER Gorgeous cashmere sweaters and scarves for men and women in every imaginable but unfailingly tasteful color.... *Tel 01-42-84-04-36. 46, rue du Bac, 7e. Métro Rue du Bac.*

See Map 25 on p. 178.

FNAC (p. 191) LOUVRE/LES HALLES A chain of large record and book stores. Service can be surly, but the selection is impressive.... *Rue Pierre-Lescot: Tel 01-40-41-40-00; www.fnac.com; Forum des Halles, 1–7, rue Pierre-Lescot (level 3), 1er; Métro Les Halles. Rue de Rennes: Tel 01-49-54-30-00; 136, rue de Rennes, 6e; Métro St-Placide. Av. des Ternes: Tel 01-44-09-18-00; 26–30, av. des Ternes, 17e; Métro Ternes. Bd. des Italiens: Tel 01-48-01-02-03; 24, bd. des Italiens, 9e; Métro Richelieu Drouot; Daily until midnight. Place de la Bastille: Tel 01-43-42-04-04; 4, place de la Bastille, 12e; Métro Bastille.*

See Map 25 on p. 178.

Free Lance **(p. 186)** ST-GERMAIN-DES-PRES Outrageous heels for party girls who don't like going home alone.... *Tel 01-45-48-14-78. 30, rue du Four, 6e. Métro Mabillon.*

See Map 25 on p. 178.

Galerie de la Java **(p. 191)** GARE DU NORD A flea market on three levels, with live jazz in the evening.... *Tel 01-42-02-20-52. 105, rue du Fauborg-du-Temple, 10e. Métro République. Fri–Sun, first weekend of the month, 10am–10pm. Admission charged.*

See Map 25 on p. 178.

Galerie Gaultier **(p. 190)** BASTILLE Sells the designer's youthful lines JPG and Gaultier Maille (knitwear), as well as his humorous and practical furniture.... *Tel 01-44-68-84-84. www.galeriegaultier.com. 30, rue du Faubourg St-Antoine, 12e. Métro Bastille.*

See Map 25 on p. 178.

Galeries Lafayette **(p. 185)** OPERA GARNIER Famed department store with an astounding variety of merchandise, including the fashions of many big-name designers. A gourmet food shop and several restaurants and snack bars are also under its roof.... *Tel 01-42-82-34-56. www.galerieslafayette.com. 40, bd. Haussmann, 9e. Métro Chaussée d'Antin La Fayette or RER Auber. Thurs until 9pm.*

See Map 25 on p. 178.

Galerie VIA **(p. 190)** GARE DE LYON The place to see the latest in French furniture design.... *Tel 01-46-28-11-11. 29–37, av. Daumesnil, 12e. Métro Gare de Lyon.*

See Map 25 on p. 178.

Galignani **(p. 190)** LOUVRE/LES HALLES English-language bookstore with fine selection of art books. Expect a mark-up over U.S. prices.... *Tel 01-42-60-76-07. 224, rue de Rivoli, 1er. Métro Tuileries.*

See Map 25 on p. 178.

Givenchy **(p. 186)** CHAMPS-ELYSEES Alexander McQueen's wild couture and impeccably tailored *prêt-à-porter* has the fashion pack moaning with pleasure.... *Tel 01-44-31-51-09. www.givenchy.com. 3, av. Georges V, 8e. Métro Alma Marceau.*

See Map 25 on p. 178.

Jacadi **(p. 188)** CHAMPS-ELYSEES A chain of classic children's clothing stores for kids ages zip to 14. Prices aren't outrageous.... *Tel 01-42-65-84-98. www.jacadi.fr. 17, rue Tronchet, 8e. Métro Madeleine.*

See Map 25 on p. 178.

Jean-Paul Gaultier **(p. 186)** LA BOURSE Fashion's favorite iconoclast has a boutique to match his image, with Roman statues as mannequins and mosaic floors inset with TV screens. The clothes are likable (unlike the staff) and wearable.... *Tel 01-42-86-05-05. www.jeanpaul-gaultier.com. 6, rue Vivienne, 2e. Métro Bourse.*

See Map 25 on p. 178.

Kabuki (p. 185) LA BOURSE High-style shoes with very high heels (and prices) by Michel Perry, Prada, Dries Van Noten, Dolce & Gabbana, Dirk Bikkembergs, Vivienne Westwood, and others. A few men's styles of a much more sober nature.... *Tel 01-42-33-55-65. 25, rue Étienne-Marcel, 2e. Métro Etienne Marcel.*

See Map 25 on p. 178.

Kyungmee J (p. 187) MARAIS Hip, young, and reasonably cheap designer looks from rising Korean-American star.... *Tel 01-42-74-33-85. 38, rue du Roi-du-Sicile, 4e. Métro St-Paul.*

See Map 25 on p. 178.

La Droguerie (p. 187) LOUVRE/LES HALLES Fine wool yarns, wonderful buttons, and all the beads and baubles needed to make your own jewelry.... *Tel 01-45-08-93-27. www.ladroguerie.com. 9–11, rue du Jour, 1er. Métro Les Halles. Closed Mon morning.*

See Map 25 on p. 178.

Laguiole (p. 190) LOUVRE/LES HALLES World-famous knives showcased in a cutting-edge boutique designed by Philippe Starck.... *Tel 01-40-28-09-42. 1, place Sainte-Opportune, 1er. Métro Châtelet.*

See Map 25 on p. 178.

La Licorne (p. 187) MARAIS Secret treasure trove of costume jewelry in the heart of the Marais.... *Tel 01-48-87-84-43. 38, rue de Sévigné, 3e. Métro St-Paul.*

See Map 25 on p. 178.

La Maison de Famille (p. 190) CHAMPS-ELYSEES Great gifts galore: kitchen stuff, housewares, clothing, accessories, and so on.... *Tel 01-56-52-00-40. 30, av. George V, 8e. Métro George V.*

See Map 25 on p. 178.

La Maison de la Fausse Fourrure (p. 187) BASTILLE Everything from fun fake-fur handbags to leopard-skin lampshades and dalmatian-spotted furniture.... *Tel 01-43-55-24-21. 34, bd. Beaumarchais, 11e. Métro Chemin Vert.*

See Map 25 on p. 178.

Lanvin (p. 186) CHAMPS-ELYSEES Boutique of the dated Lanvin fashion house with a fashion café in the basement.... *Tel 01-44-71-33-33. www.lanvin.fr. 15, rue du Faubourg-St-Honoré, 8e. Métro Concorde.*

See Map 25 on p. 178.

Le Bon Marché (p. 185) EIFFEL TOWER The oldest department store in Paris, the only one on the Left Bank. Upmarket product lines.... *Tel 01-44-39-80-00. www.lebonmarche.fr. 24, rue de Sèvres, 7e. Métro Sèvres Babylone.*

See Map 25 on p. 178.

L'Eclaireur (p. 186) MARAIS Trendy retailer carrying hip, young fashion designers ranging from Martin Margiela to Hervé Leger and Helmut Lang.... *Tel 01-48-87-10-22. 3 ter, rue de Rosiers, 4e. Métro St-Paul.*

See Map 25 on p. 178.

Le Repaire de Bacchus (p. 188) CHAMPS-ELYSEES The flagship store of a small French-owned chain of wine shops with several branches in Paris.... *Tel 01-42-66-34-12. Le Village Royale, 12 cité Berryer, 25, rue Royale, 8e. Métro Madeleine. Closed Mon.*

See Map 25 on p. 178.

Les 3 Marches (p. 187) ST-GERMAIN-DES-PRES Catherine B, the Sherlock Holmes of the fashion world, tracks down secondhand Chanel and Hermès accessories with an unerring eye.... *Tel 01-43-54-74-18. 1, rue Guisarde, 6e. Métro St-Sulpice.*

See Map 25 on p. 178.

Ligne 2 (p. 187) MARAIS Meet the men behind the clothes. This charming Franco-Japanese duo work under their shop in a basement studio and nip upstairs for coffee and a chat every now and then.... *Tel 01-42-71-70-00. 42, rue des Blancs-Manteaux, 4e. Métro Hôtel de Ville.*

See Map 25 on p. 178.

Madelios (p. 188) LOUVRE/LES HALLES Paris's first megastore for men—shop for YSL and Helmut Lang jeans, or enjoy a fabulous in-store massage.... *Tel 01-53-45-00-00. www.madelios.fr. 23, bd. de la Madeleine, 1er. Métro Madeleine.*

See Map 25 on p. 178.

Maison Kayser (p. 189) LATIN QUARTER Parisian chefs are celebrated for their baked goodies, and locals are the most demanding in the world about their fresh croissants in the morning. This boulangerie makes the best.... *Tel 01-44-07-01-42. 5, rue Basse de Carmes, 5e. Métro Maubert.*

See Map 25 on p. 178.

Malo (p. 186) CHAMPS-ELYSEES His 'n' her cashmere sweaters at film-star prices.... *Tel 01-47-20-26-08. 12, av. Montaigne, 8e. Métro Alma Marceau.*

See Map 25 on p. 178.

Marais Plus (p. 188) MARAIS A treasure trove of reasonably priced unusual gifts, toys, T-shirts, posters, and greeting cards. Also has a tea salon with scrumptious desserts.... *Tel 01-48-87-01-40. 20, rue des Francs-Bourgeois, 3e. Métro St-Paul.*

See Map 25 on p. 178.

Marché d'Aligre (p. 187) BASTILLE Pick up perfect picnic fare at this vibrant, low-priced market near Bastille.... *No phone. Place d'Aligre, 12e. Métro Ledru-Rollin.*

See Map 25 on p. 178.

Marie Mercié (p. 187) ST-GERMAIN-DES-PRES Flamboyant hats from the famous French hat queen.... *Tel 01-43-26-45-83. 23, rue St-Sulpice, 6e. Métro St-Sulpice.*

See Map 25 on p. 178.

Muji (p. 189) LOUVRE/LES HALLES The Japanese "brand with no name" that's taken Paris by storm. Shop here for kitchenware, furniture, home accessories, trendy stationery, and ultra-functional clothing.... *Tel 01-44-07-37-30. www.muji.fr. 30, rue St Sulpice, 1er. Métro St-Sulpice.*

See Map 25 on p. 178.

Nickel (p. 189) MARAIS Hot beauty salon for men that offers everything from Shiatsu massage to body waxing.... *Tel 01-42-77-41-10. 48, rue des Francs-Bourgeois, 3e. Métro St-Paul.*

See Map 25 on p. 178.

Nicolas (p. 188) CHAMPS-ELYSEES Flagship store of a chain of more than 280 wine boutiques, with bottles at all prices.... *Tel 01-42-68-00-16. 31, place de la Madeleine, 8e. www.nicolas-wines.com. Métro Madeleine.*

See Map 25 on p. 178.

Patricia Louisor (p. 187) MONTMARTRE Bohemian chic in a party atmosphere.... *Tel 01-42-62-10-42. www.patricialouisor.com. 16, rue Houdon, 18e. Métro Abbesses.*

See Map 25 on p. 178.

Printemps/Printemps Design/Printemps Homme (p. 185) OPERA GARNIER An enormous 19th-century department store in three buildings. Check out the fantastic stained-glass dome in the Café Flo.... *Tel 01-42-82-50-00. www.printemps.com. 64, bd. Haussmann, 9e. Métro Havre Caumartin. Thurs until 10pm.*

See Map 25 on p. 178.

Samaritaine (p. 185) LOUVRE/LES HALLES A classic French department store that's trying to enter the modern world.... *Tel 01-40-41-20-20. www.lasamaritaine.com. 19, rue de la Monnaie, 1er. Métro Châtelet, Pont Neuf, or Louvre Rivoli. Thurs until 10pm.*

See Map 25 on p. 178.

Sentou Galerie (p. 190) MARAIS Spot-on selection of contemporary design—everything from minimalist Japanese lamps to tableware by hip French design duo Tsé Tsé.... *Tel 01-42-77-44-79 and 01-42-71-00-01. 18 and 24, rue du Pont Louis-Philippe, 4e. Métro Pont Marie.*

See Map 25 on p. 178.

Sephora (p. 189) CHAMPS-ELYSEES A cosmetics chain that stocks more than 10,000 brands. A must for fragrance and foundation freaks.... *Tel 01-53-93-22-50. www.sephora.com. 70, av. des Champs-Elysées, 8e. Métro Franklin D Roosevelt.*

See Map 25 on p. 178.

Séquoia (p. 187) ST-GERMAIN-DES-PRES Fashionable but functional bags at surprisingly purse-friendly prices.... *Tel 01-44-07-27-94. 72 bis, rue Bonaparte, 6e. Métro Saint-Germain-des-Prés.*

See Map 25 on p. 178.

Shakespeare & Co. (p. 190) LATIN QUARTER Funky shop for used books, frequented by recently arrived American expatriates.... *Tel 01-43-25-40-93. 37, rue de la Bûcherie, 5e. Métro St-Michel. Noon–midnight.*

See Map 25 on p. 178.

Shiseido (p. 189) LOUVRE/LES HALLES Perfumes custom designed in this beautiful boutique.... *Tel 01-49-27-09-09. www.shiseido.com. 25 rue Valois, galerie de Valois, Palais-Royal, 1er. Métro Palais Royal.*

See Map 25 on p. 178.

Shoe Bizz (p. 186) ST-GERMAIN-DES-PRES The bizz here is this season's footwear trends at unbeatable prices.... *Tel 01-45-44-91-70. 42, rue du Dragon, 6e. Métro St-Sulpice.*

See Map 25 on p. 178.

Stephane Kélian (p. 185) EIFFEL TOWER Men's and women's footwear that is hip, urban, and très Parisian.... *Tel 01-45-44-02-68. 13 bis, rue de Grenelle, 7e. Métro Sevres Babylone.*

See Map 25 on p. 178.

Tartine et Chocolat (p. 188) OPERA GARNIER Contemporary French baby and children's wear light on the fuss and frills.... *Tel 01-47-42-10-68. 24, rue de la Paix, 2e. Métro Opéra.*

See Map 25 on p. 178.

Thierry Mugler (p. 186) EIFFEL TOWER The high priest of hips and bosoms is back in style with a vengeance.... *Tel 01-45-44-44-44. www.thierrymugler.com. 45, rue du Bac, 7e. Métro Rue du Bac.*

See Map 25 on p. 178.

Victoire (p. 186) OPERA GARNIER Hip designers, from Romeo Gigli to Jin Téok, in this boutique.... *Tel 01-42-60-96-21. 10, place des Victoires, 2e. Métro Pyramides.*

See Map 25 on p. 178.

Village Voice (p. 190) ST-GERMAIN-DES-PRES The best store in Paris for English-language books, with an especially good literature section.... *Tel 01-46-33-36-47. www.villagevoicebookshop com. 6, rue Princesse, 6e. Métro St-Germain-des Prés. Closed Mon morning.*

See Map 25 on p. 178.

W.H. Smith (p. 190) The most popular English-language bookstore in France, with 52 sections of literature.... *Tel 01-44-77-88-99. 248, rue de Rivoli, 1e. Métro Concord.*

See Map 25 on p. 178.

Why? (p. 190) MARAIS The kingdom of kitsch—if you like inflatable plastic furniture and glow-in-the-dark tulips, this is the store for you. There are five locations around town.... *Tel 01-44-61-72-75. 41, rue des Francs-Bourgeois, 4e. Métro St-Paul.*

See Map 25 on p. 178.

Yves Saint Laurent (p. 186) CHAMPS-ELYSEES The boutique for ready-to-wear couture.... *Tel 01-42-65-74-59. www.ysl.com. 38, rue du Faubourg-St-Honoré, 8e. Métro Madeleine.*

See Map 25 on p. 178.

NIGH

TLIFE

Map 26: Paris Nightlife

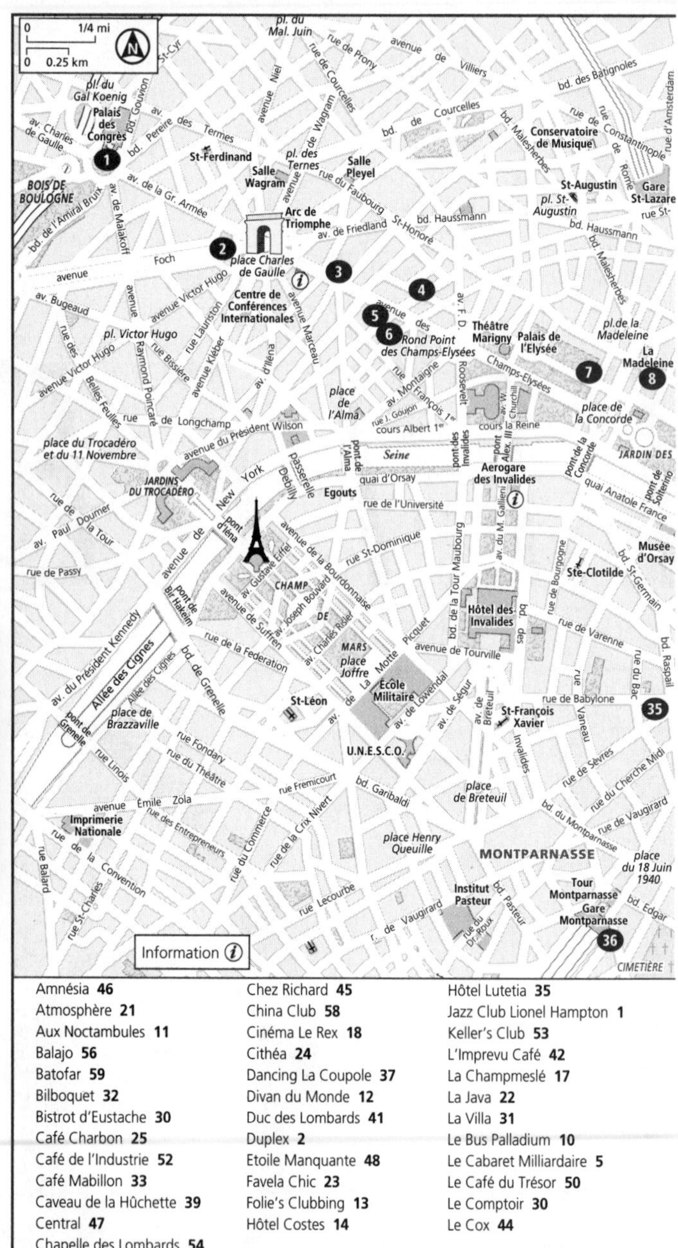

Amnésia **46**
Atmosphère **21**
Aux Noctambules **11**
Balajo **56**
Batofar **59**
Bilboquet **32**
Bistrot d'Eustache **30**
Café Charbon **25**
Café de l'Industrie **52**
Café Mabillon **33**
Caveau de la Hûchette **39**
Central **47**
Chapelle des Lombards **54**
Chez Richard **45**
China Club **58**
Cinéma Le Rex **18**
Cithéa **24**
Dancing La Coupole **37**
Divan du Monde **12**
Duc des Lombards **41**
Duplex **2**
Etoile Manquante **48**
Favela Chic **23**
Folie's Clubbing **13**
Hôtel Costes **14**
Hôtel Lutetia **35**
Jazz Club Lionel Hampton **1**
Keller's Club **53**
L'Imprevu Café **42**
La Champmeslé **17**
La Java **22**
La Villa **31**
Le Bus Palladium **10**
Le Cabaret Milliardaire **5**
Le Café du Trésor **50**
Le Comptoir **30**
Le Cox **44**

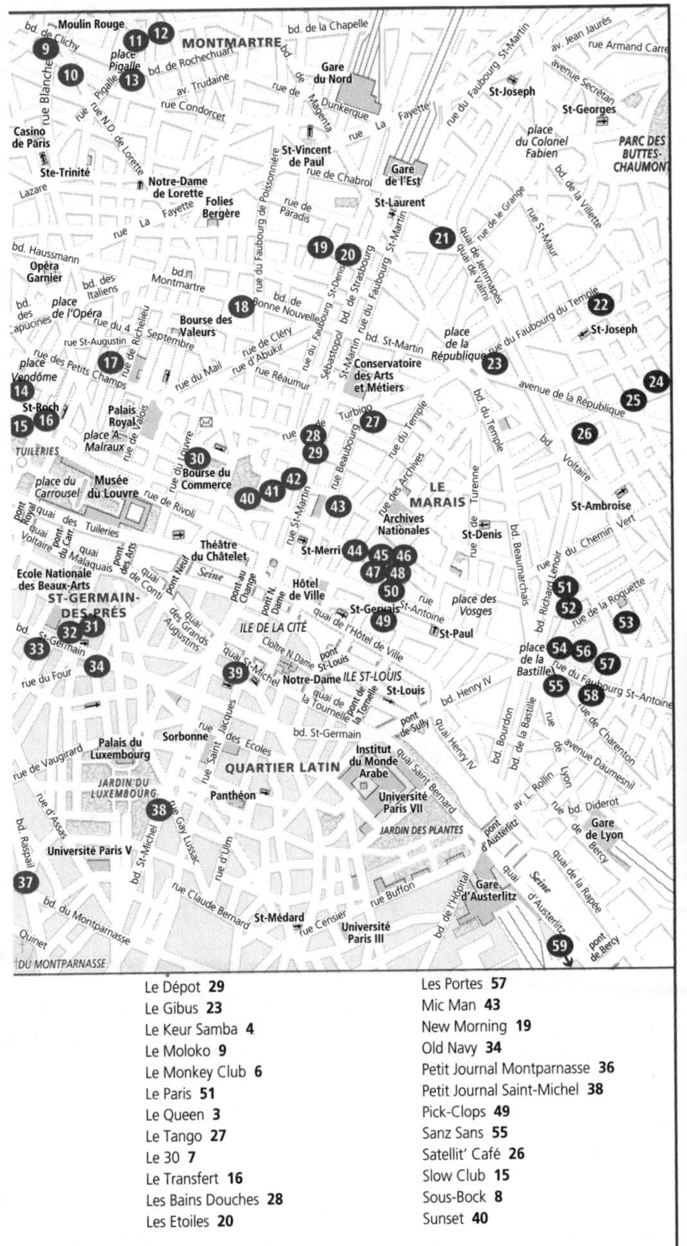

Le Dépot **29**
Le Gibus **23**
Le Keur Samba **4**
Le Moloko **9**
Le Monkey Club **6**
Le Paris **51**
Le Queen **3**
Le Tango **27**
Le 30 **7**
Le Transfert **16**
Les Bains Douches **28**
Les Etoiles **20**
Les Portes **57**
Mic Man **43**
New Morning **19**
Old Navy **34**
Petit Journal Montparnasse **36**
Petit Journal Saint-Michel **38**
Pick-Clops **49**
Sanz Sans **55**
Satellit' Café **26**
Slow Club **15**
Sous-Bock **8**
Sunset **40**

Basic Stuff

In spite of its reputation for being frisky after dark, Paris is not as naughty as one might think, and when it comes to *le dernier cri,* the nightlife scene definitely plays follow-the-leader. There hasn't been a major new nightlife trend here since World War II, and during the past couple of decades, the city's club scene, to be unfairly cruel, was barely worthy of Skokie or Saskatoon. Now, however, it does seem that most Parisians are finally starting to get over the Village People, and the music-masters of the night are taking their house and garage inspiration from London and New York, while local hip-hop, French rap, Algerian Rai, and Latin music also enjoy mounting popularity.

There are few sights more ludicrously funny than a bunch of French people at a rave—their spastic moves barely work when they're dancing to Joe Cocker (which they still do)—but house and funk music are extremely popular with 20- and 30-somethings, and many clubs regularly import British and American DJs. More decorous BCBGs (yuppies with aristocratic pretensions) continue to worship at the *Saturday Night Fever* altar in expensive 8th- and 16th-arrondissement clubs where they dance with a necktie on, but even they are getting caught up in Paris's raging love affair with Latin music, from the passionate precision of the tango to samba lines and salsa. Latin nights are immensely popular at clubs like **Les Etoiles** and **La Java.**

The Latin craze continues to entice Parisians back to the nightlife in huge numbers, and the bar scene is thriving, as exemplified by bar-restaurants like **Barrio Latino** near the Bastille. All the hot spots, like **Café Charbon** in super trendy Ménilmontant, a neighborhood that spans the border between the 11th and 20th arrondissements, have DJs spinning their vinyl.

When the lights of the Eiffel Tower, looming over Paris in the night, are unplugged—at midnight in winter, 1am in summer—it's the signal to Paris clubgoers that it's party time. In a city that is almost fetishistically concerned with appearances, it would not do to brave the velvet ropes before 1am; 1:20am is the calibratedly cool hour to first show face. Plan to stay out until dawn or until the first Métro starts in the wee hours of the morning.

Just getting your timing right is only step one, though, if you seriously want to sample some of the French capital's clubs. For starters, you're going to need a lot of money. Cover charges are stiff, averaging 18€ to 22€ ($23–$28), and drinks tend to be very pricey—a beer will set you back 16€ ($20) at the wildly popular gay club **Le Queen** on the Champs-Elysées, for example. Then, most crucially, there's the matter of how you look. Paris nightlife is very tribal, and your sartorial gaffes will be forgiven only if you're a stark raving beauty or show up on the arm of someone like Orlando Bloom or Nicole Kidman. As a general rule, black is the color of choice, but no color will save you if you make the deadly fashion mistake of showing up in sweatshirts, stonewashed jeans, or any kind of athletic footwear.

Even if you don't do clubs, Paris still offers a huge menu of after-dark activities, ranging from pool halls to jazz bars. **Georges** (p. 91 in the Dining chapter), the top-floor restaurant of the Centre Pompidou, and the latest offering from trendmasters the Costes Brothers, is one of the hippest places to be seen, even though it has no bar or dance floor. Instead, wouldn't-you-just-love-to-touch-me waiters and waitresses flounce in and out of three huge brushed-aluminum pods that hide the kitchen, toting their trays to a soundtrack of house and garage. **Le Monkey Club** is a combo bar-disco-restaurant; this place is pulling in a mix of young hipsters, fashion people, BCBGs from the rich western suburbs, foreigners, and media execs who work in the nabe. What everyone seems to like is the California-Bauhaus decor and the idea of a one-stop night out. *Cafés-concerts* are sort of an easygoing update on the cabarets for which the city was once renowned, with patrons sitting at tables where they can drink and sometimes eat while listening to live music and, depending on the venue, dance. Certain traditional cafés are also well frequented at night, including the **Select** in Montparnasse, **Café Beaubourg** next to the Centre Pompidou (see p. 88 in the Dining chapter), **Café Marly** at the Louvre, and **Café de l'Industrie** near the Bastille (see below, "Bar-hopping in and around the Bastille").

Most straight Parisians seem to marry young and stop going out regularly after they do, so nightlife is pretty much an under-30 scene. But don't worry, no one will give you a hard time if you're a frisky 40-year-old yearning for a bit of disco inferno. Gay clubs are age-mixed, as are almost all bars.

Sources

Those who understand French and want up-to-the-minute information on raves and one-night-only parties can listen at 7:45pm every Friday to the 15-minute program **"Bon Plans"** on Radio Nova (101.5 FM), the hippest radio station in town. Radio Nova also publishes a monthly magazine called ***Nova,*** available at newsstands, which has the latest word on Paris nightlife. A handy little magazine called ***Lylo,*** distributed free in many clubs, has a nightlife calendar and a list of addresses. Travelers familiar with **Minitel,** the national computer service, can find techno and rave listings at 36 15 CODA, 36 15 FG, or 36 15 RAVE (Minitel terminals can be used for free at post offices). Useful alternative magazines (*Out Soon, Liquid Leva, TNT,* and *Coda*) and fliers for raves can also be found at the following "techno" record shops: **BPM, KGB, Rough Trade,** and **Techno Import.**

On Mondays, the daily newspaper *Libération* publishes a hip, gay-oriented nightlife column called **"Nuits Blanches"** that alerts readers to weekly raves. Another good source is the **"Nocturne"** column by Sophie de Santis in the "Figaroscope," a weekly Paris entertainment insert to the Wednesday edition of *Le Figaro,* the largest French daily. De Santis covers the minutiae of the club scene, and her column is a good source of news on weekly events, raves, concerts, and club openings and closings. For English-only sources, you can consult the community monthly called the ***Paris Voice*** or ***Irish Eyes.*** *Time Out* prints a few pages in English every week in the entertainment guide **Pariscope,** which is published every Wednesday.

Liquor Laws & Drinking Hours

The French have one of the highest per capita rates of alcohol consumption in the world, in part because the official drinking age of 18 is very rarely enforced. Drinking is built into daily life—especially as an apéritif before, wine with, and a digestif after dinner. Don't drive if you've had a few, though: The French are tough on drunk drivers—more than two drinks and you're likely over the limit. Drinking hours are established by the license of each establishment; some have to close at 2am, while others can remain open all night. One way or another, there's no time of the day or night when you can't find a drink somewhere in Paris.

The Lowdown

Dance fever... **Les Bains Douches** is the best-known straight disco in town. Models and fashion folk frequent the former bathhouse not far from the Centre Pompidou. Despite a famously bitchy door policy, this place has managed, perhaps *faut de mieux,* to maintain its popularity for an amazingly long time. But you might be disappointed—where the hell's Kate Moss and did the bartender forget about the vodka in *mon cocktail?*

It's your call, but depending on your style, you're probably better off in one of the yuppie party holes in the 8th arrondissement like **Le Monkey Club, Le Cabaret Milliardaire,** and **Duplex.** Le Monkey Bar, which replaced the very popular Bash, caters to a crowd that's more likely to go on safari than to Ibiza or Aya-Napa in Cyprus, but that likes to party in spite of its good jobs and manners. Come here to play with *la jeunesse dorée* (the gilded youth) of Paris; it's actually a lot of fun and a good place to observe the phenomenon of decreasing dance ability with rising socioeconomic scale. Le Cabaret Milliardaire is another wear-a-suit-and-boogie spot, brimming with bankers, press attachés, counts and countesses, a smattering of models, and others who've mastered the art of perspiration-free dancing, while Duplex is more likely to attract the children of those who go to Le Cabaret. On any given night, Duplex is a sea of pouting Gucci-clad *Vanity Fair* wannabes and is such an absurd place that it's actually kind of fun. You might even strike up a conversation with the odd Dutch au pair girl or a Lebanese banker trainee who studied in the U.S.

If the bourgeoisie has never been your secret fascination and you want to boogie with a way-cool crowd, skip the fuss and head for **Batofar,** a club on a former lighthouse barge that's moored in the Seine. This is the most intriguing club in Paris right now, with an original mix of music that comes from a regularly changing cast of visiting DJs, including many passing through from other European cities. **Le Queen,** where the boy-girl ratio is about three to one—and most of the carefully coifed suburban pups here are sniffing after each other—still reigns as the disco supreme. And even though it's a gay club, it has become the cool night out for Xavier and Marie-Odile types from Saint-Cloud (the Gallic version of Teddy and Amanda types from Old Greenwich). For the very trendy and the very young, the places to go are the **Cinéma Le Rex** and **Le Gibus.** Cinéma Le Rex is a feisty spot with a feisty crowd of serious club-goers who love its hard-core electronic dance music, while Le Gibus, once a famous rock venue, is now a popular and very sexy mostly gay dance club specializing in house and garage.

Concert cafés... The American-style bars (actually modern versions of the French wartime cabarets), known as *cafés-concerts,* have introduced two radically new concepts to Parisian club life: live music and reasonable prices for drinks (about 6€–10€/$7.50–$13) for mixed drinks, cheaper for wine or beer). **Cithéa,** near place de la République, hosts live bands Thursdays through Saturdays, with music ranging from salsa to funk and acid jazz. **Le Paris,** a Bastille-area café, stages rock and pop concerts on Saturday nights. The Pigalle nightclub **Divan du Monde** stages shows ranging from French pop to African and Caribbean music, and the cozy little **Blue Note,** near the rue Mouffetard market, mixes Brazilian, jazz, and blues into its nightly musical calendar.

Two to tango... *Bal-musettes* live on in Paris and have come back into vogue. These dances—where old fogies have been doing the foxtrot, polka, and tango to the strains of accordions since the 1930s—are now frequented by young people. **Le Tango,** an African disco located between the Centre Pompidou and the place de la République, becomes a *musette* on Friday and Saturday afternoons. In the Bastille area, **Balajo** does the *bal-musette* thing on weekend afternoons. **La Java,** a former Belleville haunt of Edith Piaf, becomes a "dancing," as the French call it, on Friday and Saturday nights and Sunday afternoons.

All that jazz... Scores of American jazz performers have left their homeland in search of a living wage in the Old World. At Paris clubs, you pay for your jazz either with a cover charge (which usually includes a complimentary first drink) or with inflated drink prices. Many cash-poor jazz fans simply nurse a single drink throughout an entire performance.

The 10th arrondissement's **New Morning,** named for a Bob Dylan album, hosts top international jazz and blues performers. The setting—smoky and crowded—is perfect for that neo–Greenwich Village jazz club atmosphere, but it can choke you a bit, and the sightlines are less than ideal. David Bowie and Liza Minnelli have been known to pop in at **Bilboquet,** a Saint-Germain-des-Prés club with a penchant for New Orleans–style jazz. The tiny, crowded, and friendly **Bistrot d'Eustache,** near the Forum des

Halles, brings in more modern sounds on Thursday, Friday, and Saturday nights. Jazz shares the calendar with blues and Brazilian music at the **Blue Note,** a small *café-concert* near the rue Mouffetard market.

The **Petit Journal Saint-Michel** and the **Petit Journal Montparnasse** are two of the most popular clubs in the city. The first has an old-fashioned character and specializes in New Orleans jazz, and the latter, which has a bit of everything, scores higher in terms of stage visibility and acoustics. **Caveau de la Hûchette,** near Saint-Michel, swings with big-band music, and **Sunset,** a restaurant/club in the center of town near Châtelet, hosts traditional jazz groups in its basement. The nearby **Duc des Lombards** attracts many visitors with its corner location and varied cocktail-hour concerts. **La Villa,** a basement club in a chic, modern Left Bank hotel, sometimes features top American performers. The **Jazz Club Lionel Hampton,** which 6 nights a week takes over the lobby of the unappealingly modern Méridien hotel, near the Arc de Triomphe, brings in an array of well-known artists. With its medieval ceiling vaults, **Slow Club** is one of the most famous jazz cellars in Europe. The venue hosts a revolving set of artists who focus on New Orleans–style jazz. The hip folks who flock here enjoy live music Thursday to Saturday. It's recorded rock and roll on Wednesday.

From strip to hip... The Pigalle area still has its strip joints, sex shops, transsexual prostitutes, and tourist buses, but little by little it's being gentrified and hipped-up. **Folie's Clubbing,** in a former strip joint, is a disco specializing in house and garage music that attracts a mostly gay crowd. **Le Moloko** is a large, ultratrendy bar with red walls, papier-mâché devils, and a funky, free jukebox. **Aux Noctambules** has always been what it is now—a rather sleazy Pigalle café with a corny three-piece orchestra—but now its high-camp appeal is a magnet for the trendy black-leather-jacket crowd. (In the staid, bourgeois world of Paris fashion, black leather jackets are *still* a rebellious fashion statement.) Occasionally, the club's mean-looking, muscle-bound bouncer takes the mike and gets all mushy while crooning his off-key version of "My Way." **Le Bus Palladium** has become freshly popular as a funky night out for French preppies, who just love Motown, and it's actually sort of fun.

Bar-hopping in the Marais... The Marais has become the center of the gay community in Paris (see "Where the boys are," below, for Marais gay bars), but there are also many straight or mixed nightspots in the area around the rue Vieille-du-Temple. **Etoiles Manquante** is a tiny but enormously popular bar and restaurant with a zinc bar, great recorded jazz, and a mixed crowd. **L'Imprevu Café** is a pleasant, laid-back little spot with red-velvet movie-theater seats and a sort of Aladdin's cave nook that pulls an amiable crowd of students and arty types and is less aggressively looking-for-love than some of the other local watering holes. **Chez Richard** is more successfully hip and has a friendlier ambience. The young, pseudo-tough, Perfecto crowd lights up at **Pick-Clops,** a café/bar named for the sort of ne'er-do-wells who bum cigarettes (*clops*). The last word in hip in the area, though, is **Le Café du Trésor,** where ex-model Rodolphe, one of the best hosts in town, attracts an exceptionally good-looking crowd.

Bar-hopping in and around the Bastille... One of the best is the **Café de l'Industrie,** a large café with a neocolonial décor, and with the arrival of a lot of rather brash boom-boom bars targeted at a suburban crowd, the **China Club,** an old-timer with a long bar, fumoir, (mediocre) restaurant, and cabaret, has acquired a certain well-worn charm that makes its L.A./Hong Kong in the '30s decor credible. **Barrio Latino** is the latest big-deal restaurant-bar to open, and if it's got a great decor created around the central atrium of a former furniture showroom, it's also a sign that the Bastille is going mainstream, since it's huge and expensive. Pop in for a drink and a glimpse of the Paris-style pretension of hostesses wearing walkie-talkie headsets. There's a VIP seating area, but it's usually tellingly empty.

You can't really claim to have done this neighborhood without having popped into **Sanz Sans,** a pretty hip bar-club with a heavy-duty party crowd that likes to get ripped and dance on the tables to hip-hop, funk, Latin, and house music. The signature of this place is the big in-house video screen in back, which shows people what they're missing up front because the action is filmed live. **Les Portes,** with its bordello decor and nuanced naughtiness, is an equally stylish but quieter option. For dancing, try **Balajo,** which is a *bal-musette* on weekend afternoons and a terrific, mixed-age disco at night, and **Chapelle des Lombards,** a disco specializing in salsa and African music.

Where the wild things are... Just north of the Bastille, the grandmotherly Ménilmontant neighborhood has suddenly switched on, following an influx of trendies in search of cheap apartments. What many consider to be the coolest bar in town is the gorgeous **Café Charbon,** a restored Belle Epoque dance hall where an oh-so-interesting crowd vies to set up camp for the evening in one of the leatherette banquettes. **Lou Pascalou** is a perfect reflection of the area's young identity—hip but friendly. Plus, the stainless-steel toilets are a perfect place to indulge your fantasies of being a Russian astronaut.

Where the boys are... There is no shortage of gay bars and discos in Paris. The hottest one seems to be **Le Cox,** a Soho (London)-style café-bar, where you can log onto the Internet. Other popular watering holes in the Marais, the center of the gay community, include the mixed bar **Amnésia,** with its cozy armchairs; the quieter **Central;** the friendly **Duplex;** and the sleazy **Mic Man. Le Dépot** is the hot spot of the neighborhood, and it's a no-nonsense disco with decor of camouflage-netting and exposed ducts; there's more action in the cubicles downstairs, though, than on the dance floor. In the Bastille area, look up the raunchy **Keller's Club** for serious cruising (its back room is equipped with a sling and other toys). The Châtelet area is home to **Le Transfert,** a down-and-dirty leather bar. The immensely popular **Le Queen,** on the Champs-Elysées, is a large disco with go-go dancers, house music, and myriad "happenings" like the "bubble baths" at 2am on Tuesdays, when the room fills with bubbles and the partiers strip off their clothes and dance in surgical masks and swim goggles.

For girls who like girls... *Les filles qui préfèrent les filles* don't have as wide a selection of clubs as do their male counterparts, but there are a few lesbian nightspots. The easygoing Marais bar **Amnésia** has a mixed gay and lesbian crowd; **La Champmeslé,** near the Bourse, is a tranquil spot for conversation.

African/West Indian clubs... Paris has a healthy share of African dance clubs, including **Chapelle des Lombards,** upscale **Le Keur Samba,** and steamy **Le Tango.** One of the most popular African/West Indian clubs is just outside Paris, in Montreuil: **Cinquième Dimension**'s *zouk* music keeps the crowds moving until the wee hours. Race or ethnic divisions aren't an issue, but getting back home can be. If you can't afford a taxi back to the city from the Montreuil clubs, keep dancing until the Métro starts running again at 5:30am.

Latin fever... Parisians of all ages are still mad for Latin music, especially salsa. Thirty-somethings pretend they are in Havana at the crowded, smoky **Chapelle des Lombards,** in the Bastille area, while an intriguingly mixed crowd—Algerian busboys teamed up with swanky Versailles matrons, local yuppies, and lots of resident Latin Americans—fill the downstairs dance hall at **Dancing La Coupole** (yes, the same Coupole where Hemingway and other unspeakably tedious members of the Lost Generation hung out) for live Latin tunes on Tuesdays, Wednesdays, and Thursdays. A funky, hip-grinding crowd, including a multitude of young Latinos, gather on Thursday nights at **Les Etoiles,** a 10th-arrondissement dive with a roughed-up rococo decor. Just slightly less feverish is the Thursday Latin night at **La Java,** a big 1930s-vintage dance hall where you would expect to hear a socialist workers' anthem instead of a rhumba. The crowd is half dressed-down yuppies and half Bastille funksters. **Cithéa,** a laid-back bar and music venue near place de la Republique, also hosts salsa bands regularly. At **Favela Chic,** know to whom you are talking. The most beautiful girls may be...well, a beautiful girl or a Brazilian transvestite. No other nightclub in Paris is as Brazilian as this dive. Trendy young men and women come here to dance, flirt, pick each other up, and talk romance in a dozen languages. Live music alternates with recorded music.

See-and-be-scenes... Though they cop some of the nastiest and most pretentious attitude in Paris, the bar and restaurant at the **Hôtel Costes** are the epicenter of hip Paris nightlife. The lush 19th-century bordello decor, candlelight, perky soundtrack, and celeb-studded crowd are pretty dazzling, so brave the door monsters for a peek at this inner sanctuary of chic. **Café Mabillon,** a Left Bank haunt open 24 hours, draws a diverse crowd of prowling bachelors, as well as stylish young couples. Don't bother with Le Montana Fashion Bar, the jazz bar around the corner from the Café de Flore, unless your goal is to keep company with bewildered Japanese tourists. This bar-disco is the pitifully ersatz creation of fashion designer Paco Rabanne, and it is a horrible proof that nightlife cannot be willed into existence with a checkbook. **Le Comptoir,** near the Forum des Halles, is a trendy place to have drinks and tapas.

Best cozy bars... In the stately Art Deco **Hôtel Lutetia,** the red-velvet-decorated fumoir bar offers a chic option of drinks in the lobby or their darkly lit bar favored by Left Bank literati. The original bar, with its dark paneling and comfy armchairs, is a fine spot to linger over your favorite, invariably well-mixed tipple. As prices have soared in Saint-Germain's cafés, this has become the place where the locals troll by for a pop after dinner. The **China Club,** a spacious bar and restaurant near Bastille, is a place to sit and chat with friends on couches and armchairs arranged in conversational groupings; upstairs, there are smaller, quieter rooms where customers play chess and other games. Try **Atmosphère,** on the Canal Saint-Martin, for just-a-bar lack of pretension and a study in simplicity. The bar draws its name from Marcel Carné's film *Hôtel de Nord,* in which Arletty famously and disdainfully intoned, "Atmosphère, atmosphère," while standing on a bridge over the Canal Saint-Martin. Located in the heart of town, just off the place de la Concorde, **Le 30,** the bar at the Sofitel Faubourg Hotel, is a place to meet for drinks, since it has a fireplace, comfortable chairs, and a glamorous Art Deco bar.

All-night bars... Le Dépanneur, a Pigalle bar masquerading as an American diner, is open 24 hours a day and serves food to help soak up the tequila. Near Les Halles, the **Sous-Bock** (the name means "beer mat"), modeled after an English pub (right down to the dartboard), offers *moules-frites* (mussels and French fries) and a vast selection of beers until 5am every night. The loungelike **Satellit' Café,** near place de la République, is open all night on the weekend. It doesn't really get going until around 2am, but the disc jockey has a vast collection of jazz, blues, and soul records (vinyl only, please), and there are occasional live concerts. If you simply can't stop dancing when the other discos close at 5am, go to **Folie's Clubbing.** Pigalle's ultrahip bar **Le Moloko** stays open until 6am, and if you want a nightcap or two at the crack of dawn on the Left Bank, the **Old Navy,** a raucous nightclub-bar-café, pulls a strange crowd of night owls on the Left Bank and is more authentic and less posey than the nearby **Café Mabillon,** which also stays open all night.

The Index

Note on prices: Obviously, prices vary greatly when clubbing, and because in Paris prices fluctuate on selected theme nights, some places impose high cover charges—if you can get in—while others make their loot on the overpriced bottles of Johnny Walker. Nightclubs on or near the Champs-Elysées tend to be predictably steep—one pays dearly to gape at the pretty people.

Amnésia (p. 213) MARAIS Gays and lesbians mingle in this relaxed bar filled with armchairs arranged around low tables. A cramped basement dance floor gets hopping after midnight.... *Tel 01-42-72-16-94. 42, rue Vieille-du-Temple, 4e. Métro Hôtel de Ville or St-Paul.*

See Map 26 on p. 204.

Atmosphère (p. 215) GARE DU NORD Friendly, simply furnished bar alongside the Canal Saint-Martin with a youngish crowd and reasonable prices.... *Tel 01-40-38-09-21. 49, rue Lucien Sampaix, 10e. Métro Jacques Bonsargent.*

See Map 26 on p. 204.

Aux Noctambules (p. 211) PIGALLE Nightspot that hasn't changed since the 1950s, except the clientele is now younger and hipper.... *Tel 01-46-06-16-38. 24, bd. de Clichy, 18e. Métro Pigalle.*

See Map 26 on p. 204.

Balajo (p. 210) BASTILLE One of the most eclectic clubs in town. The clientele is mixed in age and not too pretentious, and the DJs spin tunes from across the decades.... *Tel 01-47-00-07-87 www.balajo.fr. 9, rue de Lappe, 11e. Métro Bastille. Cover.*

See Map 26 on p. 204.

Barrio Latino (p. 206) BASTILLE See p. 87 in the Dining chapter for a complete rundown.

See Map 8 on p. 78.

Batofar (p. 209) GARE D'AUSTERLITZ A showplace for alternative, often electronic concerts, which are usually followed by heavy DJ action. Come play with really cool young creative Parisians.... *Tel 01-56-29-10-00. Facing 11, quai Francois-Mauriac, 13e. Métro Bibliotheque. Cover.*

See Map 26 on p. 204.

Bilboquet (p. 210) ST-GERMAIN-DES-PRES Left Bank club offering New Orleans–style jazz and dinner in a handsome Belle Epoque setting.... *Tel 01-45-48-81-84. 13, rue St-Benoît, 6e. Métro St-Germain-des-Prés.*

See Map 26 on p. 204.

Bistrot d'Eustache (p. 210) LOUVRE/LES HALLES Intimate jazz bar near Les Halles that serves food until 2am. Live music Thursday through Saturday.... *Tel 01-40-26-23-20. 37, rue Berger, 1er. Métro Les Halles.*

See Map 26 on p. 204.

Blue Note (p. 210) MONTMARTRE Cozy bar near the rue Mouffetard market that specializes in Brazilian cocktails. Live Brazilian music, jazz, or blues nightly at 10pm.... *Tel 01-42-54-69-76. 13, rue Feutrier, 18e. Métro Château Rouge.*

See Map 26 on p. 204.

Café Charbon (p. 206) BASTILLE The jewel of Ménilmontant. Dress down (wear black) and come early to squeeze into a cushy banquette.... *Tel 01-43-57-55-13. 109, rue Oberkampf, 11e. Métro Ménilmontant.*

See Map 26 on p. 204.

Café de l'Industrie (p. 207) BASTILLE Large, trendy but relaxed café.... *Tel 01-47-00-13-53. 16, rue St-Sabin, 11e. Métro Bastille.*

See Map 26 on p. 204.

Café Mabillon (p. 214) ST-GERMAIN-DES-PRES Prowling bachelors, late-night couples, and kids who missed the last train gather in this 24-hour Left Bank bar for one last drink.... *Tel 01-43-26-62-93. 164, bd. St-Germain, 6e. Métro Mabillon.*

See Map 26 on p. 204.

Caveau de la Hûchette (p. 211) LATIN QUARTER Popular basement jazz club.... *Tel 01-43-26-65-05. 5, rue de la Huchette, 5e. Métro St-Michel. Cover.*

See Map 26 on p. 204.

Central (p. 213) MARAIS Convivial gay bar centrally located in the Marais. Cruisy, macho crowd. 8-room hotel upstairs (book well in advance).... *Tel 01-48-87-99-33. 33, rue Vieille-du-Temple, 4e. Métro Hôtel de Ville or St-Paul.*

See Map 26 on p. 204.

Chapelle des Lombards (p. 212) BASTILLE Salsa and merengue reign at this 20-year-old dance club.... *Tel 01-43-57-24-24. 19, rue de Lappe, 11e. Métro Bastille. Cover .*

See Map 25 on p. 178.

Chez Richard (p. 212) MARAIS Trendy bar, with a pleasant atmosphere but high prices. Serves food.... *Tel 01-42-74-31-65. 37, rue Vieille-du-Temple, 4e. Métro Hôtel de Ville or St-Paul.*

See Map 26 on p. 204.

China Club (p. 212) BASTILLE Sit on couches or play chess in the upstairs rooms.... *Tel 01-43-43-82-02. 50, rue de Charenton, 12e. Métro Ledru-Rollin.*

See Map 26 on p. 204.

Cinéma Le Rex (p. 209) LA BOURSE A brash and packed-out club with a frisky and devoted following of regulars who live for its electronic dance music.... *Tel 01-42-36-83-98. 1, bd. Poissoniere, 2e. Méro Bonne Nouvelle. Cover.*

See Map 26 on p. 204.

Cinquième Dimension (p. 213) SUBURBAN PARIS A temple of West Indian dance music, in Montreuil.... *Tel 01-42-87-38-63. Centre Commerciale de la Mairie de Montrevil, 93100 Montrevil, Métro Mairie de Montreuil. Cover (free for women on Sun).*

Cithéa (p. 210) BASTILLE A well-ventilated club with good indirect lighting. Live music Thursday through Saturday, ranging from salsa to funk and acid jazz.... *Tel 01-40-21-70-95. 112, rue Oberkampf, 11e. Métro Rue St-Maur. Cover.*

See Map 26 on p. 204.

Dancing La Coupole (p. 214) MONTPARNASSE The basement dance hall in this café-restaurant has become a happening nightspot, with live Latin music Tuesday through Thursday.... *Tel 01-43-27-56-00. 102, bd. de Montparnasse, 14e. Métro Montparnasse. Cover.*

See Map 26 on p. 204.

Divan du Monde (p. 210) PIGALLE Nightclub with concerts, fashion shows, and other events. Music ranges from jazz to rock, salsa, funk, and pop.... *Tel 01-42-52-02-46. 75, rue des Martyrs, 18e. Métro Pigalle. Cover.*

See Map 26 on p. 204.

Duc des Lombards (p. 211) LOUVRE/LES HALLES Popular Châtelet-area jazz club with occasional cocktail-hour concerts (7 or 8pm) and performances every night at 10:30.... *Tel 01-42-33-22-88. 21, bd. de Sébastopol, 1er. Métro Réaumur Sébastopol. Cover.*

See Map 26 on p. 204.

Duplex (p. 209) BOIS DE BOULOGNE This club is popular with rich 20-something Euro-boppers smoking Marlboro lights and swilling whisky and Cokes. Fun for a harmlessly trashy night out.... *Tel 01-45-00-45-00. www.leduplex.fr. 2 bis av. Foch, 16e. Métro Charles de Gaulle Etoile. Cover.*

See Map 26 on p. 204.

Etoile Manquante (p. 212) MARAIS Friendly bar-restaurant (food served until 12:30am). Always packed.... *Tel 01-42-72-48-43. 34, rue Vieille-du-Temple, 4e. Métro St-Paul or Hôtel de Ville.*

See Map 26 on p. 204.

Favela Chic (p. 214) OBERKAMPF This night club in a grungy but trendy district attracts one of the city's best-looking crowds. Samba music rules the night.... *Tel 01-40-03-02-66. 18, rue de Faubourg du Temple, 11e. Métro: République.*

See Map 26 on p. 204.

Folie's Clubbing (p. 211) PIGALLE A two-level disco featuring progressive house and techno music, go-go dancers, and a gay crowd. Turns into an after-hours club Saturday and Sunday.... *Tel 01-48-78-63-56. 11, place Pigalle, 9e. Métro Pigalle. Cover.*

See Map 26 on p. 204.

Hôtel Costes (p. 214) LOUVRE/LES HALLES The bar here is the spot for fashionable young Euro-trash and fashion types, who hungrily scan the scene in search of supermodels and actors.... *Tel 01-42-44-50-25. 239, rue St-Honore, 1er. Métro Concorde.*

See Map 26 on p. 204.

Hôtel Lutetia (p. 215) ST-GERMAIN-DES-PRES There are actually three settings here: the dark, cozy bar, the buzzy lobby hall, and the plush new fumoir.... *Tel 01-49-54-46-46. www.lutetiaparis.com. 45, bd. Raspail, 6e. Métro Sèvres Babylone.*

See Map 26 on p. 204.

Jazz Club Lionel Hampton (p. 211) PARC MONCEAU Swinging jazz club in the lobby of the Méridien hotel west of the Arc de Triomphe. Good music, pricey drinks.... *Tel 01-40-68-30-42. www.jazzclub-paris.com. 81, bd. Gouvion St-Cyr, 17e. Métro Porte Maillot.*

See Map 26 on p. 204.

Keller's Club (p. 213) BASTILLE Put on your leather before visiting this rough, tough, raunchy gay bar. Women not admitted.... *Tel 01-47-00-05-39 or 01-47-00-05-33. 14, rue Keller, 11e. Métro Bastille.*

See Map 26 on p. 204.

La Champmeslé (p. 213) LA BOURSE Lesbian bar with a quiet, conversational ambience.... *Tel 01-42-96-85-20. 4, rue Chabanais, 2e. Métro Bourse.*

See Map 26 on p. 204.

La Java (p. 206) GARE DU NORD *Bal-musette* where you can dance the waltz or tango on Friday and Saturday nights or Sunday afternoons. Live salsa groups Thursdays.... *Tel 01-42-02-20-52. 105, rue du Faubourg-du-Temple, 10e. Métro République or Belleville. Cover, free on Sun afternoon.*

See Map 26 on p. 204.

La Villa (p. 211) ST-GERMAIN-DES-PRES Basement club in the modernized Left Bank hotel of the same name. Quality jazz acts.... *Tel 01-43-26-60-00. 29, rue Jacob, 6e. Métro St-Germain-des-Prés.*

See Map 26 on p. 204.

Le Bus Palladium (p. 211) PIGALLE Rock 'n' roll is here to stay with the young crowd at this reincarnated Pigalle disco.... *Tel 01-53-21-07-33. 6, rue Fontaine, 9e. Métro Pigalle. Tues–Sun 11pm–dawn. Cover (free entry for women on Tues).*

See Map 26 on p. 204.

Le Cabaret Milliardaire (p. 209) CHAMPS-ELYSEES This disco pulls in people-column wannabes, and the surly staff cater to their every whim, which may include excluding you at the door. In spite of this, it's a good time.... *Tel 01-42-89-44-14. 68, rue Pierre Charron, 8e. Métro Franklin D Roosevelt.*

See Map 26 on p. 204.

Le Café du Trésor (p. 212) MARAIS The stylish young bar/restaurant run by former Kenzo model Rodolphe.... *Tel 01-42-71-78-35. 5, rue du Tresor, 4e. Métro St-Paul.*

See Map 26 on p. 204.

Le Comptoir (p. 215) LOUVRE/LES HALLES A mixed crowd frequents this chic Les Halles tapas spot. A DJ plugs in Thursday through Saturday.... *Tel 01-40-26-26-66. 37, rue Berger, 1er. Métro Les Halles.*

See Map 26 on p. 204.

Le Cox (p. 213) MARAIS Spacious and attractive cyber-gay bar with an arty, international crowd that spills out onto the sidewalk.... *Tel 01-42-72-08-00. www.cox.fr. 15, rue des Archives, 4e. Métro Hôtel de Ville.*

See Map 26 on p. 204.

Le Dépanneur (p. 215) PIGALLE Twenty-four-hour diner/bar.... *Tel 01-40-16-40-20. 27, rue Fontaine, 18e. Métro Blanche.*

Le Dépot (p. 213) MARAIS The latest gay hot spot is a disco with a dimly lit basement that's busier than the dance floor. Homoerotic video walls get the crowd in the mood and a heavy-duty sound system prevents idle chatter.... *Tel 01-44-54-96-96. 10, rue aux Ours, 3e. Métro Rambuteau. Cover.*

See Map 26 on p. 204.

Le Gibus (p. 209) BASTILLE A serious urban dance club with a large gay following, this place really moves to mostly house and garage music. Wednesdays are popular with trance music.... *Tel 01-47-00-78-88. 18, rue du Faubourg-du-Temple, 11e. Métro République. Cover.*

See Map 26 on p. 204.

Le Keur Samba (p. 213) CHAMPS-ELYSEES Upscale African nightclub, with a very selective door policy.... *Tel 01-43-59-03-10. 79, rue La Boétie, 8e. Métro Franklin D Roosevelt. Cover.*

See Map 26 on p. 204.

Le Moloko (p. 211) PIGALLE Funky, popular bar with good recorded music.... *Tel 01-48-74-50-26. 26, rue Fontaine, 9e. Métro Blanche.*

See Map 26 on p. 204.

Le Monkey Club (p. 207) CHAMPS-ELYSEES The latest hot spot for young bourgeois professionals and the fashion and media crowd. A pretty good, and pretty expensive, time.... *Tel 01-58-56-20-50. 65–67, rue Pierre Charron, 8e. Métro Franklin D Roosevelt.*

See Map 26 on p. 204.

Le Paris (p. 210) BASTILLE Ordinary-looking café, with live music on Saturday.... *Tel 01-47-00-87-47. 24, bd. Richard-Lenoir, 11e. Métro Bréguet Sabin.*

See Map 26 on p. 204.

Le Queen (p. 207) CHAMPS-ELYSEES Largest, most happening gay disco in Paris. Women admitted selectively. Go-go dancers set the pace.... *Tel 01-53-89-08-90. 102, av. des Champs-Elysées, 8e. Métro George V. Cover Fri and Sat.*

See Map 26 on p. 204.

Le Tango (p. 210) MARAIS The ambience is hot at this African club and the dancing intimate, to say the least. On weekend afternoons, the club turns into a *bal-musette.... Tel 01-42-72-17-78. 11, rue au Maire, 3e. Métro Arts et Métiers. Cover (free for women before midnight).*

See Map 26 on p. 204.

Le 30 (p. 215) CHAMPS-ELYSEES Bar off the lobby of this hotel is a peaceful, pleasant spot for a tête-à-tête over cocktails.... *Tel 01-44-94-14-14. Hotel Sofitel Le Faubourg, 11, rue Boissy d'Anglas, 8e. Métro Concorde.*

See Map 26 on p. 204.

Le Transfert (p. 213) LOUVRE/LES HALLES Acts, not words, count in this hot, friendly gay bar frequented by tough, raunchy leather men. Women not admitted.... *Tel 01-42-60-48-42. 3, rue de la Sourdière, 1er. Métro Tuileries.*

See Map 26 on p. 204.

Les Bains Douches (p. 208) MARAIS Star-studded disco in a former bathhouse near the Centre Pompidou. Hard to get into but easy to leave.... *Tel 01-48-87-01-80. 7, rue du Bourg-l'Abbé, 3e. Métro Arts et Métiers. Cover.*

See Map 26 on p. 204.

Les Etoiles (p. 206) GARE DU NORD Live Latin music is the draw at this club, also known for its wild rococo decor; near Strasbourg-St-Denis.... *Tel 01-47-70-60-56. www.etoilessalsa.com. 61, rue Château-d'Eau, 10e. Métro Château d'Eau. Cover (includes a main course).*

See Map 26 on p. 204.

Les Portes (p. 212) BASTILLE This popular bar has a coy 1920s bordello ambience and decor that appeals to a young clientele who'd never dream of "paying for it".... *Tel 01-40-21-70-61. 15, rue de Charonne, 11e. Métro Bastille.*

See Map 26 on p. 204.

L'Imprevu Café (p. 212) MARAIS Check out the basement for occasional jazz action at this friendly, popular café with an easygoing mixed crowd.... *Tel 01-42-78-23-50. 7–9, rue Quincampoix, 4e. Métro Hôtel de Ville.*

See Map 26 on p. 204.

Lou Pascalou (p. 213) MENILMONTANT The draw at this unpretentious but very hip bar is the pool table.... *Tel 01-46-36-78-10. 14, rue des Panoyaux, 20e. Métro Menimlmontant.*

See Map 26 on p. 204.

Mic Man (p. 213) MARAIS Videos and live action are in the basement of this rather seedy Marais gay bar. Women not admitted.... *Tel 01-42-74-39-80. 24, rue Geoffroy l'Angevin, 4e. Métro Rambuteau.*

See Map 26 on p. 204.

New Morning (p. 210) GARE DU NORD Attracts some of the best international jazz, blues, African, and South American groups.... *Tel 01-45-23-51-41. 7, rue des Petites-Ecuries, 10e. Métro Château d'Eau. Cover.*

See Map 26 on p. 204.

Old Navy (p. 215) ST-GERMAIN-DES-PRES Soldiers on leave, party girls, stumped writers, habitual local sozzlers—the gang's all here at this funky, frisky café-bar that gets harmlessly stranger as the night wears on.... *Tel 01-43-26-88-09. 150, bd. St-Germain, 6e. Métro Mabillon.*

See Map 26 on p. 204.

Petit Journal Montparnasse (p. 211) MONTPARNASSE Jazz club with good sightlines, good acoustics, and excellent musicians.... *Tel 01-43-21-56-70. 13, rue du Commandant-Mouchotte, 14e. Métro Montparnasse.*

See Map 26 on p. 204.

Petit Journal Saint-Michel (p. 211) LATIN QUARTER Club with New Orleans–style jazz.... *Tel 01-43-26-28-59. 71, bd. St-Michel, 5e. RER Luxembourg. Cover.*

See Map 26 on p. 204.

Pick-Clops (p. 212) MARAIS Smoking is de rigeur for the cool, young clientele of this Marais café-bar.... *Tel 01-40-29-02-18. 16, rue Vieille-du-Temple, 4e. Métro Hôtel de Ville.*

See Map 26 on p. 204.

Sanz Sans (p. 212) BASTILLE Well-mixed drinks and well-spun Latin, funk, hip-hop, and house.... *Tel 01-44-75-78-78. 49, rue du Faubourg-St-Antoine, 12e. Métro Bastille.*

See Map 26 on p. 204.

Satellit' Café (p. 215) BASTILLE Lounge lizards will feel at home in this bar, where a DJ plays old jazz, blues, and soul, and there are occasionally good live shows.... *Tel 01-47-00-48-87. 44, rue de la Folie-Méricourt, 11e. Métro Oberkampf.*

See Map 26 on p. 204.

Slow Club (p. 211) CHATELET The hip folks who flock here are mostly in their 30s and 40s. They know they're getting some of the best New Orleans–style jazz in Paris.... *Tel 01-42-33-84-30. 140, rue de Rivoli, 1e. Métro Chatelet.*

See map 26 on p. 204.

Sous-Bock (p. 215) LOUVRE/LES HALLES Large, English-style pub with wide selection of international beers.... *Tel 01-40-26-46-61. 49, rue St-Honoré, 1er. Métro Pont Neuf or Les Halles.*

See Map 26 on p. 204.

Sunset (p. 211) LOUVRE/LES HALLES Agreeable basement jazz club where you can dine while listening to some of France's best jazz talents.... *Tel 01-40-26-46-60. 60, rue des Lombards, 1er. Métro Châtelet. Cover.*

See Map 26 on p. 204.

ENTERTA

INMENT

Map 27: Paris Entertainment

Blancs-Manteaux **36**
Bouffes du Nord **19**
Café de la Gare **35**
Cathédrale Américaine **8**
Centre Pompidou **34**
Cinéma le Rex **21**
Cirque d'Hiver **38**
Comédie Française **22**
Crazy Horse Saloon **9**
Double-Fond **39**
Eglise Américaine **11**
Elysées Montmartre **18**
Fast Publicité **20**
Folies-Bergère **16**
La Boule Noire **17**
La Cigale **17**
Lido **4**
Madeleine **12**
Maison de Radio France **1**
Moulin Rouge **5**
Notre-Dame **30**
Odéon-Théâtre de l'Europe **27**

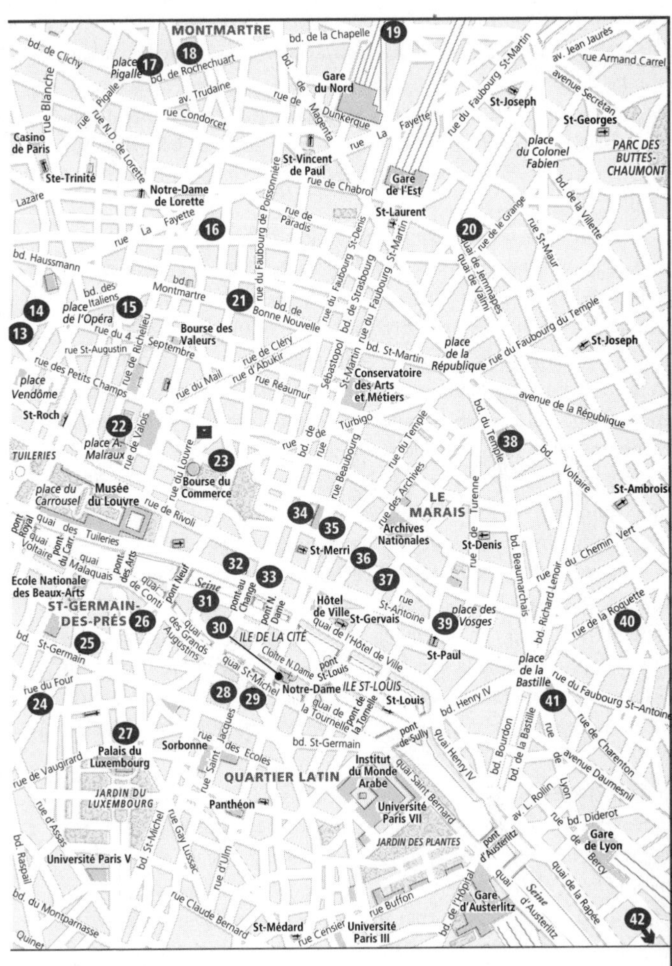

Olympia **13**
Opéra Comique **15**
Opéra Garnier **14**
Opéra National de Paris-Bastille **41**
Palais d'Omnisports de Paris-Bercy **42**
Point Virgule **37**
Rond Point Théâtre
Renaud-Barrault **7**
Saint-Eustache **23**
Saint-Germain-des-Prés **25**
Saint-Julien-le-Pauvre **29**
Saint-Séverin **28**
Sainte-Chapelle **31**
Salle Gaveau **6**
Salle Pleyel **3**
Théâtre de la Bastille **40**
Théâtre de la Ville **33**
Théâtre de Nesle **26**
Théâtre des Champs-Elysées **10**
Théâtre du Châtelet **32**
Théâtre du Vieux-Colombier **24**
Théâtre National de Chaillot **2**

Basic Stuff

Though the first image most folks have of Paris entertainment is the age-old tits-and-feathers revues, these days the city's legendary cabarets are more can't-can't than can-can. Unless your idea of a great night out is to be surrounded by heavy-breathing businessmen, take the 125€ ($156) per person you save by skipping these sorry spectacles and spend it on tickets to an opera, a ballet, or a concert.

Because of lavish government subsidies, Paris remains one of the major arts centers of the world, and even if France hasn't been producing a lot of native talent recently, it can afford to import the very best performers and companies from other cities. Unfortunately, despite government largesse, ticket prices are stiff; your best bets are the Ballet de l'Opéra de Paris, any opera, and, for French speakers, a production at the Comédie Française or the Théâtre de L'Odéon. The mainstream French theater has lost its way in feeble attempts to imitate Broadway and London's West End, but good productions of French classics, à la Molière, are generally available.

Interested in local stars? Keep your eyes peeled for performances by American soprano Jessye Norman (she lives in Switzerland but Paris is her regular performing venue); concerts by Les Arts Florissants, a popular Baroque chamber music group directed by American William Christie; and plays by Alfredo Arias, an avant-garde Argentine playwright and resident of Paris.

Sources

Pariscope and ***L'Officiel des Spectacles*** come out every Wednesday with complete listings of films, theater, music, dance, and art exhibitions. *Pariscope* includes **"Time Out Paris,"** a 12-page English-language insert that also gives instructions on how to decipher the French listings. French speakers should also pick up the *Figaro* newspaper on Wednesdays because its weekly supplement, the **"Figaroscope,"** provides not only the same listings, but also restaurant reviews, an excellent nightlife column, and a lot of general information about the trendiest places and faces. The hip monthly magazine ***Nova*** is another good source.

Getting Tickets

The major ticket outlets in Paris are **Virgin Megastore,** 52, av. des Champs-Elysées, 1er (Tel 01-49-53-50-00), and the book/record stores **FNAC** with outlets everywhere—its main location is in the Forum des Halles (1–7, rue Pierre-Lescot, 1er; Tel 01-40-41-40-00; Métro Les Halles). The **Office du Tourisme,**

127, av. des Champs-Elysées, 8e (Tel 01-49-53-53-56; Métro Etoile), can also make theater and exhibition reservations.

Half-price theater tickets are available on the day of the performance from **Le Kiosque Théâtre** on the place Madeleine (Métro Madeleine) and in the RER station at Châtelet-Les-Halles. No information is given by telephone, and a small commission is charged. Most major theaters participate, but tickets to *cafés-théâtres* are not sold. And although selection varies according to availability, it's generally fairly good.

Opera, classical music, and dance performances are often sold out well in advance, but don't despair. You can show up an hour or so before a performance, line up at the ticket window, and pray for cancellations—unclaimed tickets are put on sale a half-hour before the curtain goes up at most stages. This is risky, however, and there's a much more efficient local custom: Scrounge up a scrap of paper and pen, and make a little sign that says *"Cherche une place"* (or *"deux places,"* as the case may be). People often arrive with tickets for friends who couldn't make it, and they'll be happy to sell the extras to you, usually at face value. This might also work at a rock concert, but there you're more likely to encounter professional scalpers. By the way, *sans visibilité* (impaired visibility) tickets are often available at very low prices. About half the stage can usually be seen from these seats and sometimes the whole stage if you stand. There's also the possibility of moving to better seats that are unoccupied—it's worth a try.

Dancing in the Streets

On June 21, the summer solstice, all of Paris celebrates the ***Fête de la Musique.*** *Just step out the door and you'll hear music—anyone who wants to can perform in the street without a permit. More organized events range from rock concerts at the place de la Bastille to classical music in the place de la Concorde. Not surprisingly, it's often cacophony—imagine a classical quartet competing with a heavy-metal band a block away. You might stumble on a brilliant blues group in a back street or Renaissance choristers in the place de Furstemberg—or you might see a gyrating horde of samba dancers on the rue de Rivoli at 2am, trailing a truck blaring salsa music.*

Since 1937, the city's firemen (pompiers-sapeurs) have observed Bastille Day with shindigs in their ***fire-station courtyards*** *on July 13 and 14. Anyone can come, so long as you make a small donation. There's usually a live band (most fun are the corny ones with an accordion player) or a disc jockey, and everyone—from the oldest granny to the youngest toddler—joins in the dancing. The best parties are at the Sévigné, Vieux-Colombier, Montmartre, and Château-Landon firehouses. Watch out for flying firecrackers.*

The Lowdown

The play's the thing... The **Comédie Française,** established by Louis XIV in 1680, is the granddaddy of French theater and still the best place for classics, with top actors playing on its stage in works by Molière, Racine, Feydeau, et al. Those with even a modest understanding of French can delight in one of the sparkling productions. The same recommendation applies to the small, handsomely renovated **Théâtre du Vieux-Colombier,** a branch of the Comédie Française that presents both contemporary and classic plays.

Bobigny/MC93, located on Lenin Boulevard just outside of Paris in the "Communist Belt," or *banlieu rouge* (Red Suburbs—many Paris suburbs have elected Communist administrations), presents international productions of works by the likes of Robert Wilson, Philip Glass, and Peter Sellars, as well as homemade productions and a yearly visit from London's Royal Shakespeare Company. English-language productions are often staged at the lovely **Odéon-Théâtre de l'Europe** and at the **Bouffes du Nord.** The latter is British director Peter Brook's theater in a lovely Italianate structure once damaged by fire and purposefully left scarred despite renovations. (It's an art statement.) The seating there is highly uncomfortable, but the productions are top-notch. Another small theater that offers at least occasional English-language productions—usually of the Sam Shepard or Harold Pinter variety—is the Left Bank's **Théâtre de Nesle.**

Not to be overlooked for its French-language avant-garde productions is the **Cartoucherie,** the home, in eastern Paris, of Ariane Mnouchkine's acclaimed Théâtre du Soleil, a troupe known for daring productions of classic Greek plays and even Molière. **Théâtre des Amandiers,** located in the western suburb of Nanterre, stages excellent productions of contemporary plays in French; sometimes it hosts English-language companies like England's acclaimed Nottingham Playhouse.

Classical sounds... Classical concerts are held at a wide variety of venues all over Paris. The **Théâtre du Châtelet** was originally built by Baron Haussmann, who wanted to create a grandiose theatre worthy of his massive 19th-century urban renewal of Paris. This house seats 3,000 and looks splendid. In addition to a well-deserved reputation for opera and dance productions, Châtelet has earned acclaim in recent years as an innovative music venue, complementing its classical music program with a special series of concerts for young people, as well as lunchtime salon recitals featuring the stars of current major productions.

At the **Maison de Radio France,** the headquarters of the national radio network located near the Seine's Statue of Liberty, the good, but not great, **Orchestre National de France** and the **Orchestre Philharmonique** stage concerts, many of them free. Composer/conductor Pierre Boulez's Ensemble InterContemporain offers a heady alternative to the classics—its avant-garde sounds can often be heard at the **Centre Pompidou.** Concerts at the **Cité de la Musique** in the La Villette complex in northeastern Paris present a grab-bag of musical styles, from North African sounds to chamber music. The **Salle Pleyel,** near the Arc de Triomphe, was the site of Chopin's last public performance, but it doesn't live in the past: It's still one of the top venues for classical concerts and recitals. The big names also pop up for recitals at the **Salle Gaveau,** off the Champs-Elysées.

Many Parisian churches regularly hold concerts, from the Sunday evening organ recitals at the magnificent **Notre-Dame** to the chamber groups and quartets that play beneath the justly famed stained glass of the more intimate **Sainte-Chapelle.** The **Madeleine,** on the place de Madeleine, often presents choral music, but the church is too immense to do justice to the voices. The **Saint-Eustache,** a strange mixture of Gothic and Renaissance architecture next to the Forum des Halles, presents organ recitals on Sunday evenings. The **Cathédrale Américaine,** located off the Champs-Elysées, sometimes hosts visiting American gospel choirs or accomplished organists; don't confuse it with the **Eglise Américaine** on the quai d'Orsay, which holds less ambitious vocal recitals and solo instrumental programs. The **Saint-Germain-des-Prés,** the oldest church in Paris, may overdo Vivaldi's *Four Seasons,* but when the trumpets of the Orchestre Bernard Thomas sing in this lovely 12th-century church, it can bring tears to your eyes. Almost as ancient is the smaller **Saint-Julien-le-Pauvre,** in the Latin Quarter, which offers many of its concerts by candlelight. Nearby, **Saint-Séverin,** one of the city's most beautiful Gothic churches, presents frequent concerts by its in-house vocal ensemble.

The prima donnas of Paris... The grandest opera of all will be found at the **Opéra National de Paris-Bastille,** a massive 1989 building that has thrived despite attacks on its bland architecture, the dismissal of internationally renowned directors and conductors, orchestra strikes, constant political meddling, and frequent breakdowns of one of the most technologically advanced stages in the world. Prices are very high for what the Socialists wanted to be "the opera of the people," but you still have to book far in advance to avoid being shut out of its 2,700-seat hall. The Opéra Bastille's predecessor, the wonderfully ornate **Opéra Garnier** (where the Phantom of the Opera hung out), was decreed to be used exclusively for ballet after the unpopular new opera opened, but after a total renovation of its main theater, it's now technically just as up-to-date as the Opéra National de Paris-Bastille.

Both full-scale and light operas can also be seen and heard at the charming **Opéra Comique,** which has staged Puccini's *La Bohème,* as well as works by Offenbach, Mozart, and Gounod. More daring is the **Théâtre du Châtelet,** which has hosted many acclaimed productions, including Wagner's *Ring Cycle* and William Christie's fabulous rendering of Purcell's *King Arthur.* The **Théâtre des Champs-Elysées,** normally a dance venue, stages operas by the likes of Tchaikovsky, Rimsky-Korsakov, and Handel.

Men in tights... Parisians flock to dance performances, whether they be *Swan Lake,* flamenco, Tibetan dance, or the weirdest experimental modern contortions. The **Opéra Garnier** is now the official home of the **Ballet de l'Opéra de Paris,** considered by many to be the world's best ballet. If you don't take in a performance, you should still try to visit this bring-on-the-gilt hall, commissioned in 1875 by Emperor Napoléon III (see the Diversions chapter). Ballets are also staged at the **Opéra National de Paris-Bastille.**

Presenting works by troupes like La-La-La Human Steps, Trisha Brown, or Pina Bausch, the **Théâtre de la Ville,** on the place du Châtelet, may be the city's most important modern dance venue. Baryshnikov, Mark Morris, the Kirov Ballet, and many other famous dance companies have tripped across the stage of the handsome and historic **Théâtre des Champs-Elysées,** where Nijinsky's 1917 première of *The Rite of Spring* is said to have started riots. The **Théâtre National de Chaillot** reserves its stage between theater productions for troupes like the Ballet Béjart Lausanne. Busy **Théâtre du Châtelet** is the Paris home of William Forsythe's Frankfurt Ballet. The **Théâtre de la Bastille** showcases new companies on their way up to the big time. For something more exotic, check the program of the **Rond Point Théâtre Renaud-Barrault,** which often hosts ethnic dance troops from other countries.

Rockin' it... The mega-venues for rock concerts are the **Zénith,** an immense concert hall in the Parc de la Villette, and the **Palais d'Omnisports de Paris-Bercy,** a 16,000-seat stadium in Bercy, with grass-covered walls. Some stars also show up at the **Olympia** or the **Cinéma le Rex,** two real theaters near the Opéra Garnier that are small enough that you can actually see the stage without binoculars. Edith Piaf and Jacques Brel sang at the Olympia, and today you might see French chanteur Claude Nougaro, blues singer Paul Personne, or big-time rock acts who "want to get back in touch with their audience." Alternative and local rock groups perform at **La Cigale** and **Elysées Montmartre,** smaller theaters in the Pigalle area. The handsome 19th-century, one-ring-circus building, the **Cirque d'Hiver,** sometimes hosts concerts by French stars like pop singer Jacques Higelin (one of the best of an uninspiring bunch). Parisians are delighted by the revival of **La Boule Noire,** the intimate venue next to La Cigale in Montmartre that was a popular rock venue in the '60s.

Life is a cabaret... If you like to pay outrageous prices to watch topless Las Vegas–style showgirls and eat mediocre food while surrounded by busloads of tourists, by all means go to the **Moulin Rouge** (yes, they still do the can-can), the **Folies-Bergère,** the **Crazy Horse Saloon,** or the **Lido.** The Moulin Rouge, up in Montmartre, goes in for spectacle, boasting 1,000 costumes and 100 artists; save yourself some money by avoiding the uninspired dinner. Dancers at the Crazy Horse, just off the Champs-Elysées, have the sexiest names: Kismy Patchwork, Looky Boob, and Pussy Duty-Free.

There is another world of French cabaret. For smaller-scale shows that might feature stand-up comedy (in French), singers, sketches, or plays, try the *café-théâtres,* some of which also serve dinner. The **Blancs-Manteaux** concentrates on comedy, as does the popular **Point Virgule. Café de la Gare** offers cabaret acts, and the **Double-Fond** has magic acts. All four are in the Marais.

Just for laffs... Fast Publicité is the name of a regular series of English-language comedy gigs held upstairs at the legendary Hôtel du Nord (yes, the one where Arletty breathed "Atmosphere, atmosphere"). This can be a fun night out, since you'll likely meet a full cast of local Anglophone expats and might run into some really good contemporary British stand-up comedian like Eddie Izzard. Of the French comedians you see around, Valerie Lemercier is probably the one who's mostly likely to get a giggle out of you, while the appeal of mainstream stars like Smain and Bigard often escapes those who are perfectly fluent in French.

On the fringe... Keep an eye on the "Scenes" section of *Pariscope* for performances by the immensely popular **Zingaro,** a wild and weird circus in which muscleman Bartabas wrestles and writhes with his company, which consists mainly of horses.

The sporting life... Emotions run high when the Paris Saint-Germain football (soccer) team plays on its home turf at the **Parc des Princes.** The sleek **Stade de France,** which looks like a high-tech layer cake and seats 25,000 around a field the same size as the Place de la Concorde, is pretty stunning and can be visited even when there's nothing going on here. Rugby matches are also held at the Parc des Princes, with the Five Nations Tournament from January to March and the French national championships in late May and early June. The **Stade Roland Garros,** out in western Paris near the Bois de Boulogne, hosts the French Open tennis championship at the end of May and the beginning of June. At the **Palais d'Omnisports de Paris-Bercy,** events range from rock concerts to martial arts tournaments to the Paris Open tennis tournament and even an indoor windsurfing competition. For horse-racing fans, the **Hippodrome de Vincennes** (see p. 174) in the Bois de Vincennes is a trotter's course.

The Index

Ballet de l'Opéra de Paris See Opéra Garnier, below.

Blancs-Manteaux (p. 233) MARAIS One of the best-known *cafés-théâtres,* this venue has two small theaters presenting plays and comedy sketches in French.... *Tel 01-48-87-15-84. 15, rue des Blancs-Manteaux, 4e. Métro Hôtel de Ville.*

See Map 27 on p. 226.

Bobigny/MC93 (p. 230) SUBURBAN PARIS Impressive modern theater in one of Paris's Communist-run suburbs, where productions tend toward the experimental and international.... *Tel 01-41-60-72-72. www.mc93.com. La Maison de la Culture, 1, bd. Lénine, Bobigny, 93000. Métro Bobigny Pablo Picasso.*

See Map 27 on p. 226.

Bouffes du Nord (p. 230) GARE DU NORD British director Peter Brook puts up top-notch productions at this arty, quasi-ruined theater in northern Paris.... *Tel 01-46-07-34-50. 37 bis, bd. de la Chapelle, 10e. Métro La Chapelle.*

See Map 27 on p. 226.

Café de la Gare (p. 234) MARAIS Plays and comedy acts in French keep 'em laughing at this *café-théâtre.... Tel 01-42-78-52-51. 41, rue du Temple, 4e. Métro Hôtel de Ville.*

See Map 27 on p. 226.

Cartoucherie (p. 230) BOIS DE VINCENNES Home to Ariane Mnouchkine's Théâtre du Soleil and four lesser-known companies.... *Tel 01-43-74-24-08. Route du Champ-de-Manoeuvre, 12e. Métro Château de Vincennes; shuttle bus available from Métro for performances.*

See Map 27 on p. 226.

Cathédrale Américaine (p. 231) CHAMPS-ELYSEES Sponsors concerts ranging from American gospel to organ and choral music.... *Tel 01-53-23-84-00. 23, av. George V, 8e. Métro George V.*

See Map 27 on p. 226.

Centre Pompidou (p. 231) MARAIS Composer Pierre Boulez's Ensemble InterContemporain performs its experimental music, as well as works by other modern composers.... *Tel 01-44-78-48-43 or 01-44-78-12-33. www.centrepompidou.fr. Place Georges Pompidou, 4e. Métro Rambuteau or Hôtel de Ville.*

See Map 27 on p. 226.

Cinéma le Rex (p. 233) OPERA GARNIER A proper theater with good acoustics that attracts some big names, Bob Dylan and Ry Cooder among them.... *Tel 01-45-08-93-89. 1, bd. Poissonnière, 2e. Métro Rue Montmartre.*

See Map 27 on p. 226.

Cirque d'Hiver (p. 233) BASTILLE More likely to host a French pop singer or a Jean-Paul Gaultier fashion show than a circus these days.... *Tel 01-47-00-28-81. 110, rue Ameloqt, 11e. Métro Filles du Calvaire.*

See Map 27 on p. 226.

Cité de la Musique (p. 231) LA VILLETTE A music conservatory, musical archives, and a theater that regularly hosts classical concerts.... *Tel 01-44-84-45-00. www.cite-musique.fr. 221, av. Jean-Jaurès, 19e. Métro Porte de Pantin.*

See Map 27 on p. 226.

Comédie Française (p. 230) LOUVRE/LES HALLES The historical home of the French dramatic arts, near the Palais-Royal.... *Tel 01-44-58-14-30. www.comedie-francaise.fr. 2, rue de Richelieu, 1er. Métro Palais Royal.*

See Map 27 on p. 226.

Crazy Horse Saloon (p. 233) CHAMPS-ELYSEES Home of the most erotic cabaret show in Paris.... *Tel 01-47-23-32-32. www.lecrazy horseparis.com. 12, av. George V, 8e. Métro Alma Marceau.*

See Map 27 on p. 226.

Double-Fond (p. 234) MARAIS A cafe that stages magic acts.... *Tel 01-42-71-40-20. www.doublefond.com. 1, place du Marché Sainte-Catherine, 4e. Métro St-Paul.*

See Map 27 on p. 226.

Eglise Américaine (p. 231) EIFFEL TOWER Vocal recitals and guitar concerts are some of the musical offerings at this American church on the quai d'Orsay.... *Tel 01-40-62-05-00. 65, quai d'Orsay, 7e. Métro Invalides.*

See Map 27 on p. 226.

Elysées Montmartre (p. 233) MONTMARTRE Pigalle rock concert venue that presents international pop acts, as well as French and world music.... *Tel 01-44-92-45-36. 72, bd. Rochechouart, 18e. Métro Anvers.*

See Map 27 on p. 226.

Fast Publicité **(p. 234)** GARE DU NORD A regular series that showcases the best of mostly British young comedians passing through Paris. Shows Sunday through Tuesday.... *Tel 01-53-19-88-66. www.anythingmatters.com. Hotel du Nord, 102, quai de Jemmapes, 10e. Métro Republique.*

See Map 27 on p. 226.

Folies-Bergère **(p. 233)** OPERA GARNIER Music hall where the shows are perhaps more clever than the flesh-and-feathers norm.... *Tel 01-44-79-98-60. http://foliesbergere.com. 8, rue Saulnier, 9e. Métro Rue Montmartre.*

See Map 27 on p. 226.

La Boule Noire **(p. 233)** PIGALLE A renovated, atmospheric performance space for emerging talent and one-night dance parties and cabaret events.... *Tel 01-49-25-89-99. 120, bd. Rochechouart, 18e. Métro Pigalle.*

See Map 27 on p. 226.

La Cigale **(p. 233)** PIGALLE Reasonably sized theater for rock concerts by both new and well-known acts.... *Tel 01-49-25-81-75. 120, bd. Rochechouart, 18e. Métro Pigalle.*

See Map 27 on p. 226.

Lido **(p. 233)** CHAMPS-ELYSEES Cabaret where the dancing Bluebell Girls and even ice-skating acts entertain tourists over dinner or champagne.... *Tel 01-40-76-56-10. www.lido.fr. 116 bis, av. des Champs-Elysées, 8e. Métro George V.*

See Map 26 on p. 204.

Madeleine **(p. 231)** CHAMPS-ELYSEES Massive 19th-century church where choral recitals are often held.... *Tel 01-44-51-69-00. Place de la Madeleine, 8e. Métro Madeleine.*

See Map 27 on p. 226.

Maison de Radio France **(p. 231)** BOIS DE BOULOGNE Orchestre National de France and the Orchestre Philharmonique perform here.... *Tel 01-56-40-22-22. 116, av. du Président Kennedy, 16e. Métro Ranelagh or Passy.*

See Map 27 on p. 226.

Moulin Rouge **(p. 233)** MONTMARTRE The birthplace of the cancan is still going strong, though its topless extravaganza is seen primarily by tour groups.... *Tel 01-53-09-82-82. 82, bd. de Clichy, 18e. Métro Blanche.*

See Map 27 on p. 226.

Notre-Dame **(p. 231)** MARAIS The landmark cathedral has free organ concerts Sundays at 5:30pm and choral music on the fourth Tuesday of each month.... *Tel 01-42-34-56-10. 6, place du Parvis-Notre-Dame, 4e. Métro Cité.*

See Map 27 on p. 226.

Odéon-Théâtre de l'Europe (p. 230) ST-GERMAIN-DES-PRES Classic Left Bank theater, with a few plays in English every season, including works by Shakespeare.... *Tel 01-44-85-40-40. Place de l'Odéon, 6e. Métro Odéon.*

See Map 27 on p. 226.

Olympia (p. 233) OPERA GARNIER Excellent concert theater because of its smallish size. A place you might see big-time rock acts who are sick of arena shows.... *Tel 01-55-27-10-00, or 08-92-68-33-68 for reservations. 28, bd. des Capucines, 9e. Métro Opéra.*

See Map 27 on p. 226.

Opéra Comique (p. 232) OPERA GARNIER Lovely restored theater in the Opéra Quarter, presenting light opera and an occasional play.... *Tel 01-42-44-45-40. Place Boieldieu, 2e. Métro Richelieu Drouot.*

See Map 27 on p. 226.

Opéra Garnier (p. 232) OPERA GARNIER This opulent 19th-century landmark is now the home of the Ballet de l'Opéra de Paris.... *Tel 01-44-61-59-65, or 08-92-89-90-90 for reservations. www.operadeparis.fr. 8, rue Scribe, 9e. Métro Opéra.*

See Map 27 on p. 226.

Opéra National de Paris-Bastille (p. 232) BASTILLE The city's controversial modern opera house. Dance too.... *Tel 01-44-61-59-65 for information, or 08-92-89-90-90 for reservations. www.operadeparis.fr. 2 bis, place de la Bastille, 12e. Métro Bastille.*

See Map 27 on p. 226.

Orchestre National de France See Maison de Radio France, above.

Orchestre Philharmonique See Maison de Radio France, above.

Palais d'Omnisports de Paris-Bercy (p. 233) BOIS DE VINCENNES Rock concerts, exhibitions, and sporting events.... *Tel 01-40-02-60-60. 8, bd. de Bercy, 12e. Métro Bercy.*

See Map 27 on p. 226.

Parc des Princes (p. 234) BOIS DE BOULOGNE National team soccer and rugby matches.... *Tel 08-25-07-50-78. 24, rue du Commandant-Guilbaud, 16e. Métro Porte d'Auteuil.*

See Map 27 on p. 226.

Point Virgule (p. 234) MARAIS *Café-théâtre* featuring comedy acts and sketches.... *Tel 01-42-78-67-03. 7, rue St-Croix-de-la-Bretonnerie, 4e. Métro Hôtel de Ville.*

See Map 27 on p. 226.

Rond Point Théâtre Renaud-Barrault (p. 233) CHAMPS-ELYSEES Plays and ethnic dance performances from around the world are held in this round, 19th-century building.... *Tel 01-44-95-98-00. 2 bis, av. Franklin D. Roosevelt, 8e. Métro Franklin D Roosevelt.*

See Map 27 on p. 226.

Sainte-Chapelle (p. 231) LOUVRE/LES HALLES This jewel of a chapel is the site of frequent classical concerts.... *Tel 01-53-73-78-51. 1, quai de l'Horologe, 1er. Métro Cité.*

See Map 27 on p. 226.

Saint-Eustache (p. 231) LOUVRE/LES HALLES Free organ recitals are held Sundays in this Gothic church.... *Tel 01-42-36-31-05. 2, impasse St-Eustache, 1er. Métro Les Halles.*

See Map 27 on p. 226.

Saint-Germain-des-Prés (p. 231) ST-GERMAIN-DES-PRES The oldest church in the city hosts frequent classical concerts.... *Tel 01-55-42-81-33. 3, place St-Germain-des-Prés, 6e. Métro St-Germain-des-Prés.*

See Map 27 on p. 226.

Saint-Julien-le-Pauvre (p. 231) LATIN QUARTER Sweet, ancient little Left Bank church that often holds candlelight classical concerts.... *Tel 01-43-54-52-16. 79, rue Galande, 5e. Métro St-Michel.*

See Map 27 on p. 226.

Saint-Séverin (p. 231) LATIN QUARTER A gorgeous Gothic church, with a choral group that performs regularly.... *Tel 01-42-34-93-50. 1, rue des Prêtres-St-Séverins, 5e. Métro St-Michel.*

See Map 27 on p. 226.

Salle Gaveau (p. 231) CHAMPS-ELYSEES A hall for classical recitals and small concerts by both renowned international stars and lesser-known talents.... *Tel 01-45-62-69-71. 45, rue La Boétie, 8e. Métro Miromesnil.*

See Map 27 on p. 226.

Salle Pleyel (p. 231) CHAMPS-ELYSEES Top-level classical concerts and recitals in a hall near the Arc de Triomphe.... *Tel 01-45-61-53-00. 252, rue du Faubourg-St-Honoré, 8e. Métro Ternes.*

See Map 27 on p. 226.

Stade de France (p. 234) SUBURBAN PARIS This state-of-the-art stadium in the Métro-accessible suburb of St Denis is a tour de force of *Star Trek*–style modern architecture.... *Tel 01-55-93-00-00. www.stadedefrance.fr. Rue Francis de Pressense, St. Denis. Métro St-Denis–Porte de Paris. Entrance through Porte H.*

See Map 27 on p. 226.

Stade Roland Garros (p. 234) BOIS DE BOULOGNE The star-studded French Open tennis tournament takes place at this stadium in late spring. Write or fax well in advance for tickets.... *Tel 01-47-43-48-00. Fax 01-47-43-04-94. 2, av. Gordon-Bennet, 16e. Métro Porte d'Auteuil.*

See Map 27 on p. 226.

Théâtre de la Bastille (p. 233) BASTILLE Theater known for taking chances on young dance and theater companies. The spring is for theater, the fall for dance.... *Tel 01-43-57-42-14. 76, rue de la Roquette, 11e. Métro Bastille.*

See Map 27 on p. 226.

Théâtre de la Ville (p. 232) MARAIS Top venue for modern dance, chamber music, and recitals, in the heart of the Right Bank.... *Tel 01-42-74-22-77. 2, place du Châtelet, 4e. Métro Châtelet.*

See Map 27 on p. 226.

Théâtre de Nesle (p. 230) ST-GERMAIN-DES-PRES Small Left Bank theater that sometimes produces English-language plays.... *Tel 01-46-34-61-04. 8, rue de Nesle, 6e. Métro Odéon.*

See Map 27 on p. 226.

Théâtre des Amandiers (p. 230) SUBURBAN PARIS Theater in a western suburb that sometimes hosts visiting English-language troupes.... *Tel 01-46-14-70-70. www.nanterre-amandiers.com. 7, av. Pablo Picasso, Nanterre. Métro La Défense, then bus 159, or RER Nanterre-Préfecture, then free shuttle bus.*

See Map 27 on p. 226.

Théâtre des Champs-Elysées (p. 232) CHAMPS-ELYSEES Many famous dance companies have appeared at this handsome, historic theater. Also hosts opera productions.... *Tel 01-49-52-50-00. 15, av. Montaigne, 8e. Métro Alma Marceau.*

See Map 27 on p. 226.

Théâtre du Châtelet (p. 230) LOUVRE/LES HALLES Fine opera, classical music, and occasional dance performances are staged in this beautiful theater.... *Tel 01-40-28-28-00. 1, place du Châtelet, 1er. Métro Châtelet.*

See Map 27 on p. 226.

Théâtre du Vieux-Colombier (p. 230) ST-GERMAIN-DES-PRES A branch of the Comédie Française in a small, handsomely renovated Left Bank theater.... *Tel 01-44-39-87-00. 21, rue du Vieux-Colombier, 6e. Métro St-Sulpice.*

See Map 27 on p. 226.

Théâtre National de Chaillot (p. 232) BOIS DE BOULOGNE Plays by Edmond Rostand, Marguerite Duras, Bertold Brecht, and occasional dance performances.... *Tel 01-53-65-31-00. www.theatre-chaillot.fr. 1, place du Trocadéro, 16e. Métro Trocadéro.*

See Map 27 on p. 226.

Zénith (p. 233) LA VILLETTE A mega-rock-concert venue in the Parc de la Villette.... *Tel 01-42-08-60-00. 211, av. de Jean-Jaurès, 19e. Métro Porte de Pantin.*

See Map 27 on p. 226.

Zingaro (p. 234) An amazing circus—actually equestrian theater. Look for announcements of appearances in *Pariscope* or *L'Officiel des Spectacles.... Tel 01-48-39-18-03. www.theatrezingaro.com. 176, av. Jean Jaurès, 19e. Métro Fort d'Aubervilliers.*

See Map 27 on p. 226.

HOTLINES & OTHER BASICS

Airports... Two international airports serve Paris: **Roissy-Charles-de-Gaulle** (referred to as Roissy, pronounced "rwah-*see*" by natives) and **Orly.** Orly is closer to town than Roissy and is increasingly used for domestic flights. Roissy is enormous but fairly easy to get around; signs tend to be clearly marked and easy to understand, even for first-time visitors. For flight information, call **Orly** at Tel 01-49-75-15-15 or **Roissy** at Tel 01-48-62-22-80.

Airport transportation into town... A taxi is usually the most convenient way to travel, but it can be a nightmare if traffic is a mess (which it often is). Avoid taxis like the plague if you are in a rush, if it is raining or snowing, during daily rush hours, and on Friday evenings, when most Parisians are trying to get the hell out of town. The ride from Orly to central Paris will cost about 35€ ($44); the ride from Roissy costs an average of 40€ ($50), plus 1€ ($1.25) for each piece of luggage you put in the trunk. The **RER** suburban train line (see "Trains," later in this chapter) has a Roissy stop, connects to the Métro (subway) at the Châtelet, Gare du Nord, Saint-Michel, and Denfert-Rochereau stations, and second-class fare costs 13€ ($16).

It's great if you are arriving at Terminal 20, but to get to or from any other terminal you have to schlep your baggage onto a shuttle bus. That may be a bit of a hassle, but the shuttle is free and the trip takes only about 40 minutes on one of the RER trains that run non-stop to Roissy from the Gare du Nord station. The **Roissybus** costs 8.20€ ($10) and leaves from rue Scribe (Métro Opéra) and Terminals 2A (Gate 10), 2C, 2 (Gate 12), 2D, as well as Terminal 3 (Gate A) and Terminal 1 (Gate 30, arrival level) every 15 minutes.

Getting to and from Orly is even more complicated. By public transportation, you can take the **Orlybus** (11€/$14) from Gate H, Platform 4, at Orly Sud; or Gate J, Level O, at Orly Ouest, which leaves you at the RER station at Denfert-Rochereau in Paris, from which you can take the Métro. Going to the airport, the Orlybus leaves from outside the Denfert-Rochereau RER station every 13 minutes. The train line to Orly, **Orlyval** (9€/$11), seems designed to be inconvenient. The airport stations are on the first floor of Hall 2 in Orly Ouest and gates E/F on the ground floor of Orly Sud; trains take you to the Antony-Orly station, from which you must take RER line B to Paris, then the Métro to your destination. From Paris, take RER line B in the direction of Saint-Rémy-les-Chevreuses and get off at Antony-Orly, where you pick up Orlyval to Orly Sud or Ouest.

Air France provides **bus service** to Roissy and Orly from several locations around the city (10€/$13) to Roissy; 11€/$14 to Orly, both one-way). The buses may be used by anyone, and they are more convenient than public transport—if you are located near one of the stops—but more expensive. For details in English, call Tel 01-41-56-89-00.

American Express... Amex operates a 24-hour phone line (Tel 01-47-14-50-00) that handles questions about American Express services (banking, wire transfers, or emergencies including lost or stolen Amex cards). Mail drop, money exchange, and wire-transfer services are available at 11, rue Scribe, 9e (Tel 01-47-14-50-00; Métro Opéra), and a smaller branch at 38, av. Wagram, 8e (Tel 01-42-27-58-80; Métro Ternes). Both are open for banking services Monday to Saturday from 9am to noon and from 2 to 5pm. Foreign exchange is available Monday to Saturday from 9am to 6pm, and Sunday at the rue Scribe branch only from 10am to 4:30pm.

Babysitters... **Kid Services** (Tel 01-47-66-00-52), provides English-language babysitting services. It claims to have experienced, reliable tot wranglers.

Buses... Paris has a good bus system that's easy to use and much more pleasant than the Métro because you can watch the city go by while you travel. (You can also watch it sit still if you get stuck in a traffic jam.) At each bus stop there is an easy-to-understand diagram of the routes served and the time schedule, and bus shelters also display a citywide map of the bus system. Tickets are the same ones used on the Métro (see "Subways," later in this chapter) and can be purchased on board from the bus drivers. (They even make change!) One-use tickets must be validated by punching them into the apparatus behind the driver's seat. Most passes (see "Subways") are good for bus travel; simply show your pass to the driver.

There is no free map that includes all of Paris's labyrinthine streets, but bus maps are included in the *Plan de Paris par Arrondissement,* and similar street guides are available at all newsstands and bookstores. A handy little book called *Le Guide Paris Bus,* some of which is in English, will tell you everything you need to know about the bus system.

The major drawback to taking the bus is that you often can't. Many do not run after 8:30pm or on Sundays. The late-night **Noctambus** service doesn't start until 1:30am, and it runs just once an hour (till 5:30am) from rue Saint-Martin and avenue Victoria at Châtelet. In theory, you can flag down any Noctambus and the driver will pick you up and let you off anywhere along the route, as long as you're willing to pay more than daytime fare and share the bus with a variety of drunks and unsavory looking characters.

The **Balabus** is a sightseeing bus that runs between the Gare de Lyon and La Défense on Sundays and bank holidays. It runs from noon to 9pm, from the beginning of April until the end of September. Métro tickets can be used to pay the fare, which varies according to how far you go (maximum three tickets).

Car rentals... Renting a car can be expensive in France. You can save money by booking a car from home; ask your travel agent about fly/drive packages. If you end up renting in France, you can go through **Avis** (Tel 08-20-05-05-05;

www.avis.com) or **Hertz** (Tel 01-42-05-05-43; www.hertz.com), which have counters in the airports and train stations. Reliable companies with lower prices include **Ada** (Tel 01-45-54-63-63; www.ada.fr) and **Europcar** (Tel 08-25-35-83-58; www.europcar.com). A hip option for those in the know is **EasyCar** (Tel 09-06-33-33-33; www.easycar.fr), which started out renting very cool Smart cars for very little and now possesses a wide variety of low-cost vehicles.

Tip: When you pay in advance for a car rental from **Auto Europe,** the company locks in the exchange rate and sends you a voucher that covers all the (hidden) expenses. Call Tel 888/223-5555 in North America, Tel 0800/89-98-93 in the U.K., Tel 08-00-90-17-70 in France, or Tel 800/12-64-09 in Australia; or visit www.autoeurope.com.

Consulates and embassies... **U.S. Consulate:** 2, av. Gabriel, 8e, Métro Concorde (Tel 01-43-12-22-22; www.amb-usa.fr). **Canadian Embassy and Consulate:** 35, av. Montaigne, 8e, Métro Franklin D Roosevelt (Tel 01-44-43-29-00; www.dfait-maeci.gc.ca/canadaeuropa/france). **British Embassy and Consulate:** 18 bis rue d'Anjou, 8e, Métro Madeleine (Tel 01-44-51-33-00; www.britishembassy.gov.uk). To locate other embassies and consulates, check www.embassyworld.com.

Currency... The euro became the country's only recognized currency in February 2002, making the franc obsolete. Like the dollar, the euro is divided into 100 centimes, but is distributed in coins of 1, 2, 5, 10, 20, and 50 cents. The euro also comes in coins of 1 and 2 euros, and notes of 5, 10, 20, 50, 100, 200, and 500. At press time, 1€ equaled $1.25.

There are commercial currency exchanges (*bureaux de change*) in train stations and airports, and all over the city, especially in areas frequented by tourists such as Champs-Elysées and rue du Rivoli. Many, but not all, banks will exchange currency—look for the sign CHANGE. A commission is usually charged. **The Banque de France,** 31, rue Croix-des-Petits-Champs, 1er (Tel 01-42-92-42-92; Métro Palais Royal) usually has the best exchange rate. **American Express,** 11, rue Scribe, 9e (Tel 01-47-14-50-00; Métro Opéra), also offers currency exchange, plus special services for cardholders.

Before you leave home, make sure to give your credit card company a call (the appropriate number should be on the back of your card) and let them know where you're traveling—otherwise, depending on your company, your account may be frozen when foreign charges are detected. Do the same for your bank if you plan on using ATMs in France—most ATMs have fair exchange rates, but there will be a fee of about 1.50€ ($1.86) every time you withdraw. If you lose your Visa card, call Tel 08-36-69-08-80; for American Express, call Tel 01-47-77-72-00; and for MasterCard, call Tel 01-45-67-84-84.

Dentists... **SOS Dentaires,** 87, bd. de Port-Royal, 13e (Tel 01-43-37-51-00; Métro Gobelins), has dentists available on weekdays from 8pm to 11:40pm and on weekends and holidays. Call first for a same-day appointment. The **American Hospital,** 63, bd. de Victor-Hugo, Neuilly (Tel 01-46-41-25-25; www.americain-hospital.org; Métro Pont de Levallois or Pont de Neuilly; bus 82), has 24-hour bilingual emergency dental services.

Doctors... If you need a doctor to make a house call, call **SOS Médecin** at Tel 01-47-07-77-77. For an **ambulance,** call Tel 15 or 01-45-67-50-50. Hospital emergency rooms (*urgences*) will treat you with no questions asked, but you should check your health-insurance policy before you travel to be sure you'll be covered for treatment abroad. The **American Hospital** 63, bd. de Victor-Hugo, Neuilly (Tel 01-46-41-25-25; www.americain-hospital.org; Métro Pont de Levallois or Pont de Neuilly; bus 82), has English-speaking doctors and 24-hour emergency services, but it can be expensive.

Driving around... If possible, avoid driving in Paris. Traffic is extremely heavy and French drivers aren't known for their patience or *politesse.* You can drive legally in France with an American or Canadian driver's license for up to a year; though an international license isn't required, it's strongly recommended that you have one. An international license can be purchased through the American Automobile Association (www.aaa.com) for $10.

The most important rule of the road is that the car coming from the right in an unmarked intersection has the right of way, so always slow down at intersections and let any car coming from the right pass ahead of you. However, almost as significant is to take the priority if it's yours. This is not a matter of polite manners; it's the rule of the road. Seat belts are required for every passenger, even in the back seat. Failure to buckle up can set you back 130€ ($163).

Drugstores... French law requires that each neighborhood have at least one pharmacy open all night; look in drugstore windows for the address of the nearest *pharmacie de garde.* Two or three pharmacies in each neighborhood are open on Sunday. **24-hour Pharmacie les Champs-Elysées,** 84, av. des Champs-Elysées, 8e (Tel 01-45-62-02-41; Métro George V) is centrally located.

Electricity... In general, expect 200 volts AC (60 cycles), though you'll encounter 110 and 115 volts in some older establishments. Adapters are needed to fit sockets. Many hotels have two-pin (in some cases, three-pin) sockets for electric razors.

Emergencies and hotlines... For an **ambulance,** dial Tel 15 or 01-45-67-50-50. For the **police,** dial Tel 17. In case of **fire,** dial Tel 18. In case of **poisoning,** call Tel 01-40-05-48-48.

SOS Help (Tel 01-47-23-80-80; open 3–11pm) is an English-language crisis line. **FACTS** is an Anglo-American association set up to help residents and travelers with concerns about AIDS, sexuality, and reproductive health issues. It maintains a helpline in English at Tel 01-44-93-16-69, available on Monday, Wednesday, and Friday from 6 to 10pm.

Festivals & Special Events

For exact dates and locations, consult the weekly events rag ***Pariscope*** or the Paris Convention and Visitors Bureau, 25, rue des Pyramides, 1er (Tel 08-92-68-30-00; www.paris-info.com; Métro Pyramides).

JANUARY: **La Grande Parade de Montmartre** (Tel 01-42-64-64-60), Montmarte; January 1, American-style parade complete with pom-pom girls.

MARCH: **Salon de l'Agriculture** (Tel 01-49-09-60-00), Parc des Expositions, Porte de Versaille; farm animals and machinery on display and farm-fresh foods to eat. **Banlieue**

Bleues (Tel 01-49-22-10-10), Saint-Denis; jazz festival. **Foire de Trône,** Métro Château de Vincennes; late March–May, amusement park.

APRIL: **Poisson d'Avril** (April Fool's Day), all over town; April 1, fish images and practical jokes rooted in the Middle Ages tradition of poking fun at a particularly infrequent bather by pinning a fish to his back and letting it stay there until it reeked worse than the wearer (today they use paper fish). **Martial Arts Festival** (Tel 01-44-68-44-68), Palais d' Omnisports de Paris-Bercy, 12e; competition and demonstrations of various techniques. **Paris Marathon** (Tel 01-41-33-15-68); 26.2-mile footrace through the streets of the city, ending on the Champs-Elysées.

MAY: **French Open** (Tel 01-47-43-52-52), Stade Roland Garros, Métro Porte-d'Auteuil; professional-tennis championship tournament. **Fêtes de Versailles** (Tel 01-39-59-36-22), Château de Versailles; every Sun through Oct, musical fountains at Louis XIV's château. **Braderie de Paris** (Tel 01-42-97-52-10), Parc des Expositions, Porte de Versaille; gigantic garage sale.

JUNE: **Grand Steeplechase de Paris** (Tel 01-49-10-20-30), Hippodrome d'Autoteuil; famous horserace. **Grand Prix de Paris** (Tel 01-43-57-21-47), Hippodrome de Longchamp; another famous horserace. **Fête de la Musique,** throughout the city; summer solstice music free-for-all on the streets, in restaurants and cafés, including major rock concert on the place de la République (festival guides available at newsstands). **Course des Garçons de Café;** mid-month, waiters and waitresses race through the streets of Paris wearing their uniforms and balancing a bottle and a glass on a tray as they run. **Gay Pride Parade** (Tel 01-53-01-47-01); annual parade, party, and expo for lesbian, gay, and bisexual celebrants.

JULY: **Festival du Cinéma en Plein Air** (Tel 08-03-30-63-06), Parc de la Villette; mid-July to late August, free outdoor films nightly at 10 (go early and bring a picnic). **Bastille Day,** in fire stations and public squares all over Paris; July 13–14, the French equivalent of America's Fourth of July celebration. **Paris Quartier d'Eté** (Tel 01-44-83-64-40), various venues throughout the city; mid-July to late August, a cultural festival including concerts, dance, circus, and theater.

AUGUST: **Tour de France** (Tel 01-41-33-15-00), Champs-Elysées; final leg of the world's oldest and most prestigious bicycle race.

SEPTEMBER: **La Villette Jazz Festival** (Tel 08-03-30-63-06; www.villete.com), Parc de la Villette, early September Live jazz in huge park right next to Métro Porte de Pantin. **Festival d'Automne** (Tel 01-53-45-17-00), various locations; mid-September to late December, cultural festival including dance, theater, music, cinema, and plastic arts. The **Techno Parade,** mid-September; a giant celebration of clubbing, with an emphasis on techno music. **Journée de la Patrimoine;** third weekend, monuments and historic buildings are open to the public. **Biennale Internationale des Antiquaires** (Tel 01-44-51-74-74), Carrousel du Louvre; antiques show.

OCTOBER: **Paris Auto Show** (Tel 01-43-95-37-00), Parc des Expositions, Porte de Versaille; new cars on display. **Fêtes des Vendanges à Montmartre** (Tel 01-46-06-00-32), Montmartre; first week, grape harvest parade.

NOVEMBER: **Festival d'Art Sacre** (Tel 01-44-70-64-10); November–December, Christmas music concerts in churches throughout the city. **Mois de la Photo,** the Month of Photography (Tel 01-44-78-75-01), staged every other year (2006, 2008, and so on) and features themed photography exhibits at the Maison Européenne de la Photographie in the Marais and museums and galleries all over town.

DECEMBER: **Braderie de Paris** (Tel 01-42-97-52-10), Parc des Expositions, Porte de Versaille; gigantic garage sale.

Gay and lesbian services... The **Centre Gai et Lesbien,** 3, rue Keller, 11e (Tel 01-43-57-21-47; Métro Bastille), provides information on activities and events in the gay community; it's open Monday to Saturday from 2 to 8pm and Sunday from 2 to 7pm.

AIDES (Tel 08-00-84-08-00, toll-free) is an AIDS hotline, and **SOS Homophobie** (Tel 01-48-06-42-41; open Mon–Fri 8–10pm) provides assistance to victims of antigay aggression.

Internet access... Almost every arrondissement is home to at least one cybercafé, whether it be a mom-and-pop establishment or a conglomerate; check websites like **www.cybercaptive.com** or **netcafes.com** for locations. For more specific suggestions, see "Plugged-In Cafés," on p. 60.

Mail... Most post offices in Paris are open Monday through Friday from 8am to 7pm and Saturday from 8am to noon. The

main post office (PTT) for Paris is at 52, rue du Louvre, 75001 (Tel 01-40-28-76-00; Métro Louvre). It's open 24 hours a day, with limited hours (Mon–Fri 8am–5pm and Sat 8am–noon) for services like purchasing money orders. Stamps can usually be purchased at your hotel reception desk and at cafés with red TABAC signs.

Airmail letters within Europe cost .50€ (65¢); to the United States and Canada, .75€ (95¢); and to Australia and New Zealand, .85€ ($1.05). You can have mail sent to you *poste restante* (general delivery) at the main post office for a small fee; take ID to pick up mail. American Express also offers a *poste restante* service, but you might have to flash an American Express card or traveler's checks.

Maps... If you're staying more than 2 or 3 days, buy an inexpensive little book that includes the *plan de Paris* by arrondissement, available at all major newsstands and bookshops. If you can find it, the forest-green *Paris Classique l'Indispensable* is a thorough guide to the city and its suburbs.

Newspapers and magazines... Most newsstands carry the *International Herald Tribune, USA Today,* the *Wall Street Journal Europe,* the *Financial Times,* and sometimes other major British dailies. The major French dailies are *Libération* (left-wing and hip, but much more mainstream now than at its Maoist beginnings); the highly conservative *Le Figaro;* and the staid, well-written, left-leaning *Le Monde.* The top French magazines are *L'Express, Le Point,* and *Le Nouvel Observateur.*

Opening and closing times... Cafés open early, at around 7am, and stay open until at least 8pm and in some cases until 2am. Restaurants are usually open from noon to 3pm and 7:30 to 11pm. Boutiques open at around 10am and close at 7 or 7:30pm. Smaller shops may close at lunchtime, usually between 1 and 2:30pm. Many boutiques are closed Monday mornings. Major department stores are open from about 9:30am to 7pm, and most stay open until 10pm one night of the week. Most banks are open from 9am to 4:30pm, except on Friday when they stay open an extra hour in the afternoon. Small branches are often closed between 1pm and 2pm. Many businesses close during all or part of August (some prefer July).

Parking... On-street parking is almost impossible to find, and you're in for a nightmarish experience if you're unlucky enough to have your car towed (if that happens, go to the nearest police station to find out where it's been taken). Parking lots are marked by a square blue-and-white P sign; just a few of the large in-town hotels have their own. Centrally located lots include **Parking Notre-Dame,** place Parvis-Notre-Dame, 4e; **Parking Saint-Germain-l'Auxerrois,** 1, place du Louvre, 1er; and **Parking Saint-Sulpice,** place Saint-Sulpice, 6e. For on-street parking, don't look for meters at each spot; look for one meter on the street that either takes coins or a parking card with time embedded on a smart chip (sold at *tabacs,* tobacco shops). These meters spit out a tab of paper, which you display on your dashboard.

Passports and visas... Visas are not required for citizens of the United States or Canada for visits of less than 90 days. If your passport is lost or stolen, report to the consulate of your embassy immediately to have it replaced (see "Consulates and embassies," earlier in this chapter).

Pets... If you have certificates from a vet and proof of rabies vaccination, you can bring most house pets into France.

Radio stations... Every 10 years or so someone flirts with the idea of English-language radio in Paris, but we're still waiting. In the meantime, the airwaves are full of British and American pop hits. Foreigners love the commercial-free station **FIP** (105.1 FM), which mingles rock with classical and jazz and has soft-spoken female announcers. **Radio Nova** (101.5 FM) plays hip-hop, funk, acid jazz, and reggae (you can get a taste of it before you leave home at www.novaplanet.com); **Radio ADO** (as in "adolescent," 97.8 FM) also plays hip-hop and rap. **France-Info** (105.5 FM) has 24-hour news in French. **Skyrock** (96 FM) plays mainstream pop music, and **RFM** (103.9 FM) specializes in rock 'n' roll. **Radio Classique** (101.1 FM) has classical music. **Radio Montmarte** (102.7 FM) airs French oldies.

Restrooms... The self-cleaning streetside toilets of Paris are the envy of the Western world—for .30€ (40¢), you get the use of consistently clean facilities. Be sure to accompany small children, though, or they may be undetected by the sensors and swept along when the entire toilet-sink apparatus, including the floor and wall, lifts up and disappears into a separate area to be cleaned and sanitized. Large department stores generally have non-life-threatening public restrooms. At cafés, most French people order a coffee at the bar and then leave it there while they run to the toilet (usually downstairs). All eating establishments are required to have restrooms, but the law doesn't say they have to be clean, so they usually aren't. Don't be shocked to discover a squat toilet, little more than a porcelain-covered hole in the ground; they're still common in cafés. Some curse at these, others find them character-building.

Safety... Paris is generally safer than most American cities, but don't drop your guard completely. Robbery at gun- or knife-point is still uncommon but not unknown, so be careful. Be especially aware of child pickpockets: They roam the city, preying on tourists around attractions like the Louvre, Eiffel Tower, and Notre-Dame, and they also often strike in the Métro, sometimes blocking a victim from the escalator. A band of these young thieves can clean your pockets even while you try to fend them off. Their method is to get very close to a target, ask for a handout (sometimes), and deftly help themselves to your money or passport.

Smoking... If you're bothered by smoke, ask for a table in the *zone non-fumeur* at a restaurant—they're required by law to provide them—but don't be surprised to find neighboring diners puffing away on their Gauloises or Marlboros. Except in some of the large, expensive restaurants, the non-smoking law is widely ignored. In the Métro, on the other hand, most people respect the ban against lighting up.

Sports hotlines... **Allo Sports** (Tel 01-42-76-54-54) provides dates and ticket information on sporting events in the Paris area. **Paris Guide Direct** (Tel 08-36-69-90-83) has info in English.

Standards of measure... The metric system is used in France. Hand gestures are often more useful for indicating what you want in a shop, but for basic conversions, see the inside front cover of this guide.

For clothing, *taille unique* means one-size only. T-shirts and knitwear are often size 1, 2, or 3 (small, medium, or large). Children's clothes are sized by age. Otherwise, follow these conversions:

Size Conversion Chart

Women's clothing							
French	36	38	40	42	44	46	
American	6	8	10	12	14	16	
Women's shoes							
French	36	37	38	39	40	41	
American	5	6	7	8	9	10	
Men's Suits							
French	44	46	48	50-52	54	56	58-60
American	34	36	38	40	42	44	46
Men's Shirt							
French	35	36-37	38	39-40	41	42-43	44
American	14	14½	15	15½	16	16½	17
Men's Shoes							
French	42	43	44	45	46		
American	9	10	11	12	13		

Subways... The Paris subway, the **Métro,** is easy to use, with maps in every station. Métro lines are numbered but are also known by the end stations; line 1 is the La Défense–Château de Vincennes line, for example. Métro service begins at 5:30am, and the last trains leave either end station at 12:30am. The cost of an individual ticket is 1.40€ ($1.75), but you can save by buying in bulk: a *carnet* (10 tickets) is 11€ ($14). The **RER** suburban train network is sometimes handy for getting around Paris more quickly than by Métro because it has fewer stops. Most RER stations are also Métro stops, so transferring from one to the other is easy. Within the city, you can use a Métro ticket for the RER. Unlike the Métro, you'll need your ticket to both enter and exit the turnstiles of an RER station.

A **Carte Orange** provides an unlimited number of trips on the Métro, on buses, and on RER within the city during a week (weeks run Mon–Sun); the cost is 11€ ($14). These passes require a passport-size photo; most stations have photo machines. Don't try to validate the Carte Orange on buses (the cartes look a lot like the regular tickets); just show your card to the driver. The **Paris Visite** card is good for 1, 2, 3, or 5 days in Paris and the Ile-de-France (the surrounding region) on all forms of Paris public transportation; Paris Visite also makes you eligible for discounts at certain sightseeing attractions. The cost ranges from 8.35€ ($10) for 1 day to 27€ ($34) for 5 days. The 1-day Mobilis card (5.30€/$6.65) works on the same principle but doesn't include sightseeing reductions.

Tickets can be purchased in any station or *tabacs.* Validate your ticket by inserting it in the turnstile, which will spit it out again; hold onto your ticket until you've left the Métro—if a *controlleur* asks to see your ticket and you don't have a valid one, you'll be fined on the spot.

Taxes... France's VAT (value-added tax) is 19.6%, levied on all goods and services except for books and newspapers, which carry a VAT of only 5.5%. See "Sales Tax," in the Shopping chapter for information on reclaiming this tax on purchases of more than 182€ ($228). For customs information, call Tel 01-49-28-54-55.

Taxis and limos... Except during rush hours, finding a taxi is fairly easy, unless it's raining or there is a Métro strike. Taxis can be hailed on the street, or you can line up at one of the many *stations de taxi,* clearly marked with a large T. A taxi is available if the entire light on its roof is glowing; if just the bulb in the center is lit, the cab's occupied. Don't get angry if a driver refuses to take you after asking where you are going: A half-hour before the end of a shift, a homeward-bound cabbie has the right to turn down any passenger who's trying to catch a ride in the opposite direction. Drivers expect about 10% tip; there are extra charges for pickups at train stations or other transportation terminals, for luggage weighing more than 5 kilograms, for a fourth person in the cab, and for an animal. Drivers can refuse to take more than three people or an animal (except a Seeing Eye dog). Fares are higher at night and outside city limits (marked by the *périphérique,* or ring road circling the city).

Radio-dispatched taxis turn on their meters when they receive a call, so don't be surprised when yours arrives with a hefty sum already on its meter. For a radio-dispatched taxi, call **Alpha-Taxis** (Tel 01-45-85-85-85), **Artaxi** (Tel 08-25-16-10-10), **G7 Radio** (Tel 01-47-39-47-39), or **Les Taxis Bleus** (Tel 01-49-36-24-24). Chauffeured limousines are available from **Prestige Limousines** (Tel 01-42-53-00-74), which has multilingual drivers.

Telephones... There are hardly any coin-operated phones left in Paris, except in cafés. You have to buy a **Télécarte** in a post office or *tabac* to use a pay phone. Follow the instructions on the phone's screen: *"Décrochez"* means "pick up the receiver"; *"insérez votre carte"* means "insert your card"; *"numerotez"* means "dial the number"; *"raccrochez"* means "hang up." In some cafés, you have to ask at the bar for the use of the phone and then pay the cashier when your call is completed. The first thing you'll hear after dialing is rapid clicking sounds, followed by long rings when the connection is made, or a faster signal if the line is busy.

France is now divided into five regions with different area codes. All Paris region numbers begin with 01. The other codes are 02 for the northwest, 03 for the northeast, 04 for the southeast, and 05 for the southwest. All numbers have 10 digits.

For international calls, dial 00, followed by the country code (U.S. and Canada 1, U.K. 44, Australia 61, New Zealand 64), the area code, and the number. To reach American long-distance operators, dial Tel 08-00-99-00-11 for **AT&T,** Tel 08-00-99-00-19 for **MCI,** and Tel 08-00-99-00-87 for **Sprint.**

For French directory assistance, dial Tel 12. For international directory assistance, dial Tel 00-33-12, followed by the country code or 11 for the United States or Canada. Toll-free calls begin with 0800. Other numbers beginning with 08 carry an extra charge.

To call from outside of France, first dial the international access code (U.S. and Canada 011, U.K or New Zealand 00, Australia 0011), then France's country code, 33. There should be a 10-digit number that follows—fixed lines in Paris begin with "01," and cellular phones begin with "06."

Time... France is usually 6 hours ahead of Eastern Standard Time and 9 hours ahead of Pacific Standard Time in the United States. French daylight saving time lasts from around April to September, when clocks are set 1 hour ahead of the standard time.

Tipping... A service charge of at least 15% is included in all restaurant and hotel bills. If you are happy with the service, leave some change for the waiter or the hotel maid. Many French people never leave anything extra, so service people won't be shocked (though they might not be pleased) if you don't either. Give taxi drivers about 10% of the fare if they've been agreeable and helpful.

Trains... The **SNCF** is the national train system. There are six major train stations in Paris: the Gare de Lyon (trains going to the southeast of France and to Italy), the Gare du Nord (Brussels, London via the Eurotunnel, and other northern destinations), the Gare de l'Est (destinations to the east), the Gare Saint-Lazare (the northwest, including Normandy), the Gare d'Austerlitz (Spain and the southwest), and the Gare Montparnasse (the west, including Britanny). Suburban trains also leave from these stations. Each station has a Métro stop with the same name. For **train information and reservations,** call Tel 08-36-35-35-35 from 7am to 10pm; for suburban lines, call Tel 01-53-90-20-20. Always remember to *composter* (validate) your ticket in the orange machines near the quays in the station before boarding your train; if you don't, you'll be fined by the conductor.

The RER is the suburban train network. Inside Paris, it can be used almost as an express Métro line (see "Subways," above). For destinations outside the city, purchase RER tickets at the ticket counters or vending machines in each station.

Travelers with disabilities... Paris is not easily accessible for those who have difficulty moving around. All Métro stations have stairs; only bus line 20 (between Gare Saint-Lazare and Gare de Lyon) has wheelchair-accessible buses. Though most hotels have elevators, they're often too small to accommodate a wheelchair, and bathrooms can be extremely cramped. The large, modern hotels are the best bet for anyone in a wheelchair, and taxis (whose drivers are required to help with a wheelchair) offer the only convenient way to cover a lot of ground. Thankfully, the sidewalks have ramps at every street corner. More attention has been paid to the needs of the blind. There are bumps on the edge of the quays in the Métro, and elevator buttons have tactile numbers.

A good source of information is **Association de Paralyses de France,** 22, rue du Pere Guerin, 13e (Tel 01-40-78-69-00; www.apf.asso.fr). **Paris Convention and Visitors Bureau,** 25, rue des Pyramides, 1er (Tel 08-92-68-30-00; www.parisinfo.com; Metro Pyramides), open Monday to Saturday 10am to 7pm, has information on the accessibility of transportation, museums, and monuments. A pamphlet published by the national railway, the SNCF, is available in train stations.

TV stations... If your hotel room has TV but no cable, you will be able to watch channels 1, 2, 3, 5, and 6. You may get a kick out of seeing reruns of some old American series in French, especially on Channel 6. Channel 5 is Arte, a high-brow French-German collaboration with obscure films, documentaries, and musical programs. On cable, you may or may not have Canal+, a movie channel, but you probably will get CNN Europe, BBC Prime (a mix of BBC programming), MTV Europe and MCM (music videos), Eurosport, Planète (nature and science documentaries), RAI Uno (Italian), TVE 1 (Spanish), and Euronews in both English and French on different channels. Canal J has children's programming until 8pm.

Visitor information... The Paris Convention and Visitors Bureau is at 25, rue des Pyramides, 1er (Tel 08-92-68-30-00; www.parisinfo.com; Metro Pyramides). Open Monday to Saturday, 10am to 7pm.

Helpful websites include www.paris.fr/EN, www.ratp.info (up-to-date transportation information), www.pagesjaunes.fr (handy for addresses and maps), and www.paris-anglo.com (a directory of companies and services for English-speakers).

GENERAL INDEX

Accommodations

Restaurant & Cafe Index

Notes

Notes

Notes

Notes

Notes

Frommer's® Complete Travel Guides

Alaska
Amalfi Coast
American Southwest
Amsterdam
Argentina & Chile
Arizona
Atlanta
Australia
Austria
Bahamas
Barcelona
Beijing
Belgium, Holland & Luxembourg
Belize
Bermuda
Boston
Brazil
British Columbia & the Canadian Rockies
Brussels & Bruges
Budapest & the Best of Hungary
Buenos Aires
Calgary
California
Canada
Cancún, Cozumel & the Yucatán
Cape Cod, Nantucket & Martha's Vineyard
Caribbean
Caribbean Ports of Call
Carolinas & Georgia
Chicago
China
Colorado
Costa Rica
Croatia
Cuba
Denmark
Denver, Boulder & Colorado Springs
Edinburgh & Glasgow
England
Europe
Europe by Rail
Florence, Tuscany & Umbria
Florida
France
Germany
Greece
Greek Islands
Hawaii
Hong Kong
Honolulu, Waikiki & Oahu
India
Ireland
Italy
Jamaica
Japan
Kauai
Las Vegas
London
Los Angeles
Los Cabos & Baja
Madrid
Maine Coast
Maryland & Delaware
Maui
Mexico
Montana & Wyoming
Montréal & Québec City
Moscow & St. Petersburg
Munich & the Bavarian Alps
Nashville & Memphis
New England
Newfoundland & Labrador
New Mexico
New Orleans
New York City
New York State
New Zealand
Northern Italy
Norway
Nova Scotia, New Brunswick & Prince Edward Island
Oregon
Paris
Peru
Philadelphia & the Amish Country
Portugal
Prague & the Best of the Czech Republic
Provence & the Riviera
Puerto Rico
Rome
San Antonio & Austin
San Diego
San Francisco
Santa Fe, Taos & Albuquerque
Scandinavia
Scotland
Seattle
Seville, Granada & the Best of Andalusia
Shanghai
Sicily
Singapore & Malaysia
South Africa
South America
South Florida
South Pacific
Southeast Asia
Spain
Sweden
Switzerland
Texas
Thailand
Tokyo
Toronto
Turkey
USA
Utah
Vancouver & Victoria
Vermont, New Hampshire & Maine
Vienna & the Danube Valley
Vietnam
Virgin Islands
Virginia
Walt Disney World® & Orlando
Washington, D.C.
Washington State

Frommer's® Dollar-a-Day Guides

Australia from $60 a Day
California from $70 a Day
England from $75 a Day
Europe from $85 a Day
Florida from $70 a Day
Hawaii from $80 a Day
Ireland from $90 a Day
Italy from $90 a Day
London from $95 a Day
New York City from $90 a Day
Paris from $95 a Day
San Francisco from $70 a Day
Washington, D.C. from $80 a Day

Frommer's® Portable Guides

Acapulco, Ixtapa & Zihuatanejo
Amsterdam
Aruba
Australia's Great Barrier Reef
Bahamas
Berlin
Big Island of Hawaii
Boston
California Wine Country
Cancún
Cayman Islands
Charleston
Chicago
Disneyland®
Dominican Republic
Dublin
Florence
Las Vegas
Las Vegas for Non-Gamblers
London
Los Angeles
Maui
Nantucket & Martha's Vineyard
New Orleans
New York City
Paris
Portland
Puerto Rico
Puerto Vallarta, Manzanillo & Guadalajara
Rio de Janeiro
San Diego
San Francisco
Savannah
Vancouver
Venice
Virgin Islands
Washington, D.C.
Whistler

Frommer's® Cruise Guides

Alaska Cruises & Ports of Call
Cruises & Ports of Call
European Cruises & Ports of Call

FROMMER'S® DAY BY DAY GUIDES

Amsterdam
Chicago
Florence & Tuscany
London
New York City
Paris
Rome
San Francisco
Venice

FROMMER'S® NATIONAL PARK GUIDES

Algonquin Provincial Park
Banff & Jasper
Grand Canyon
National Parks of the American West
Rocky Mountain
Yellowstone & Grand Teton
Yosemite and Sequoia & Kings Canyon
Zion & Bryce Canyon

FROMMER'S® MEMORABLE WALKS

Chicago
London
New York
Paris
Rome
San Francisco

FROMMER'S® WITH KIDS GUIDES

Chicago
Hawaii
Las Vegas
London
National Parks
New York City
San Francisco
Toronto
Walt Disney World® & Orlando
Washington, D.C.

SUZY GERSHMAN'S BORN TO SHOP GUIDES

Born to Shop: France
Born to Shop: Hong Kong, Shanghai & Beijing
Born to Shop: Italy
Born to Shop: London
Born to Shop: New York
Born to Shop: Paris

FROMMER'S® IRREVERENT GUIDES

Amsterdam
Boston
Chicago
Las Vegas
London
Los Angeles
Manhattan
New Orleans
Paris
Rome
San Francisco
Walt Disney World®
Washington, D.C.

FROMMER'S® BEST-LOVED DRIVING TOURS

Austria
Britain
California
France
Germany
Ireland
Italy
New England
Northern Italy
Scotland
Spain
Tuscany & Umbria

THE UNOFFICIAL GUIDES®

Adventure Travel in Alaska
Beyond Disney
California with Kids
Central Italy
Chicago
Cruises
Disneyland®
England
Florida
Florida with Kids
Hawaii
Ireland
Las Vegas
London
Maui
Mexico's Best Beach Resorts
Mini Las Vegas
Mini Mickey
New Orleans
New York City
Paris
San Francisco
South Florida including Miami & the Keys
Walt Disney World®
Walt Disney World® for Grown-ups
Walt Disney World® with Kids
Washington, D.C.

SPECIAL-INTEREST TITLES

Athens Past & Present
Cities Ranked & Rated
Frommer's Best Day Trips from London
Frommer's Best RV & Tent Campgrounds in the U.S.A.
Frommer's Exploring America by RV
Frommer's NYC Free & Dirt Cheap
Frommer's Road Atlas Europe
Frommer's Road Atlas Ireland
Retirement Places Rated

FROMMER'S® PHRASEFINDER DICTIONARY GUIDES

French
Italian
Spanish